How to Start and Manage your own Vacation Rental

by James Dorgan

Table of Contents

Prologue

People I personally know routinely contact me for advice on how to find, start up, and successfully manage a vacation rental. We meet for lunch, and in a no nonsense, simple to understand way, I explain the basic 'rules' to follow in selecting, setting up, and marketing a vacation rental. I then teach them how to self-manage the vacation rental, after the system is initially set up, on less than an hour a week.

Without fail after our discussions, these same people later say that everything that I taught them was spot on. Every time, the conversation ends with encouragement for me to put it all down in a direct, easy to understand and follow, video course or a book.

After many years of encouragement, I created both.

My online video course is available at

www.vacationrentaltrainingcourse.com

which **shows** prospective owners how to set up and successfully self-manage a vacation rental, while this book **tells** prospective owners how to do it.

So here we go –

SECTION I – BUYING YOUR FIRST VACATION RENTAL

Chapter 1

Where should I buy a vacation rental?

The best place to buy a vacation rental is typically a place that you are familiar with and have vacationed before. If the area or location is attractive enough for you to travel and vacation there, then it may be similarly attractive to other vacationers to go there as well.

If you or your family love sugar white sand beaches, emerald green waters, or Florida sunshine, then a vacation rental in Panama City Beach may be an option to consider.

If you are an avid snow skier, and spend every winter on the slopes, and return to the Rockies each summer for hiking and mountain biking, then maybe a condo in Breckenridge, Colorado may be an option.

If you travelled to Gatlinburg, Tennessee as a child and have magical memories of pancake houses, cute brown bears, Smoky Mountain streams, and the excitement of Pigeon Forge, then maybe a cabin may be something to consider.

If you are a Disney fanatic, and visit the Magic Kingdom every year, and want to continue a family tradition of Orlando vacations for years to come, then a short-term vacation rental house in Orlando may be something to look into.

Ask yourself, where do I vacation? Then imagine that you own a vacation rental there. It is possible.

The main thing to prioritize is that you *know* the vacation destination. You know what draws people there. You know what fun things there are to do there. You also enjoy being there, as it is a place you feel comfortable and feel at home. It is also a place you *like* to visit and *want* to visit for years to come.

One of the coolest things about owning a vacation rental in a place that you love is that you get to go on vacation there whenever you want, and stay in your own place, for free. So, you might as well establish your vacation rental in a place that is both familiar, loved, and enjoyed by you and your family.

RULE: Buy somewhere you love to vacation.

Chapter 2

How far away should my vacation rental

be from my home?

My wife and I have always dreamed of having a small condo on the slopes in downtown Breckenridge. We could fly out at Christmas with the kids, ski in and ski out, and walk to town for delicious dinners each night. During the summer, we could mountain bike, hike, and fish the mountain streams. It seemed to be the perfect place to have a vacation rental.

After finding several options that were within our budget, we flew to Colorado to check them out.

The trip was a long, tiring, and complicated process to just get there, which included airport parking, flights, shuttles, and a rental car. There is no hopping in the car for a weekend of fresh powder. If we owned a Breckenridge vacation rental, there would be no quick weekend getaway for me to replace an inoperable TV.

A good rule of thumb would thus be for your vacation rental to preferably be within driving distance of your home, eight to ten hours away at the most. Having to fly to your vacation rental complicates things immensely. It is possible, but the distance eliminates a degree of spontaneity and last-minute use – a critical enjoyment factor to owning a vacation rental.

RULE: Focus on securing a vacation rental that is within a reasonable driving distance of your home.

Chapter 3

Should I risk buying a vacation rental

based on the MLS listing alone?

Follow my advice: do not buy a vacation rental without first making the trip there, knowing the vacation destination, and staying in the unit, or if unavailable, at least stay in the same resort.

Allow me to provide an example which underscores the importance of this concept.

The MLS described the vacation rental as a ski in and ski out studio, which boasted heated and covered underground parking, with a dedicated parking space. The description sounded promising. However, we needed to be able to handle the entire vacation rental process remotely, i.e., from the opposite side of the country, and a plane flight away.

Upon arrival, I realized that the parking garage was only accessible by using a physical magnetic card key, that if lost, was a $500 fee and a huge hassle to replace. This presented the first major challenge. How do I get that parking magnetic strip card to every guest checking in, and then get it back from the departing guest, before getting it to the next arriving guest?

Never ever rely on a guest to get anything right. Remember that. The system you set up for logistics of stay must be simple, dummy proof, and cannot rely upon a guest's diligence. It also needs to be as automated as humanly possible.

To get in the unit, a physical key was required. None of the units on the hallway had an electronic lock. I later learned that physical door keys were required in the complex.

Physical keys that could be misplaced or mishandled are the opposite of efficiency and simplicity. Avoid physical keys in your vacation rental like the plague.

The issues of being bound by a magnetic card parking key and an actual physical key to get in the door ruled out this resort, as I self-manage our units from afar. A physical key is only used for an emergency backup. It is never the primary means of entry. I will talk more about that later.

But it only got worse from there.

On my first morning, I realized that the unit faced north, and that sunlight, throughout the day, would *never enter the unit*. The unit in no way resembled the bright and airy photos that I had seen on the MLS with the pretty mountains in the distance. This condo was a cave, literally.

I also kept waking up to a bang and swishing sound. I realized that it was the hallway trash chute, directly next to the unit. Just terrific.

Again, this is not something one would pick up if basing a decision to buy or not exclusively on an MLS listing.

It is a successful trip when one realizes things like this *before* they buy, rather than realizing these things after they have already bought the unit.

RULE: Never buy a vacation rental sight unseen – always stay in the unit or in the resort before buying. By actually staying in the vacation rental, you will realize the good, the bad, and the ugly with both the quality of stay, and the potential logistical difficulties of actually renting the vacation rental.

Chapter 4

Focus on 'Bang for the Buck.'

Some vacation properties make money like ATM machines. While others, even when expertly managed, marketed and furnished beautifully, make significantly less, *for the same amount of money invested.*

It is at this point that one must detach from the emotional attachment to a particular condo, cabin, dream, or even a particular area of the country. Allow me to explain.

I had a $400,000 budget for a vacation rental. The money was gathered from rental income from other vacation properties I owned, and a large legal related project that had been in the works for over ten years, which finally materialized.

The first step is to take your budget, and not put it down as a down payment on a million-dollar property, but rather find a vacation rental that you can pay cash for, without financing. Never ever use 'found money' to bind you to a mortgage you cannot afford if a hiccup occurs (pandemic, an oil spill, a hurricane, or perhaps your own unemployment). Simply take what you have and pay <u>cash</u> for whatever you can afford.

Florida's Panama City Beach consistently has amazing vacation rental revenue numbers that are just astonishing. We had the opportunity to buy a beautiful 1400 square foot fully furnished beachfront condo, that sleeps nine guests, with a huge 9th floor balcony Gulf front view, in a recently built, concrete Gulf front resort, with average gross rental revenues in the $50k's and up. It has a kid's onsite waterpark, lazy river, hot tub, gorgeous beach, and a dream location.

However, we already owned two condos in Panama City Beach, and needed some diversification (remember Hurricane Michael?), so Panama City Beach was not an option. Our goal was to instead find 'bang for the buck' as good or better than that location. We were thinking of getting off the beach – like way off the beach – to help diversify and reduce risk.

I ran the numbers on a series of ski in and ski out condos in Colorado, Utah, and Wyoming.

A $400k budget in Breckenridge, Colorado bought at best a studio with less than $30k in gross rental revenues. Our $400k literally would buy a shoebox producing less than $30k a year, in a best-case scenario. We would also have to fly there, as it was too far to drive from Alabama.

I then ran the numbers on Pigeon Forge / Gatlinburg, Tennessee cabins.

For the same $400k, we could get a 1200 square foot, three story authentic log cabin, log furnishings, cathedral ceilings, amazing mountain top views, game room, loft, hot tub, full size dining table and an outdoor grilling area, that could sleep 12 guests, with rental revenues between $60k and $70k per year, and within an eight-hour driving distance of our home.

It is at this point when you have narrowed down your choices, one should focus on the property that produces the most 'bang for your buck,' both with what you end up with, and the amount of rental income it produces.

The choice was clear.

By getting an accurate reading of the gross rental revenues for each potential location, and comparing the properties on size, sleeping capacity, amenities, and accessibility from your home, it became increasingly clear that the best 'bang for the buck' option was the cabin in Tennessee, and it also fulfilled our goal of having a variety of vacation rental properties to reduce risk.

RULE: Zero in on buying a vacation rental property with the highest comparable rental revenues, and gives you the best overall 'bang for your buck.' Why buy a studio when the same money could buy a three-story cabin that makes twice the rental income?

Chapter 5

Ask lots of questions.

After narrowing down the vacation rental to a particular region, area, condo resort, or neighborhood, start asking a lot of questions.

Secure a realtor to assist you with the buying process. This realtor can then research the 'comps' or comparable sales over the past year. This would then give you a non-emotional platform to offer a reasonable amount for the property, without paying too much.

Contact the HOA and secure minutes from the last few years of annual meetings. These minutes are helpful to get a feel for whether the resort is rental friendly or not, whether major repairs are being put off, whether a large assessment is coming down the pipeline, if a general hostility exists toward vacation rentals, or other critical information that would affect your decision to buy.

For instance, if it was debated and was narrowly voted down to ban short term vacation rentals at the resort the year before (i.e., to make it a condo rule that all rentals must be at least 30 days or longer), perhaps that resort shouldn't be considered for your next vacation rental property.

Ask questions about how often the area is hit by hurricanes and how to insure against it. Ask questions about forest fires and how to insure against them. Ask questions about possible pandemic restrictions that might block your access to guests being able to come and stay at your property. How would most guests get to your property, do they drive in or fly in? What is the main selling point of why guests stay at this particular property?

For the cabin, how often does a winter storm shut down the roads? How do you protect against termites in an all-wood cabin? How many forest fires have there been? Does the cabin rely on a well? Does the cabin have its own septic system? Are there below ground power lines? How often does the cabin lose power during the winter? How often is the cabin inaccessible? Does a guest have to have four-wheel drive to get to the cabin?

When staying on the property, find another property owner and take them out for drinks or dinner to get them talking. After some libations, they will share with you the good, the bad, and the ugly of owning in the resort, and it won't be sugar coated.

Contact the property manager, introduce yourself, and tell them which unit you are interested in purchasing, and just see what they say.

One time I called the property manager of a beach condo resort that we had narrowed down to and found what we thought was an awesome deal. The vacation rental was a completely renovated, pristine Gulf front unit that was turnkey ready (and the photos were just epic). I told him that I was thinking of making an offer on that specific condo.

The property manager immediately said, 'Don't do it Dorgan." He knew that condo well as it had been vacant for years, although he wasn't sure why, *and during that entire time it was without power and air conditioning.* He said that up until the renovation, no one was allowed near that unit due to the toxic mold that had developed.

No matter how much paint is used to freshen a place up, toxic mold is a serious issue and is extremely hard to get rid of. I couldn't believe it and had no idea, so we bailed. Never ever buy into a vacation rental that could harm you, your family, or your guest's health. Ever.

At another beach resort, I introduced myself to a lady reading a book by the pool. I explained that I was interested in buying in the resort and wanted to do short term vacation rentals. The older lady literally sighed, put her book down, crossed her arms, looked past the readers perched on the end of her pointy nose, and told me, "Most everyone here are year-round retired residents. Renters, if they come, are not welcome here." End of that visit.

I found another amazing property, and it was so inexpensive. I was far along in the process and had always assumed that the property could be used as a vacation rental. Never assume that any given property is vacation rental authorized. Indeed, the condo was restricted – no short-term vacation rentals were permitted. Guest stays had to be 30 days or longer – no exceptions. Even though it was a solid 30% per square foot less than comparable properties that allowed short term rentals, we could never afford it without having the short-term vacation rental income. It was a nonstarter. The place was also full of retirees. If there is a rule that says no short-term rentals, don't try and do it anyway or sneak around or try to circumvent the system. They will catch you and shut you down. Renters stand out like sore thumbs in resorts like that, and the neighbors will literally wage war on this issue.

I found another lower priced condo on the beach and could not believe that it was so much cheaper than comparable Gulf front units. The place had everything – a new resort, direct Gulf front, amazing pool area, lazy river, wave pool, waterpark, and covered parking.

When checking out a specific resort, a good rule of thumb is to always review the VRBO listings for the resort that you are looking at buying, as it offers a treasure chest of valuable information from other owners, doing the same thing that you hope to be doing. See what their nightly rates are. See how busy their calendar looks. Read all the reviews, good bad and ugly.

We quickly learned through the vacation rental listings (and mainly through the negative reviews) that the pool amenities of the resort were owned by an entity separate from the resort. Guests had to pay $50 per day per person to access the pool and waterpark, *which was directly in front of the condo, and were the resort's only amenities*. This meant that the guest would first have to rent the unit, and then shell out daily entrance fees to simply enjoy the resort amenities each day.

Indeed, the rental reviews were brutal. Guests felt that they were unfairly surprised that there was no pool or resort amenity for them to enjoy, unless they purchased the expensive daily pass, which for a family of four, was astronomical. The inexpensive stay suddenly got very expensive for renters, and they were unhappy. None of the odd or unusual amenity ownership was mentioned in the stock MLS listing.

We found another amazing property, a condo right on the beach. It checked all the boxes - concrete gulf front, plentiful covered parking, amazing views, beautiful pool, and beaches. At the front desk, we asked whether short term vacation rentals were allowed. We learned that short term rentals were indeed allowed, but all vacation rentals were required to be *run through the front desk*. Specifically, our vacation rental would be managed by the front desk – no self-management was permitted in the building.

Even if that were fine, and the rental numbers were really strong, and you were comfortable with a management company handling your vacation rental, we had a difficult time with financing because the resort was considered to be a 'condo-tel,' a hybrid word combining condo and hotel. Many lenders simply will not lend on that type of property. Unless you are paying cash, investing in what is a 'condo-tel,' may present financing challenges.

RULE: Tell everyone what you plan to do, ask a lot of questions, review other existing vacation rental listings in the resort you are looking for, actually visit and stay at the property, and absorb all of that information before making a final decision.

Chapter 6

Lessons learned from our first vacation rental.

Please, do not repeat my mistakes.

In view of how badly I bludgeoned my first attempt at a vacation rental, I would recommend that you start off small with your first vacation rental. 'Get your feet wet' first, and then forge ahead with larger properties and larger investments as you get more experienced and in turn, more confident with the process.

You also need to make sure that you can tolerate vacation rental management, as it may or may not be for everyone. There is some thick skin needed occasionally when dealing with unhappy guests, which unfortunately happens even under the best of circumstances. By starting off small, it is easier and less expensive to escape, if necessary, if the vacation rental management experience turns out poorly.

In addition, even with the power of vacation rental apps, templates and automation, there is still some time commitment needed to self-manage your vacation rental, which may fall at random times on any given day. This may also present an issue for you depending upon your circumstances.

For those reasons and more, maybe start off small.

Our first condo was a tiny studio across the street from the beach, and only an hour from our home, in Orange Beach, Alabama. We spent $150,000. We financed it as a second home. It was as close as our income to debt ratios barely allowed, but we somehow qualified for the note.

After bank approval for the loan, there was this euphoria of finally being able to get our proverbial 'foot in the door' at the beach, and it seemed at that moment a great way to start. We finally could stay at our second home rather than having to drive back home each night after a long day at the beach. We would rent it out to cover the note and expenses. It was across the street from the beach, but we didn't care. It was going to be the proverbial 'crash pad,' that we could also rent out.

In our jubilation, and initial euphoria of being approved to buy, we overlooked a few shortcomings that I now realize are important.

First, it was an older building built in the 1970's, with our unit only accessible by two flights of stairs. This immediately knocked out a sizeable chunk of potential renters, including the handicapped, those with mobility issues, and older guests. It was also a huge pain getting one's luggage, groceries and belongings up and down two flights of stairs.

RULE: Do not buy a vacation rental that is not handicapped accessible, or at minimum, that does not have an elevator. A couple of stairs is fine. Two or more flights of stairs – not good.

Second, it was a wooden structure at the beach. We lucked out and the few hurricanes we endured did not knock it down. It also never burned down, but an older, all wood multi-unit resort just like ours burned down just a few blocks away. Do not buy wooden structures at the beach – way too much risk on many different levels.

RULE: If buying along the beaches, buy concrete.

Third, the unit was across the street from the beach, with a limited view. When we did get an inquiry, the first question was whether it was Gulf front and how far it was to the beach. It thereafter took a lot of salesmanship to convince someone to stay there. Fast forward to present day, and we own two Gulf front units, the number of inquiries, views and website traffic is nearly 100x that of our little studio across the street from the beach. Gulf front sells itself. Everything else is distant runner ups. Buy something that sells itself.

RULE: If buying on the beach, buy Gulf or Ocean front. There are exceptions in certain circumstances (look at 30-A in the Florida panhandle), but that's the general rule.

Fourth, it was a fixer upper. We put nearly $25,000 in hard improvements, but it took months to complete, and was a huge investment of my personal time and missed work. I also nearly killed myself hauling appliances, materials, and furniture up and down the two flights of stairs. This was a mistake. Do not buy fixer uppers – buy units which are 'turnkey' ready to be rented. Your time is valuable. You want the unit to be able to be rented and accept reservations the day you close, or at worst, within a few weeks of closing. You want a vacation rental immediately generating substantial rental income, with you doing very little to nothing. Having to renovate a place violates that general rule of vacation rental success. Your goal is a small investment of personal time and resources for a large monetary return. Be patient and wait for a vacation rental that is already redone and is turnkey ready – they are out there – and will come along. Simply be patient.

RULE: Buy turnkey / rental ready properties.

In retrospect, the studio did get our 'foot in the door' at the beach and was at least a good start. We loved the studio, and we were so excited to be getting $15k+ a year in rental revenues, which we thought at the time was a fortune. It's not. We learned a lot of crucial lessons from that experience, which led to better decisions down the road.

We were finally able to sell the studio and sold it for just over what we had invested in it.

Looking back, we in fact way overpaid and priced ourselves way too high in that resort. We bought on emotion. We also bought it during the summer – a big mistake when buying at the beach. Never buy a vacation rental in the middle of peak season. Buy a beach condo when it's a ghost town and 20 degrees out. It's the same mentality when buying a motorboat. Always buy a boat in the dead of winter, never the week before Memorial Day.

I also do not remember ever looking at comps on the other units recently sold in the resort. I look back now and wonder - what were we thinking?

We put way too much into fixing it up and as a result, were 'upside down' in value for nearly our entire term of ownership. Our rental revenues were nominal at best. It was, however, a good first step, and not too expensive. We got a taste of how sweet a successful vacation rental could be, learned a lot of valuable lessons, and we wanted more of it.

RULE: Risk as little as humanly possible on your first vacation rental, as mistakes are inevitable. Think of the first vacation rental as something you can 'cut your teeth on' to learn the vacation rental trade and get situated.

Chapter 7

How do I finance the purchase of a vacation rental?

The easiest way to finance a purchase is to have solid employment income, and then reach out to your lender to get a mortgage for a second home if you can qualify. You then have a note to pay, along with monthly HOA dues, taxes, insurance, power, and any other miscellaneous expenses. When financing your vacation rental, the margins are incredibly thin. You will likely be able to stay at your own property for free a few weeks each year, but in the end, you will likely not 'net out' any money. It is incredibly tight to keep from having to go 'out of pocket' on the property if it is financed. You are doing well if you simply break even and get to use it when it isn't rented.

Ideally, use a lump sum of cash to buy the vacation rental, or money that has been inherited, or gifted to you. Even better, it is a property that has been in the family and has long ago been paid off, and you now are looking at renting it out. Setting up a vacation rental in a paid off property gives you dramatic cash flow and a healthy return on investment. There is always plenty of money flowing in and 'netting out' cash each year is a cinch. By having substantial cash flow, it is a lot easier to weather income disruptions caused by storms, something as unexpected as an oil spill or pandemic, or your own unemployment.

RULE: Paying cash for an investment property is the ideal way to go as it gives you a ton of breathing room, even if your rental income is unexpectedly interrupted. If it's too close for the numbers to work, don't do it. You must be able to sleep at night.

Chapter 8

Can I buy a vacation rental through my IRA?

Another option is to purchase the vacation rental through your IRA.

Before I begin, this is an overview of how to do it. Do not move around IRA money, buy property, or do any of this without first securing appropriate tax and legal advice from a professional, as there are many rules involved with this process.

Now that the disclaimer is out of the way, allow me to give you a broad stroke overview of the process.

Let's say you have $400k in your brokerage managed IRA. Simply liquidate the assets in your IRA and transfer the cash proceeds to an IRA trust company, such as Equity Trust Company (ETC).

Moving the IRA money from the brokerage to the trust company is a sideways transfer between two similar IRA's so there are no tax consequences triggered in the sideways move across the same types of IRA's.

After you locate and place under contract your vacation property, you then instruct ETC to wire the recently deposited IRA funds to purchase the property, for your benefit. The property is then placed in ETC's name, *for your benefit.* You do not own the vacation rental personally. Your IRA trust, ETC, owns it, but it is held for your benefit, and at your sole control, management, and or direction. It is akin to owning it individually, but simply titled in a different way.

You then self-manage the investment property through VRBO. You accept reservations and manage income and expenses through the ETC online bank account, also in ETC's name but set up for your benefit.

You cannot touch or spend or place in your own personal non-IRA account the rental income from the vacation rental. The net rental income must flow back into the Equity Trust Company IRA bank account as rental income. It is not a contribution. It is the asset producing net rental income, akin to a stock dividend. The net rental income from the vacation rental simply flows back into the IRA.

Think of the vacation rental as a stock your IRA bought. A stock produces dividends, which then flow back into your IRA. The stock value may go up or down. It may or may not produce a yearly dividend. All the net income or dividends stays within the IRA.

The vacation rental is like owning a stock.

Akin to stock ownership, the vacation rental will hopefully go up in value, and if it does, the appreciation that is ultimately realized when the vacation rental is sold flows back into the IRA. When the vacation rental nets out rental income above expenses, that rental income flows back into the IRA, just like a stock dividend would.

On the downside, and pursuant to IRS rules, you are not permitted to stay in the investment property that is held within a self-managed IRA. It truly needs to be set up as an investment property that you cannot stay in or live in or even visit for the weekend.

You are not even allowed to personally complete repairs to the vacation rental. All repairs and or improvements must be handled by a third party (but at your direction).

The vacation rental cannot be in your name and then sold to your IRA, and you cannot buy from your IRA the investment property. This reduces the risk of sham transactions. It must be an 'arm's length' transaction between your IRA and someone else other than yourself.

ETC then allows you to use the rental income to pay regular expenses, such as HOA dues, lodging taxes, cleaning fees, utilities and so forth, through the ETC account set up for your benefit.

In other words, if you rent through VRBO, the rental income flows from VRBO directly into the ETC account. You then pay bills from those funds through their online banking account.

At the end of each year, there may be net proceeds sitting in the ETC rental income account. You can then invest that net income through

ETC's brokerage account to further build your IRA worth or transfer the net income out to another IRA brokerage account. Transferring out the rental income to another IRA brokerage is not a contribution. It is IRA dividend income that is simply converted from cash into stocks or other investments, all within the IRA.

In the end, your IRA gets the benefit of the capital appreciation of the vacation rental, and then the rental income flows back into the IRA, which you then reinvest into stocks, bonds, or other securities. The income is tax deferred in that income tax is not paid until you start taking distributions from the IRA account.

This is an excellent way to build wealth over the long run.

The downside of this arrangement, however, is that you are not supposed to step foot or spend the night in the investment property. That's a major drawback.

It is possible to have a rental management company or a third party managed bank account that is not disqualified (the account handling the rental income cannot be in your name, your spouse's name or your children's names), that can handle the income and expenses of the vacation rental, rather than running that income and expenses through Equity Trust Company. The net income at the end of the year from that account is then sent to ETC as a dividend or rental income or return on investment (not a contribution).

Yes, there are specific IRS rules that must be followed on exactly how the rental income and rental expenses are handled when doing a vacation rental IRA. Get the assistance of a knowledgeable accountant to stay in compliance with all tax rules. Also, contact Equity Trust Company – they will tell you exactly how to do it and assist you with staying in compliance with the IRS rules on doing something like this. Their website also clearly explains the rules of ownership. You simply follow the guidance of ETC, your attorney, and accountant, and it can be legally done.

I firmly believe that owning a vacation rental is significantly less risky than owning stock in any given publicly traded company. I feel so much more confident picking my own vacation rental, than having money managers gamble my money in the stock market.

Assuming you follow the rules in this guide, you will know the area, you will know the resort, the vacation rental market, the rental revenues, the risks, and arguably have much more knowledge about your vacation rental than you otherwise would have in any given stock pick. You will get solid advice on what a good purchase price is. You will have done your homework on your vacation rental investment. That alone is more research than hoping and praying that some random stock pick in a company you really don't know much about works out in the long run.

Under the IRA approach to vacation rental ownership, you plan to benefit in the long run from both capital appreciation of the property your IRA owns and netting out yearly rental income to reinvest. The more vacation rentals you own in your IRA, the faster the rental income will grow to buy more vacation rentals, all within the IRA.

When you reach retirement age, you then start taking your minimum distributions, and that draw from your IRA is then taxed as income. Hopefully, the rental income will be sufficient to pay you the minimum monthly distribution and tax, without you having to sell the vacation rental. This in turn could then provide you with years of steady retirement income.

RULE: You never will get rich off your income. You will only get rich from your investments. Set up a system where your investment produces vacation rental income, that is then reinvested and diversified back into your IRA. This is how you build wealth.

Chapter 9

Should I use a real estate agent when

I buy the vacation rental?

You know the vacation destination as you have been going there your whole life. It is within driving distance of your home. You have stayed at the property many times. You have asked the requisite questions. You know the rental income numbers. You know the vacation rental is literally an ATM machine, so you are now ready to buy.

For first time vacation rental buyers, the most important thing you can do is to hire an experienced and local real estate agent to be your buyer's agent. What does this mean? How do I afford that?

When a seller lists their property, they typically list it through a real estate agent on a 6% commission, and the realtor then puts the listing on the Multiple Listing Service or MLS. This means that if the property is sold, the seller's real estate agent will get 6% of the purchase price, and the net then goes to the seller, after the mortgage and other costs are paid.

If there is not a buyer's agent, the seller's real estate agent will solely receive the full 6% commission.

If you have a buyer's agent, the seller's real estate agent then has to split that 6% commission with your agent, the buyer's agent, at no cost to you. It would absolutely be foolish to buy a property through a real estate agent without employing your own buyer's agent. It costs you nothing to have a buyer's agent. Their fee comes out of the sale proceeds and simply reduces the amount of commission the seller's agent would otherwise receive. In addition, the fee, or cost to the seller, is the same either way, so you are not prejudiced in any way by having a buyer's agent.

So why is having a buyer's agent so important?

First, the buyer's agent can save you time. Instead of looking up comps on similar sales prices in the past year, the agent does that for you. Instead of figuring out what the rental numbers are, the agent does that for you. Instead of coordinating visits and showings, your agent does that for you and can set up a half dozen showings in a day. Your time is valuable. Your agent will save you time. Use one.

Second, the agent is not emotionally attached. The agent will tell you based on comparable sales, market trends, and other factors what is or what is not a good offer. You cannot let emotion overcome reason when buying your dream vacation rental. Listen to your real estate agent's advice.

Third, the agent will know what boxes to check on the purchase and sale agreement and what concessions are typically available in the state and or region that the transaction is taking place. They will know whether it is customary for the seller to pay closing costs or the other way around. They will know how to draft the offer of purchase in such a manner as to allow you leeway to escape if something unexpected pops up on inspection, and still get your earnest money back.

Fourth, the agent will go to bat for you if the seller pulls some type of last-minute shenanigan. If the sales contract said, 'as shown,' and the seller at the last minute, tries to take with them the refrigerator and washer dryer set, your agent will firmly inform them that the contract will be enforced as written and that they do not have a leg to stand on. That is more forceful than you as an unrepresented buyer simply letting it slide, as you don't want to lose the purchase. The agent will help keep you from being unfairly taken advantage of.

Fifth, ask your realtor to attend closing with you. At a minimum, ask the realtor to look over the closing paperwork, well in advance of closing. It is a lot easier to negotiate or change the closing paperwork in advance, as opposed to trying to get it reprinted or adjusted when everyone is already at the table signing away. Get that closing paperwork done and reviewed in *advance* of closing. Get your agent to go over the closing paperwork, and if you have a lawyer friend, or an accountant friend, get them to review it too, as mistakes do happen.

RULE: Use a buyer's agent if the property is being sold through a realtor.

Chapter 10

What is the best way to buy a vacation rental

in a hot real estate market?

During COVID, cruise lines temporarily halted, and international travel plummeted. Demand for short term vacation rental housing within driving distance of major population areas around the country exploded. People were not cruising, not traveling internationally, and they wanted a place to themselves that was safe. Traditional hotels with enclosed shared hallways or indoor amenities were risky.

At the same time, the government stimulated the economy with an enormous amount of money, coupled with low interest rates, to supercharge the economy and get the country back on track. Housing prices soared accordingly, and unfortunately, a lot of other prices went up as well.

After you have decided upon the region you want to be in, or even the city, or resort, or housing community, visited there, researched everything that I have mentioned in this guide, and absolutely know exactly what you want, you then start watching the local MLS hot sheet. This list shows you the vacation rental properties being listed for sale on the day they are listed. You then watch for that specific condo or cabin or vacation rental that you hope gets listed for sale. Hopefully, you have already stayed in that resort or area, and know what you are looking for.

However, in a hot market, nearly every MLS listing quickly gets listed as 'pending.' The cabin or condo switches from available to pending typically within 24 hours of listing. One quickly realizes that one must be 'on go' and submit a written offer, typically higher than the list price. List price offers simply were not working. It was literally a bidding war. Forget visiting the property in advance. Forget contingencies of inspections and subject to financing. The seller in a hot market could pick and choose the best offer for them, as so many offers would come in on the first day. The seller would typically accept a (verified) cash offer, albeit subject to inspection, and for closing to occur in a short amount of time.

Such an expedited pace and completely blind approach places enormous risk on the buyer's shoulders, and in my opinion, is an extremely risky and expensive means to do business from the buyer's perspective.

What is the solution?

The short answer – contact the owner directly.

Simply go into the local online tax records, and find that cabin, or vertical stack of units (i.e., all of the condos in a Gulf front high rise in the '04' stack that are all 1 bedroom -104, 204, 304 etc.). You then look up the owner's name and their billing address listed in the tax records, and simply write them a letter, asking the owner if they want to sell.

After researching for nearly a year and weighing the pros and cons of buying a vacation rental along the Gulf Coast, or Orlando, or in the Rocky Mountains, the French Quarter, or Pigeon Forge, and actually visiting each of these locations, checking out rental revenues, and simple vacation rental logistics in each location, we narrowed down our search to a specific cabin development located near Pigeon Forge and Gatlinburg, Tennessee. As most cabins were very expensive, we focused on the smallest - the one-bedroom cabins.

We felt that this specific sized cabin in that development had the most 'bang for the buck' of anything we could find anywhere within driving distance of our home.

In the form letter to the owners, I simply introduced our family, and indicated that we were interested in purchasing a one-bedroom cabin in The Preserve. We wanted to negotiate directly with the owner and pay a fair and reasonable price, without the assistance of a realtor, potentially saving the seller a 6% commission. By avoiding that commission, the seller could potentially increase their net proceeds on sale – an alluring prospect.

The first response was from another owner, who also rented their cabin. He wanted us to stay in touch as it is good to have owners that know each other in the development. Yes, a promising beginning.

The second response was from a vacation rental property owner who told me how well their cabin does. Another promising response.

I then received a telephone call from an owner willing to sell.

This cabin owner was just about to list his Preserve cabin with a realtor for $475,000. I knew instantly that this was an extremely reasonable price for this cabin in a hot market. I contained my excitement and played it cool.

The owner liked the idea of saving the 6% commission and wanted the closing to occur after the New Year. I too did not feel the need to have an agent between us take a $28,500 plus commission out of the seller's pocket. We both agreed that since we were able to find each other without an agent, there was no need to get an agent now.

I know this recommendation is completely opposite from what I said in a previous chapter. Use a buyer's agent realtor if you are buying from an agent listed property sold through the MLS. You can skip having a real estate agent in the transaction and its accompanying commission if you and the seller can make a deal without a realtor's involvement. That's the difference.

During the call, I pulled up the vacation rental cabin, which was marketed online with breathtaking pictures and rented through a local vacation rental company. Pictures speak volumes. Within minutes of the call, I knew I had found a true gem.

After only minor negotiations, we landed at $455,000 for the cabin, as that would be the owner's gross amount, without the realtor commission, and was some $7,500 or more than he would have netted if he had listed through a realtor and got his full asking price. Boom. Win Win.

To seal the deal, he invited me up to stay in the cabin, for free. I was beside myself in gratitude. I reimbursed him for the cleaning fee, and even bought a nice bottle of wine for him and his wife. His rental agency squeezed me in between two existing rentals, as the cabin was booked solid with vacation rentals through the end of the year (another good sign). We both agreed that if a renter damaged anything between now and closing, we would simply work it out.

I found a simple form online for a Tennessee Offer of Purchase. We sat down on the picnic table outside the cabin, on a clear alpine sunny day, literally on top of a mountain, and signed off on our agreement.

Unlike other buyers submitting bids in a frenzied manner on nearby cabins sight unseen, I had the gift of time, and no other competition for this owner's attention. I could inspect every inch and get a professional to do the same for me. The peace of mind of knowing what you are getting into is a priceless feeling. The process was slow, deliberate, and methodical for both of us. There was no drama, and no disagreement. The process could not have been any more perfect.

RULE: Especially in a hot real estate market, contact the owner of the vacation rental directly, and you may just luck out.

SECTION II - CRITICAL TASKS TO COMPLETE WHILE THE PROPERTY IS PENDING

Chapter 11

What is the first thing I should do after my vacation rental goes under contract / is pending?

There are a lot of steps to take to transition the vacation rental from the prior owner to your own ownership. This list is not exhaustive, but hits the highlights of what, at a minimum, must be done during the time.

The first step is to immediately scour the existing online vacation rental listing on the property for occupancy and rates for the preceding year (if one exists). This information is priceless to you, as you will need it to set your rates for your first year of business. You do not want to underprice the vacation rental, but at the same time, not overprice it and end up with too much vacancy. The prior year's occupancy and rental rates will be instrumental to you in setting your own rates. Secure it. Print it off, and do not assume that the listing will remain up for long. As soon as the vacation rental agency of the seller realizes that you plan to self-manage the unit through VRBO and or Airbnb, they will likely remove it.

Secure permission from the seller for you to use the owner's existing photos of the vacation rental. Download and save those photos.

Secure (i.e., print it, copy, paste it, and save it) the language of the description of the property, the disclaimers, their logistics on the rental process, area attractions, resort amenities and other information in the description of the vacation rental. You could use that as a template or guide when creating your own vacation rental description. Don't recreate the wheel – stand on their shoulders and polish it up a little bit better.

RULE: Document the nightly rates and occupancy from at minimum, the past year from the prior owner's vacation rental management company and the seller's VRBO or Airbnb listing. This information will be instrumental in you setting your rates for your first year.

Chapter 12

Should I get a professional inspection?

Ideally, the best inspection you can complete is by you staying in the vacation rental for a few days between the time the property goes under contract, and before closing.

Let's go back to the Tennessee cabin example.

With plenty of time before closing, the owner allowed me to stay in the cabin and hire a professional inspector to survey the cabin. I literally spent hours going over every inch of the property.

The inspector focused on things that were outside my expertise or comfort zone – checking for termites, hidden defects, electrical or plumbing concerns, structural or foundation issues, bed bug infestations, getting up on the roof, inspecting crawl spaces, etc. It's the best couple hundred dollars one can spend – believe me.

Finding a material defect in the inspection process could allow a buyer to back out of the purchase and get the earnest money back. But this may be the opposite of what the buyer wants in a strong seller's market (when prices are going up). This is because when a dispute arises over inspection defects, the sale will be canceled, earnest money returned, and the property is then relisted for more than what was your agreed upon price.

In a seller's market, it may be tough for the buyer to get the seller to assist with paying for and or fixing any defects found in the buyer's inspection. The seller simply says, 'take it or leave it' and the buyer usually balks and buys it anyway with defects, as they do not want to lose the vacation rental and end up having to pay more for a different property.

In a buyer's market (where prices are dropping), finding a list of material defects is a boon or bonanza for the buyer. The seller very much wants to sell the property and they are faced with the potential risk the sale could fall through if they don't either reimburse the buyer for the defects or spend their own money remedying them. In view of that, the buyer should find as many things as possible that need fixing and let the seller fix them.

RULE: Always get a professional inspection before buying any vacation rental. If possible, try to visit the vacation rental immediately prior to closing as well.

Chapter 13

How do I quickly and affordably get my vacation rental up to the quality that I want?

As soon as the property is under contract, prepare a list of everything that you plan to fix, replace, or toss out. In doing so, you can shop without pressure and have everything assembled and ready to be put in the vacation rental immediately following closing, and all at once.

Focus on the obvious things. If something is broken, damaged or worn out, replace it. If something is in desperate need of updating, update it. However, everything does not have to be perfect. You want to get up and running. You will have time later to decorate to your own style, so don't overdo things right out of the gate. I would focus on spending a small amount of money on things that make a huge difference, rather than spending a lot of money on things that might not be noticed, if possible.

By inspecting the vacation rental, and preferably, staying in the vacation rental at least one or two nights between the time of offer of purchase and closing, compile the list of needed items on your phone, and add to the list throughout your stay as needed. You will reach a stopping point, and then you can go through the list and order everything off Amazon (or similar shopping source) all at one time. Do this early, so that you have plenty of time for everything to arrive and be sorted through. Do your best to stay out of crisis mode scrambling at the last minute to get needed items.

When the new items arrive, inspect them for accuracy and quality, and set them all aside for easy (preferably via your own car) transport to the vacation rental immediately upon closing, so that you get a lot done quickly, rather than constantly running back and forth to Walmart or a hardware store, prices of which, may or may not be as competitive as Amazon.

It is always convenient to have an owner's closet at a vacation rental, where you can store needed items such as bulbs, air filters, batteries, bottle openers, game supplies, bromine, or other supplies. The owner's closet will need a simple lock system for you, maintenance, and your cleaning team to access it as needed.

If your cleaning crew knows there are extra light bulbs sitting in a supply closet, it is a quick fix to replace the bulb with little or no hassle. If you do not have needed supplies on hand, and it requires a trip to the store every time something needs to be replaced, like a battery, bulb or air filter, then it's less likely to get timely serviced.

RULE: Prepare an initial inventory of things that absolutely have to be replaced or updated and cannot wait. Stock your owner's closet with replacement items such as bulbs, batteries, air filters, and other supplies that need routine replacement.

Chapter 14

Who pays for utilities?

Immediately contact all applicable utilities and set up the date for everything to be switched over to you, preferably within a day or two of closing. This process sometimes takes time.

For example, our previous cabin owner had to box up and ship back all their Xfinity equipment, and then we had to have Xfinity mail us the routers, remotes, and boxes, all of which took time. As our selling owner had his unit booked solid through the date of closing, this is yet another reason to block off the first two weeks, at minimum, from rental availability, so you can complete tasks like this that take time and logistics. As this was a standalone cabin, we also had to transfer over the power, water, sewer, and pest control.

However, at our beachfront condo, the HOA provided free cable as part of the HOA dues, as well as water, sewer, garbage, and pest control. The only utility we had to transfer over was power, a much simpler process than the cabin.

Depending upon the circumstances, transferring utilities immediately on or after closing sometimes takes time, so be patient.

RULE: Block off, at minimum, the first two weeks of ownership to allow time for utility transitions, improvements, and so forth.

Chapter 15

What is an HOA?

Beachfront vacation rentals and or vacation rental developments that share common areas typically have a Homeowners Association (HOA). The HOA collects dues, handles casualty insurance on the building, provides water, sewer, Wi-Fi, all resort amenities, and maintaining the common areas – the grounds, pools, and parking areas. Basically, everything outside the sheetrock of your condo is the HOA's responsibility. You will need to contact the HOA to set up payments to get the dues paid. They may send you a booklet with tear out sheets to mail in each month, or perhaps provide you with access to an online owner only portal for monthly payments.

The HOA also will provide you with resort rules that should be provided to each guest you have. Simply scan the HOA guest rules to a PDF file or ask the HOA to email them to you in PDF. You will need that PDF file later when you set up your email templates within your listing.

HOA rules can be as mundane as not hanging beach towels over the railing, to more serious rules, like no fireworks. If the guests know the rules, they are less likely to accidentally break a rule and run afoul of resort security, and thus, have a better vacation experience. Perhaps even print a summary of the HOA rules, laminate them, and post them in the vacation rental.

While communicating with the HOA, confirm the amount of the monthly HOA dues, and confirm that there are no declared, but not yet due, assessments coming down the pipeline after your closing. If there are, you need to work that issue out with the seller prior to closing.

For example, the HOA board declares that an assessment is due by all units in the resort, to help share the cost to renovate the exterior of the entire resort. Rather than requiring owners to pay it all at once, as some assessments can be substantial, the HOA then offers interest free payments over several years. So, the assessment has been declared, but is not yet due. You want to make sure the balance of that declared assessment is paid by the seller at closing, so that you do not then have to pick up the installments still pending on the financing of any given past assessment.

RULE: Always provide your guest a copy of the resort rules and have a laminated copy in your vacation rental. Informed guests are less likely to get in trouble with security, leading to a better vacation rental experience. Always confirm with the HOA the amount due monthly, and whether there are any declared, but not yet due, future assessments on the vacation rental that you are buying.

Chapter 16

What is the best way to handle guest parking?

If you have your own standalone vacation rental house, or cabin, then parking is typically on your own property. I would recommend a specific limit on the number of guest cars, to help prevent guest overcapacity.

To enforce that rule, I recommend some type of video camera or Ring doorbell system that is tied to your smart phone to keep an eye on the parking lot and disclose that to the guests. If guests know that parking is actively being watched by cameras, they are much less likely to try and have a party, exceed guest capacity limits, or sneak in pets.

A lot of vacation rentals rely on the resort parking garage for guest parking. This removes the control over guest parking from the owner's hands.

HOA's typically charge each vacation rental guest a parking fee. Typically, it is an income generating machine for the resort. Fortunately, most HOA's have a front desk on site to handle parking passes. When you set up your system to handle guest reservations, you will instruct the guest to simply visit the HOA desk upon arrival and pay for and secure their parking pass on site. The parking pass fee and process will need to be explained on your property description, in your acceptance email, and in your check in instructions. There is nothing worse than 'surprising' a vacation rental guest with fees and costs upon arrival that they were not aware of.

Disclose parking pass fees everywhere and often.

I do not recommend collecting the parking fee, and then somehow paying the HOA for each parking pass. That's too complicated. Stay out of the parking pass business. It is the guest's responsibility to pay for, secure, and display a parking pass. Do not get in a situation where you are in the middle of a dispute between a guest and the HOA over a parking issue. Simply provide the guest the contact information, how the process is handled, and stay out of it. If their car is booted due to their not having a parking pass, it is not your fault and is something outside your control. If the guest wants to bring a golf cart, or motorcycle, or motorhome or boat, simply give them the phone number of the HOA and you as the owner, stay out of it. Don't make any promises about something that is not within your control. Your job is to provide a nice place to sleep – that's it.

RULE: Never be the liaison between the HOA and your guest on resolving issues such as parking, boats, motorcycles, or motorhomes. Otherwise, when a glitch happens with the HOA, the guest will blame you, and will be looking for a refund or credit.

Chapter 17

What guest amenities should I include with stay?

As you plan for your vacation rental to be up and running, and accepting reservations within two weeks of closing, you need to go ahead and set up and secure all resort amenities in advance, so that they are 'on go' for the first guest.

Most of the time, the outdoor pools, slide, lazy river, indoor pools, gym, putting green, tennis courts and other amenities at a typical HOA run resort are all free to guests of the resort, if they secure a complimentary wristband from the front desk (who verifies that the guests are indeed staying in the resort).

However, on occasion, some amenities of the resort may require compensation separate from HOA dues for guests to be able to use the resort amenities.

For example, some beachfront condos have a beach chair and umbrella service. This is typically an outside vendor who contracts with the HOA for permission to conduct a service on the beach in front of the resort, and charge guests for their services. The HOA then gets a percentage of beach service revenues in return. The daily beach service fee may be roughly $35 per day plus tax. However, the beach service sells an annual pass for all guests of a vacation rental unit to use for around $1100 per year, significantly less than the daily rate if purchased piecemeal. This annual pass is a terrific selling point for your unit. Free beach chair and umbrella service included – a $35 per day value! This perk may be a significant decision between a guest booking your unit and another unit that does not include that service. Yes, it is an additional annual cost. However, I have always found that the increased rental revenues more than offset the additional cost, as you can then charge more per night, and you also have more bookings and or demand as a result.

On occasion though, a large percentage of other vacation rentals may also offer that same perk, which may put you in the position to do it simply to keep up with the competition in the resort. So that you don't stand out as the only unit who does include the perk with stay - a competitive disadvantage, you may have to include an amenity with the rental. Keep an eye out for that situation as well.

Whatever that additional guest amenity may be at your vacation rental, sign up and pay for it, and advertise the amenity on your listing. You want your guests to simply pay you up front for their stay, and then get to use all the amenities that the resort has to offer, even if that separate amenity results in you having to pay an annual subscription for it.

An example from our Tennessee cabin - the resort offers a mountain top pool, jacuzzi tub, pavilion, and fireplace, all with epic views. The photos of the pool, jacuzzi and fireplace pavilion overlooking the valley below were simply breathtaking. They also have a state-of-the-art gym, sauna, and steam room. Unlike most HOA's, the Preserve's amenities are only available if the cabin owner pays an additional annual fee, separate from minimum Preserve HOA dues, for their guests to use those amenities.

Researching other vacation rentals in the cabin development, I realized that very few other vacation rentals in the cabin development included those amenities with their stay. I quickly signed up for the annual amenity pass for all my guests. At this resort, providing those amenities to guests set our listing apart and was money well spent since so few other cabins included The Preserve's amenities with their guests' stay.

Also, I noticed in some of the reviews of my competition at the resort that their guests tried to access the pool in the development during the summer, only to be turned away. They had assumed that use of the pool was included with their stay, a reasonable assumption in this circumstance, as the pool and jacuzzi amenities were all in the middle of the cabin development. Those guests, whose owner had not signed up for the annual membership, not only were turned away, but there also wasn't even an option for them to pay a daily use fee, which was brutal.

We highlight in the description of our vacation rental listing that the resort amenities are included with the stay, on a complimentary basis, and warn the shopping guest that other cabins may not necessarily have similar access.

Here is a sample description in the VRBO listing from our Splash Resort beachfront unit in Panama City Beach, which tells guests this additional perk is complimentary and free with stay, a major perk that may separate our unit from the others that do not include beach chair service with stay:

FREE BEACH SERVICE, including two beach loungers, with cushions, small table and giant umbrella, for all stays in this unit between March 1 and October 31 - a $35 per day value!

Here is a sample description in the VRBO listing from Appalachian High, our vacation rental cabin in Pigeon Forge:

ALL PRESERVE RESORT AMENITIES INCLUDED WITH STAY: The Appalachian High cabin is in The Preserve, a high-end cabin resort community with first class guest amenities. Check out the mountain top huge outdoor pool and jacuzzi tub with amazing views of the Smoky Mountains (open approximately from Memorial Day to Labor Day each summer, weather permitting), a fitness center with steam room and sauna (open 24 hours), all of which are perched atop a mountain with incredible blue vistas of the Great Smoky Mountains National Park. The Preserve's guest amenities are complimentary for guests staying at 'Appalachian High.' Simply provide your cabin confirmation at the Hearthside front desk, located adjacent to the pool, for key code access to all resort amenities.

If you do spend that additional expense for an amenity that comparable vacation rentals may or may not do, then make sure that you 'toot your own horn' by listing that perk in your description, in your inquiry template response email, your template keycode email, and take lots of pictures of the amenities and include them in your listing with a description that it is free / complimentary with stay.

RULE: If an additional perk, amenity, or resort attraction is available to you on an annual rate, rather than having the guest having to pay a full daily use fee for it during their stay, pay for the annual cost and advertise it on your listing. Never skimp or skip guest amenities if they are otherwise available for a reasonable price. The included, complimentary amenity will more than offset the annual fee, as you will be able to charge a consistently higher nightly rate and get more bookings.

Chapter 18

How to take great photos, and sequence them for success.

As you want to be able to make your VRBO or Airbnb listing go public within minutes of the closing papers being signed, you will need to go ahead and secure photos of the vacation rental, resort amenities, and area attractions. You will need, at a minimum, no less than 50 high quality photos for your vacation rental listing. As discussed in an earlier chapter, you may have already downloaded or copied all the photos from a prior VRBO or Airbnb listing, or the previous owner may have photos that were provided to you incidental to the sale of the property.

The bulk of these photos will not be the final photos, as you plan to replace dated furnishings, remove clutter, update quilts and spreads, update flooring, paint, and replace artwork immediately following closing.

Remember, these are temporary photos, which are designed to simply be an overview of the property and get you by until you finish all your improvements after closing.

If you plan to photograph the unit yourself, in lieu of using the photos from the old VRBO or Airbnb listing, I recommend that you use an updated iPhone equipped with a wide-angle lens, or a comparable Android should be sufficient to get you by, at least temporarily.

When taking the photos, the vacation rental will need to be in a presentable rental ready condition – beds made, fresh towel sets placed out, vacuumed, spotless bathrooms, a clean kitchen and so forth.

At this point, you simply keep the furnishings that are there - furniture, paint color and appliances that exist, the existing flooring - as these photos simply need to get you through from when the listing goes live on the date of closing, and through the first few weeks.

After you get the vacation rental updated to your satisfaction during the time following closing - fresh paint, new furnishings, new artwork, new flooring, etc., you will then hire a professional photographer to photograph the unit <u>after</u> you have made 95% of your improvements, including major renovations, if needed. The same photographer may also be able to make a couple minute video, or virtual tour as well.

Until the professional shots are ready, you will still need photos to get by. Let's assume that either the prior listing photos are so poor that you are embarrassed to use them, or perhaps, the vacation rental has never been rented before, so photos may not be available, or you are not allowed to even use the photos used to advertise the property for sale.

Before personally photographing the vacation rental, follow these suggestions.

1   Vacation rental must be in its 'rental ready' condition.

2   All toilet seats should be down.

3   Games should be on / lit up.

4   The pool table racked and ready for play.

5   Every light in the entire vacation rental should be on.

6   The hot tub water should be clear and clean, not foamy.

7   Hide the cumbersome hot tub cover and do not include those in the photos. Do the same with an outdoor grill cover, or a pool table cover, or other protective type items. Why would you want a picture of an outdoor grill in your listing that has a giant tarp over it?

8   The mirrors and glass should be sparking clean.

9   There should be no fingerprints on the stainless appliances.

10 Every shade should be open for as much natural light as possible.

11 All ceiling fans should be off.

12 No bulbs should be burned out.

13 All shower curtains and shower doors should be open.

14   The more spacious one can make the photo, the better.

15   Visible vacuum lines should be present on the carpet – not footprints.

16   No personal items should be in any of the photos. It needs to be void of any personal items - especially your toiletries, suitcases, groceries, drinks, clothes, dirty towels, or dirty dishes.

The vacation rental needs to appear in the photos as it would appear when a guest checks in.

For interior photos, it may be best to use the wide angle setting to capture as much of the room as possible. Back yourself as close as possible to the walls, or corners, making the room look as big as possible, from a typical adult height vantage point, and take the photo.

Periodically, clean the camera lens of fingerprints, smudges or streaks, a common oversight.

You should also take photographs on a 'blue bird' or super sunny, bright, and blue-sky day, for the best views, and the best light for the vacation rental. Yes, timing is difficult. This is why it would be helpful if you stayed in the vacation rental prior to closing over a few days, so you can catch the perfect light for great photos at varied times and under varying conditions during your stay. For instance, the view at noon may be great, but the view at sunset may be spectacular, so take a variety of shots.

As most guests already know the area, you do not need many shots of area attractions. Nevertheless, secure a photo of the top five tourist draws to the area. Make sure they present the most ideal perfect day for the visit. Carpe Diem – Seize the Day! Take a break and enjoy a day in the city of your vacation rental destination taking photos of the top five major attractions. However, pick a good day to do it.

For instance, a rainy, cloudy dark day of a shoulder-to-shoulder gridlocked pedestrian sidewalk, and vehicle gridlocked Gatlinburg main street, may not be the best photo to use. Likewise, cloudy, cold, or rainy-day photos of the beach are not recommended.

You will also need to secure photos of resort amenities, such as the pool, gym, lazy river, beach chair and umbrella service, or any other vacation rental amenity. Again, you are trying to portray the best possible scenario for a guest's use of these amenities. Minimal crowds. Sunny skies. Organized. Clean. Well maintained.

If you bought a beach condo during the winter, it may be a few months before you get the ideal pool and beach photos, but eventually, you need to secure stellar amenity photos at some point during your first year of ownership, at minimum.

Yes, absolutely. Use filters. Artificially brighten every photo. At minimum, use the 'auto' enhance iPhone function for every photo that you take. The photos will be brighter and have more pop than a photo without being digitally enhanced. Use every available technology that you know how to use to create the most incredible photos ever. Note though, overdoing the enhancements could backfire, so the enhancements need to be subtle, and not too obvious.

Most of your photos will be of the vacation rental itself. The photos should be arranged with the first photos being the main driver of guests to the vacation rental – the amazing view for instance. The photos then go to the living areas, balcony areas, exterior, kitchen, dining, game room, then follow with the sleeping accommodations - master bedroom and bath, guest bedroom and bath. Finish the rental photos with technical photos, such as the washer and dryer, appliances, parking, closets etc.

The 50 photos should capture, in a photo sequence, the entire vacation rental interior, then exterior, then the resort or neighborhood, then resort amenities, and then finally, at least the top 5 area attractions, all in that general sequential order.

A good way to think about how to order the photos is by putting them in the same sequence that a guest would experience your vacation rental during any given stay. The guest does not typically go straight to the beach upon arrival. They first go to the vacation rental to get situated, and then head down to the beach or start enjoying amenities.

The photo carousel will thus start with breathtaking views from the balcony. It then highlights the living area, kitchen, dining area, and then moves to the bedrooms, followed by the baths. Technical photos of the washer and dryer, the grill, rollaway, and other useful items are last.

The photo carousel then moves to resort amenities (that are closest to the vacation rental), and then finishes with the top five general attractions in the area.

This sequence is designed for the guest to subconsciously map out their stay while they go through your camera carousel. They are then 'picturing' each experience, associated with each photo, so it needs to be a coherent chronological 'story' for the guest to follow as they work sequentially through your camera carousel.

I dare say that 99% of guests will make their decision to book with you or not after they have gone through your photo carousel just one time.

Remember, the prospective guest always goes through the photos, even before they read the description. **The photos are probably the most important selling point of your convincing a prospective renter to choose your vacation rental over all the rest.** If you do not have a good camera, or smart phone with a good camera, buy an updated one and expense it.

Ultimately, when you hire a professional photographer, and they come out and shoot your vacation rental after you get it all redone to your satisfaction, you can then cherry pick the best of the two batches.

For instance, you may have an amazing sunset photo from the balcony that your professional photographer was not able to take due to their brief, midday shoot, or whatever given time of the day their photography shoot appointment was scheduled.

Where do you find a professional photographer?

Ask your real estate agent if they have one. If not, call several area real estate companies and ask them who they use for their MLS photos. The expense for professional photography is money well spent. Hire a professional whose primary job or occupation is to take high quality MLS shots – not just a friend or neighbor with a fancy phone or camera.

If possible, get the professional photographer to also take photos of the resort amenities, and perhaps see if they have some stock photos of the region's top tourist destinations. With a large batch of photos from both what you took originally prior to closing, and what the professional shot after you finished all your improvements and or renovations, you should then end up with some great photos.

If the professional photographer can also shoot a short three-minute promotional video, do it. It's worth its weight in gold too. We will explain how to add a video to your vacation rental listing later.

Your beachfront condos pretty much show an endless summer, as it doesn't get that cold in Florida, and your resort has heated pools. However, if your vacation rental is in Tennessee or the Rocky Mountains, you may have to dedicate more photos to showing the resort amenities in different seasons – summer and winter.

For instance, the fall leaves in Tennessee are a major attraction to that area around Thanksgiving, so include a variety of seasonal photos as well.

For your ski in and ski out condo, photos of snow, ski lifts and snow skiing would be essential, but also include summertime photos of hiking and mountain biking, and perhaps some photos of the leaves changing colors as well.

Even after you have completed all your renovations, hired a photographer, and gotten to the point that you have 50 of the most amazing photos on the planet, you may need to do more.

On no less than an annual basis, peruse your competition's photos for vacation rentals in the same resort. If their photos are better than yours, it's time to redo them. You *must* have the best photos of any listing for the resort. It's that important.

When a guest states in their review of your vacation rental that they loved the vacation rental, and it was exactly as shown by the photos, you are doing it right.

RULE: Photos will make or break your vacation rental and are the single most important selling point for prospective renters. Your photos must be dramatically better than your competition. Hire a professional. Buy a great camera. Do whatever it takes to have amazing, bright, sunny photos that absolutely showcase your vacation rental in a variety of seasons. Your photos need to depict what appears to be a slice of heaven at any given time of year. They also need to be updated whenever the vacation rental is updated, so that the pictures match the latest décor or look.

Chapter 19

Should I secure pest control? Does standard pest control prevent bed bugs?

Most HOAs provide monthly pest control, which may or may not include bed bug control. Standard pest control services typically do not include monitoring for and treating bed bugs.

If bed bug control is not included, I recommend that you see if you can find a local bed bug control specialist who can periodically inspect for bed bugs. Bed bug services typically have a specially trained K-9 dog that can detect bed bugs quickly and pinpoint their exact location. The specially trained K-9 is well worth the $12,000 purchase price for this type of specialty animal. You simply get a subscription for periodic bed bug inspections, and or preventative treatment, akin to a standard pest control company.

Fortunately, the bed bug inspection team is low key, and arrives in unmarked vehicles, for obvious reasons. You do not want any type of stigma or suspicion out there that your vacation rental may have bed bugs. Indeed, the preventative inspection for bed bug monitoring should be done when the cabin is vacant. Imagine staying somewhere and in comes a K-9 looking around for bed bugs. That would freak anyone out.

Also, go ahead and purchase the expensive bed bug protectors that are waterproof but not crinkly, and zip in and Velcro shut the entire mattress and box spring. Yes, it is expensive to have a $75 bed bug proof mattress protector on every bed and box spring, but it's worth it. Place on top of the zipped bed bug protector an inexpensive, standard cotton bed protector that can easily be removed, washed and or bleached by your cleaning crew on an 'as needed' basis. Sometimes the inexpensive bed protector gets stained, and you just throw it away, so don't spend a lot of money on the bed protectors placed on top of the zipped in full mattress bed bug protector.

The zipped in bed protector will not prevent a bed bug from crawling out of a guest suitcase and into your vacation rental – that is something that is impossible to ever prevent. But what it will do is make it easier to spot the bed bugs if they get into your unit, and in turn, get rid of them, as there will be less places for bed bugs to hide (as the entire mattress and box spring will be encased leaving few spaces for bed bugs to hide).

If you are buying a standalone cabin or home, you will likely need to handle pest control for both standard pests like spiders, scorpions and or roaches, and then a separate service specifically for bed bugs.

Go ahead and contact several area reputable pest control services to come out to the property, before you close, to inspect for termites and bed bugs, and to give you a quote for termite control for both types of pests.

Most pest control companies are willing to come out for free, and confirm the absence of an active termite issue, and then offer you a termite bond and monthly pest control, which would commence after you close.

If during this free process, which you arrange to happen before closing, termites are discovered, you would cancel the purchase agreement, get your earnest money back, and look for a different vacation rental.

The same scenario may happen if your bed bud inspector found bed bugs in the vacation rental you were purchasing. If you find bed bugs in the vacation rental you are purchasing, this may be the reason why the sellers are selling. Their rental history may also show where prior guests had an issue, so the reputation of the location may be tarnished, and may be a serious reason to consider backing out of the deal. Further, bed bug treatments can cost thousands of dollars, which you would want the seller to pay for, a significant expense which may derail the sale of the vacation rental.

So, take advantage of that inspection and get a quote for termite control, pest control, and bed bug control. Get it done prior to closing so that if an issue is found, you can then exit the purchase and get your earnest money back, depending upon what is found.

Yes, pest control is essential.

A guest texted me directly (thankfully and not through a review), that she spotted a tiny mouse running across our kitchen floor in our newly purchased cabin. It was not a big deal to her, and she just wanted me to know. I immediately contacted our pest control service, and they came out, set traps, and got rid of them, or at least we thought we did.

Several months later, the stove stopped working. Lowe's came out with a replacement and discovered a burned-up mouse inside the stove on the electrical panel. The mouse could literally have caused a fire and burned our cabin down. It was that close. The pest control company came back out again.

Now, the pest control company treats for mice preventatively, instead of after a complaint, and so the mice are thankfully no longer around. Some pest control services also preventatively treat for bed bugs. If that is available, it's worth every penny.

There is a new bed bug product out that is very expensive and must be kept cold prior to application and is only available to licensed bed bug pest control outlets. It is called Apprehend, and it is a product applied directly to bed frames and is effective for three months.

Apprehend is about the only preventative bed bug product on the market today that works. Apprehend causes the bed bugs to get a skin fungus and die. Bed bug powder products and sprays do not work, unless they happen to be applied directly to a bed bug, which is nearly impossible to do. This is why Apprehend is so effective, as it is applied to the bed frame and when the bed bug touches it, it gets a skin fungus and then dies.

Taking these steps for bed bug prevention and detection are a small price to pay compared to the potential liability if a guest is bitten. If this happens, the cost of refund, cleaning, and or damage that a bed bug related review could do to your business needs to be avoided under all circumstances.

For the vacation rentals where pest control is provided by the HOA, you simply list the HOA phone number in the guest's paperwork to contact them if there is a pest control issue. This helps prevent getting the midnight text from a guest that there is a dead roach on the floor and wanting to know how you plan to address the issue. Simply put in your paperwork that pest control is handled by the HOA and provide them the telephone number.

Monthly pest control is provided by the HOA. In the exceptionally rare case of a pest control issue, please contact xxx-xxx-xxxx for assistance.

This disclaimer immediately reduces or eliminates a guest complaining to you directly about a roach they found in the vacation rental. Renters are freaked out about spiders, bugs, or roaches so make sure you do everything you can to make sure they are dealt with accordingly on a routine preventative basis.

If you have a standalone house, or standalone vacation rental cabin, put in your paperwork the contact information for the pest control company, which typically has free follow-ups and remedial measures if there is a pest control issue:

Monthly pest control is provided by ABC Pest Control. In the exceptionally rare case of a pest control issue, please contact xxx-xxx-xxxx for assistance.

This process removes you from getting in the middle of the issue. You simply directly connect the guest to the pest control company and try and stay out of it.

If a guest alerts you to a bed bug issue, this is a much more serious situation. Fortunately, a bed bug issue is very rare, but can and does happen sporadically for anyone in the lodging business. We will talk about how to handle a bed bug issue more when dealing with issues that may arise after you are up and running.

RULE: Make sure you have pest control in place for your vacation rental, and preventively and proactively do everything you can to prevent and or to detect a bed bug issue.

Chapter 20

What type of casualty insurance

do I need for my vacation rental?

Most vacation rentals have an HOA that provides casualty insurance on the building, which is paid for through your monthly HOA dues, and is typically, one of the larger expenses of the HOA.

Your mortgage company will want confirmation that the HOA has casualty insurance and will require that you provide an annual certificate showing that there is coverage in place.

Our Splash Resort HOA provides casualty insurance on the beachfront resort. The insurance is paid for through our monthly HOA dues.

When Hurricane Michael hit Panama City Beach, our Splash Resort HOA simply assessed each unit what it took to pay the hurricane deductible (around $1,500 per unit). The insurance company was then responsible for nearly $10,000,000 (ten million) dollars in hurricane related repairs to the resort. The entire building exterior ended up being completely redone (the resort now looks brand new). Compared to so many other properties who were devastated by Hurricane Michael, we were very fortunate, in part, due to the HOA having excellent insurance, and hiring smart adjusters to negotiate the adjustment of the massive claim.

If you are purchasing a standalone vacation rental, cabin, or beachfront home, you will need your own separate casualty insurance. If you finance your vacation rental, casualty insurance is required, and the mortgage company added as a loss payee. The casualty insurance, as well as property taxes, are both then paid by your mortgage company through your escrow account.

If you pay cash for your vacation rental (the preferred alternative), casualty insurance is not required, but it would be foolish not to protect your cash investment.

A fire started in a community adjacent to our cabin, and burned for nearly a week, destroying hundreds of cabins.

I could see the burning woods from my Ring Doorbell camera in the distance each night. It was one of the most sleepless weeks in my entire life.

The only consolation was that I had full coverage on both the cabin and personal property. Due to favorable wind currents, the fire only came within a mile of our development, and we were spared. Several hundred other cabins in the same valley though, were not as fortunate.

Whether it is hurricanes along the beaches, forest fires in the mountains, or a tornado that comes through the lake regions, there are multiple casualty risks that you need to insure against, if your vacation rental is not otherwise covered by an HOA casualty insurance.

Recent reports suggest that approximately ninety percent of US counties suffered a weather disaster between 2011 and 2021.

In view of such risks, I recommend that you secure multiple casualty insurance quotes from reputable, A+ or higher rated insurance companies. Surprisingly, the prices and what is or is not covered in the respective policies vary wildly.

Also, focus on securing the type of insurance that rebuilds your property up to $5 million or a higher amount, versus insuring just the current value of your vacation rental. This helps ensure that your vacation rental can be rebuilt, no matter how much materials may cost when the casualty event occurs.

RULE: Make sure your vacation rental is fully insured in the event of a fire, hurricane, or other natural disaster.

Chapter 21

Should I get homeowner's insurance or form an LLC to shield myself from liability?

A terrific perk of having guests rent through VRBO is that the service provides $1M of liability insurance coverage for guest injuries on property, if the reservation was booked and paid for through the VRBO platform. If a guest is injured, the VRBO policy will cover the injury claim and the insurance will defend you from the lawsuit.

The VRBO policy also covers a guest negligently causing damage to another unit. For instance, the guest leaves the tub running in your high-rise vacation rental, and floods multiple units below. The VRBO coverage would cover the damage caused by the renter's negligence as well.

Airbnb, or other independent websites offering vacation rental services, may or may not offer similar liability insurance with every booking through their platform. If they do not, I feel that having that available $1M liability coverage is a huge benefit of going with VRBO over the others. That liability coverage is that important.

However, you should not rely solely on the $1M in liability coverage that VRBO provides, and then skip traditional homeowner's insurance on your vacation rental (to save money).

Indeed, you may have an 'off the books' stay at your condo, such as a family member or friend staying last minute, long term, or you have a multi-month annual snowbird staying during the winter, all of whom may not have necessarily booked through VRBO. Therefore, the $1M VRBO liability coverage would not apply to them, as their stay was not booked through VRBO.

As such, it is important to secure homeowner's insurance to cover an accidental injury of a guest at the vacation rental, who may be there even though they did not book through VRBO, and in turn, would not be covered by that VRBO policy, leaving you exposed to potential personal injury liability.

Further, if one reads the fine print of the VRBO $1M liability policy, it is a co-insurance policy with an owner's homeowner's policy and co-contributes with that owner's policy to cover a claim.

If you don't have that homeowner's policy, and the VRBO policy solely handles the guest liability claim, the VRBO policy administrator then charge a 25% deductible on any given damage claim – which can be a considerable amount of money if the liability claim is substantial. You want your own homeowner's insurance working with the VRBO insurance 'tag teaming' the defense of any liability claim, and equally paying a settlement or judgment, if necessary, without you having to pay a substantial deductible for the coverage.

The homeowner's insurance would not only supply the requisite liability insurance if a guest were injured on the premises and defend any claims brought against you but may typically also have additional coverages for loss of contents or lost rental income in the event of a natural disaster, fire, loss, or theft. These are additional reasons to secure a homeowner's insurance policy.

Remember this though – it is critical that you inform your insurance agent that you are renting the property through VRBO and or Airbnb. Make sure your insurance agent knows that they are insuring a vacation rental, not just an ordinary residence, or second home, as some homeowner's policies cover vacation rentals while others don't. It is not a standard homeowner's policy. The policy must include coverage for guests staying in your vacation rental.

The premium for the insurance coverage is not cost prohibitive, as the HOA is covering the casualty insurance on the building. The separate homeowner's policy that you secure is only covering personal liability, and (usually) not the casualty side of coverage, therefore the premium is significantly lower than it otherwise would be. Since it is so affordable, you should get it.

If it is a standard homeowner's policy where you provide casualty insurance for the cabin or structure, then simply make sure the policy also includes coverage for renters staying in your vacation rental.

In sum, you should always have several layers of liability insurance for a guest injury, just in case it may happen, and happen unexpectedly, even despite all our best intentions.

Some may chime in at this point that one should put their vacation rental in an LLC for protection against liability, in order to shield an owner from guest lawsuits. I disagree.

An LLC stands for Limited Liability Company. A limited liability company is a hybrid form of business organization that combines the benefits of pass-through tax status (no double taxation), like how a partnership is taxed, with the limited liability aspects of a corporation. One could quickly, easily, and inexpensively form an LLC in their home state, and then place the vacation rental property in the LLC name, rather than their own personal name. The purpose would be to shield the member / owner of the LLC from personal liability, or liability beyond the amount of their investment in the LLC / vacation rental.

However, simply because you form an LLC and put the vacation rental in the LLC name, does not mean that you will have insurance to cover a claim, or that anyone will step up to defend the liability claim for you (i.e., where an adjuster, and eventually a team of attorneys step in to defend you).

In addition, an LLC incurs expenses of formation, annual privilege taxes, company formalities to follow, and additional annual tax returns. That initial and annual expense would be better spent on insurance, not an LLC.

If you nevertheless put the property in an LLC, you still need to hire an attorney to defend any type of liability claim. If you don't have homeowner's insurance, then you would need to personally hire an attorney to defend the renter's claim(s) against you and your LLC. Your LLC would then have to pay any settlement or judgment entered. You are not versed in the defense of lawsuits. You do not have 'reserves' laying around to pay an unexpected settlement or judgment. This is what insurance is for. It would be better if your insurance company covered liability claims and the defense thereof – not you or your LLC at your own expense.

The best way to defend against a liability claim is to have insurance, which would then pay an adjuster or attorney to defend you against any liability claim, and pay a liability claim if deemed appropriate.

Rather than forming an LLC and putting your property in the name of the LLC, simply use what you would have spent on an LLC and pay for and secure homeowner's liability insurance sufficient to cover any liability claims and be responsible for the defense thereof. Investing in liability insurance will help you sleep at night.

There is yet another reason not to put a vacation rental in the name of your LLC.

I am not a tax professional and cannot give tax advice.

However, several accountants have advised me at various times over the years to not hold a vacation rental property in an LLC due to the negative tax consequences when it comes time to sell the vacation rental.

In addition, the property tax may be higher if it is in an LLC instead of being held in someone's individual name. I have had owners hire me to move their vacation rental out of an LLC name and into their sole names, because of property tax reasons.

Finally, the long-term net tax downside of having a vacation rental in an LLC versus the vacation rental being held in one's own sole name(s) is yet another reason for not putting your vacation rental in an LLC.

Yes, there are times where it is appropriate to put a property in an LLC, perhaps when you have non-immediate family members or a group of investors owning a vacation rental together, or you have a situation where each vacation rental owner has a disproportionate interest in the ownership of the vacation rental. For instance, one member will contribute and own 70% of the vacation rental and the other member only 30%.

If that is the case, or there is ever a situation where the ownership interest in the vacation rental is anything other than dividing the interest equally among all persons involved, one must put the vacation rental in the LLC and have a fully executed and detailed operating agreement. The operating agreement would detail the varying ownership interests in the LLC, which owns the vacation rental. All vacation rental income and expenses, and net proceeds of eventual sale, are then divided according to the percentages as listed in the LLC operating agreement.

Remember, unless there is a written agreement to the contrary, ownership of a deeded property with multiple owners is presumed equal, unless specifically disclaimed in writing. The same is true for an LLC. The members own an equal interest unless the operating agreement says otherwise.

So yes, an LLC would be appropriate when you have multiple non-immediate family members or disproportionate ownership interests.

Even if the LLC is used as a vehicle to hold the vacation rental, still get homeowner's insurance.

RULE: Secure multiple layers of overlapping insurance coverage to cover a guest injury at your vacation rental, rather than trying to shield yourself from liability by putting the vacation rental in an LLC. Remember that the $1M in renter's insurance through VRBO only works for guests who booked through VRBO and is a co-insurance plan to be coupled with your own separate homeowner's insurance policy.

Chapter 22

Should I self-manage my vacation rental

or hire a rental manager to handle it for me?

You will need to decide whether you plan to turn your vacation rental over to a management company and allow them to market, rent out and handle all the logistics of your vacation rental, or rather, handle the entire vacation rental yourself.

Should you use a professional rental manager for your first year?

The short answer is that you should manage it yourself.

If you can manage it yourself, and follow all my suggestions in this book, then you will likely gross two or three times the amount of rental revenues than if you had a rental manager taking care of your property.

How do I know this? Let me explain.

Early in our experience, we had never bought a vacation rental before out of state. We took the plunge and bought a unit outside our home state at Splash Resort, in Panama City Beach Florida. Splash has a two tower, 21 story Gulf front resort directly on the beach, with a giant parking garage across the street, accessed by a skybridge. The resort boasts an onsite kid's waterpark, lazy river, pools, and the beautiful sugar white sands that Panama City Beach is famous for.

Rather than renting it myself, as it seemed to be a daunting task, and out of the secret hope that by having a vacation rental manager handle it for me, that it would make more money than if I handled it myself, we initially went with a rental management company.

The onsite vacation rental company, which had a desk in the lobby, was open 24 hours, and had the most units under their management than any other rental management company at Splash. They seemed to be the best fit, as they had an office right in the resort, and had so many vacation rentals under management.

The rental management company would handle all reservations. They would pay the lodging taxes. They would handle the website. They would take the photos. They handled the guests. They took care of the cleaning. They did everything. I simply could sit back and do nothing and wait for my net rental income check to occasionally appear in my mailbox. It sounded very appealing, so we decided to use them, at least for the first year.

Our first task was to purchase all the items that they had in their inventory checklist – sufficient pots and pans, dishes, silverware, fire extinguisher, vacuum, coffee pot, extra air filters, and so forth. Easy enough. As we were new to the vacation rental concept, this guidance was helpful.

If we wanted to block off the unit, and come and stay, we simply called their front desk, and the staff would block off the time we wanted to stay. That was easy and convenient too. Upon arrival, they would generate a door code for us to use during our stay – simple enough.

We also were provided with a monthly accounting. They charged around 30% of revenue for their vacation rental management services, and multiple other service fees, which seemed endless, but let's not digress.

During that first year, it seemed like every month, there was some management expense that kept eating away at the few bookings we were receiving.

I also monitored the bookings on the online calendar, and it seemed that our unit was consistently not being booked, or was vacant, when most other units at Splash were booked. Out of 200 units, 70 or 80 percent were booked, while ours sat empty.

I also noticed that the rates set by the management company were static, even when last minute, set months ahead of time and never changed, leading to a dramatic nightly rate gap versus owner managed condos who discounted their rate last minute.

Stated simply, our unit was not being booked as it was way overpriced compared to comparable units in the resort. The rates appeared to have been set by the management company, and then never changed. The 'over pricing' worked great when everything sold out during June and July, but for the rest of the year, our unit was typically empty.

We ended up grossing around $25k that first year, with the bulk of that income coming from just June and July – our two peak summer months. The net income was nearly non-existent, having nearly all been eaten up in management fees, cleaning fees, dues, maintenance fees, and so forth.

The following year we switched to self-managed and listed our unit through VRBO. I created our listing and handled the reservations myself. I basically did everything that I am telling you to do in this book. I secured a dependable cleaning team from a recommendation of another owner in the resort, hired the onsite maintenance team to a yearly contract, and never looked back.

The first year I self-managed, we more than doubled gross revenues. The unit now makes no less than $60k per year – a huge difference from the $25k gross from the 'professionally managed' first year of business.

In addition, the amount of time that it took me to self-manage the unit was minimal - an hour a week at the most. Again, I will teach you how to do this in this book. It can be done.

I strongly recommend that you self-manage your unit, rather than farming it out through a rental management company. I firmly believe that no one can market, sell, and fill your vacation rental better than you, the owner.

While the rental management company worked 9-5, you could be busy answering inquiries at 8 o'clock at night.

Yes, it would at first glance seem that managing your own vacation rental would be a time-consuming thing to do, but with vacation rental apps, the latest technology, and automation, and if you follow the rules of this book, you can literally manage a $60k per year vacation rental on just an hour a week. I kid you not. This book will teach you how to do that.

RULE: As long as you follow the rules in this book, and set up the system as I suggest, I firmly believe that a self-managed vacation rental will likely make substantially more rental income than using a management company. With automation, a vacation rental app, and technology, you can manage a vacation rental property on an hour or less a week (after the initial system is set up).

Chapter 23

If I self-manage my vacation rental, should I use VRBO, Airbnb, an Independent, or a combination of all of them?

Years ago, well before being bought out by Expedia, VRBO started off as one of the first and most well-known privately owned online vacation rental resources, which organized listings not only in the area, but also into vacation rental resorts. The platform made it easy to find the condo resort where they wanted to stay. It then listed all the units within that resort for easy comparisons on price and quality.

Initially, VRBO charged owners a flat yearly fee, and connected the guest with the owner, and payment for the stay was made independently of the platform. Most owners simply accepted checks while others had their own credit card machine for their vacation rental.

Later, VRBO started offering different levels of yearly membership. The higher the flat fee paid (around $1500 per year), the more likely the vacation rental would end up at the top of the search results. You could buy a gold, silver, or bronze membership, and depending upon which one you got, would determine where your listing landed in the vacation resort's search results. Just like Google search results, it is best to be on or near the top of that list for best results.

VRBO was bought and sold several times and is now owned by Expedia and is one of the most popular vacation rental platforms on the market today.

VRBO now charges a flat yearly fee for an owner to list their vacation rental on their platform, currently around $500.

VRBO now handles all credit card transactions for reservations.

The VRBO platform is incredibly efficient to use for those who wish to self-manage their vacation rentals. I now self-manage all four of our vacation rentals from the VRBO app, and spend only a few hours each week, at the most, handling all four vacation rentals. With practice, one can literally manage a single vacation rental in well under an hour each week, no matter how busy it gets.

Airbnb is a similar online vacation rental resource, and like VRBO, has an online calendar, a reservation system, and handles all guest payments. They too have an owner phone app which makes things easy for the owner to market and manage their vacation rental.

The biggest difference between VRBO and Airbnb is that VRBO offers standalone vacation rental homes or condos only, while Airbnb offers shared spaces and hotel rooms, in addition to vacation rental homes.

From a marketing standpoint, VRBO seems to attract guests who are wanting to book a vacation rental house or beachfront condo.

Airbnb seems to be more eclectic. It's a shared room in the French Quarter, treehouse along the river, hotel room, or a Seattle houseboat – something a little bit more unique than a cookie cutter condo resort on the beach. The type of property alone may steer you into one platform or the other, regardless of which one seems better than the other.

Finally, state based, or regional based mom and pop managed online vacation rental systems are available as well. Typically, the owner pays an annual fee, and they get their listing, with a calendar and so forth, lots of photos. Some sites assist with online payment processing, while others do not. I have seen some owners move away from both VRBO or Airbnb, as they wanted that direct connection with the guest, and get VRBO out of handling 'their money.' Some of the independents may have phone apps, while others don't. I could not imagine using a service that does not have a solid phone app to handle the vacation rentals. I have also yet to see any of these independent services market like VRBO or Airbnb - a huge disadvantage.

In the end, every single vacation rental owner that moved away from VRBO or Airbnb, came back. No site fills the calendar like VRBO and Airbnb.

I prefer VRBO over Airbnb as the phone app makes the entire listing process super easy (you can create your entire VRBO listing on your phone in under an hour). VRBO also makes the reservation system fully automated. They process the money and provide easy summarized accountings. Finally, the efficiency of the phone app is simply stellar.

I did try Airbnb for a cookie cutter typical beachfront condo.

Like VRBO, I created the Airbnb online listing easily, and appreciated the gigantic, sensual photos, and 'sophisticated feel' of the listing. Admittedly, the look and feel of the listing was 'chic' when compared to the more 'functional' VRBO listing.

I then integrated the calendars of both VRBO and Airbnb so that if I have received a booking on one service, the calendar would show that stay blocked on the other, to avoid double bookings.

That was cool.

However, I learned a couple things, some of which are not necessarily Airbnb's fault, and other things that were major issues that may have been updated since the time I was on Airbnb's platform, so let's give that service the benefit of doubt.

First, nearly 80% of my business came from VRBO versus Airbnb, despite providing the same description, and the same photos and same nightly rates on both listings. VRBO brought me a ton more reservations than Airbnb. Again, this was for a 'cookie cutter' Gulf front condo, not an eclectic treehouse, or luxury campsite.

Second, each Airbnb reservation took at least an hour of my time to process from beginning to end. In contrast, VRBO has readily accessible and customizable email templates that are built into the app. These are fully customizable email forms that once created, can be reused easily with every guest with a click of a button on the app. All guest emails are then saved under the guest's reservation, as they are sent and received within the app.

At the time (as this was several years ago), Airbnb did not have a similar email template system within their app for me to set up and use, so I had to find time to sit down on my laptop or desk top computer, transfer over the guest's email, dates of stay, and so forth, and then open a couple of windows, copy and paste, and create from scratch all guest correspondence, and their accompanying attachments, for every reservation, and then send the guest correspondence through my Gmail account.

The record of stay and correspondence was then not preserved inside the Airbnb app. The process was slow, time consuming, and prone to errors, as inevitably there would be a typo in the dates of stay, or email address, typing out the keyless entry code, or some other human error in the convoluted process.

Airbnb has likely updated that shortfall, as the lack of email templates within the app was incredibly inefficient when compared to VRBO.

Another big difference between the two – while I could adjust rates last minute on the fly from my VRBO listing, I was not able to adjust last minute rates on Airbnb as quickly and easily. I had to find time to pull up the listing on my laptop, instead of being able to adjust the rates on the fly in the Airbnb phone app – another disadvantage.

Airbnb may have also made that easier since that time on this issue as well, but I am not sure. Every single Airbnb issue that I had may have since been resolved, but the fact remained, the VRBO app at the time was 'leaps and bounds' ahead of the Airbnb app in terms of efficiency. I have nothing against Airbnb and want them to succeed. Again, these are issues that they may have since improved upon or resolved, so let's give them the benefit of the doubt, and assume that Airbnb's app is now just as efficient as VRBO's.

Third, when booking through two different platforms, taxes became a major issue. Our handy summary provided by VRBO of reservations and rental income grids allowed us to pay taxes easily, if they were our only booking platform. On some properties, VRBO paid all the taxes for us. On other properties, we accessed our summary to pay the taxes that VRBO did not pay for us at a specific time each month.

Airbnb was similarly set up, but may have handled taxes differently, depending upon where each vacation property was located.

For example, we collect from the guest and pay all lodging taxes on our Orange Beach condo, but if the Orange Beach unit is booked through the Airbnb app, that service may do the opposite – Airbnb collects the tax and then pays all lodging taxes on that particular stay.

With multiple vacation rental properties in multiple states, it quickly became a labyrinth of work to figure out which taxes were being paid by which service, and that we were supposed to pay taxes on one set of reservations, but not pay taxes on the other set of reservations booked through Airbnb.

At the year end, we then provided two sets of accounting on income, one from each service, instead of one, and their summaries were not the same, requiring additional reconciliation from our tax preparer, for each separate property.

In the end, it was simply way too much work, especially with getting taxes paid, to have both vacation rental services going at the same time on any given property.

If your vacation rental is busy enough with just using one service or the other, then stick with the one that works for you. Keep it simple. Since 80% of our business was coming from VRBO versus Airbnb, it was an easy decision.

I have never personally tried an online booking platform other than VRBO or Airbnb. Others I know have tried independent vacation rental listing services but with minimal success to make it worthwhile to fool with two or more instead of using just one.

In addition, most 'mom and pop' vacation rental sites do not offer an app, which is essential to efficient vacation rental self-management, and no independent ever advertises as aggressively as VRBO or Airbnb – another huge disadvantage.

The simpler you keep things, the better.

If Airbnb books your treehouse on the river like crazy, stick with it and exclusively use their site and run all payments through that service. Do not accept 'off the books' reservations outside the platform, even for a friend. You can charge them less, or next to nothing, but still run every stay through whichever platform you end up using.

If VRBO books your condo on the beach like crazy, stick with VRBO and run everything through their platform every time. Do not accept 'off the books' reservations or stays outside the platform. This is especially true if you are relying on the $1M in guest liability coverage provided by VRBO for stays booked through their site. For that to apply, the stay must be paid for through their platform.

In that way, each vacation platform's summaries on rental income are the *one source* you need to accurately pay lodging taxes and provide your accountant a summary for annual taxes as well, all from the one service.

By having more than one online booking service marketing your vacation rental, the multiple listings lead to a lot of inefficiency. This is the opposite of what this entire book is about.

Unless working with a snowbird or long-term guest you personally know, never ever take a check for a reservation. Taking checks is the opposite of vacation rental efficiency. You want money in the bank, instant payment by credit card as soon as the vacation rental is booked. Checks floating back and forth, or bouncing checks, are the opposite of that efficiency, and may lead to being scammed at some point.

Resist the temptation to list your property on more than one service, and always, always, run all reservations through the system you have set up, to avoid taxation issues, problems with guests not obeying your rules, avoiding scam transactions, and having a single source for summaries which you will need for your accountant and to easily pay taxes. Your goal is efficiency, organization, and stability – not inefficiency, chaos, and uncertainty. More is not necessarily better in this area, especially if the one service consistently books out your property.

RULE: VRBO is the most cost effective and efficient online vacation rental platform available today, for those with standard types of vacation rentals - a standalone home, a condo on the beach, or a cabin in the mountains.

Airbnb is also an excellent platform, but better suited for more unique or eclectic vacation rental properties - shared spaces, unique locations, or rooms to rent. Find the service that works for your property, resist the temptation to list it in more than one place, and run all stays through your system of choice, every time.

Chapter 24

When should I start building my VRBO Listing?

You want to start building your VRBO listing as soon as the deed is signed and have it ready to go 'public' the minute you walk out of closing.

Please allow me to explain this concept through a great story on the condo that we had bought in Panama City Beach, Florida.

Prior to closing, there were a few days of pretty weather, and the seller allowed me to drive over for the day and access the unit during a brief vacancy to get some photos.

With the new photos, I began to populate our newly created VRBO listing, so that I could make the listing live on the same day we closed. I would be ready to hit the publish button to make the listing public, within hours of closing, an exciting prospect. Imagine having reservations for Spring Break or summer, within 24 hours of buying the vacation rental. The possibilities were intoxicating.

When I would buy a vacation rental, I would simply block off any stays for the first month after closing to allow for plenty of cushion to get everything ready or leave extra time if the closing was unexpectedly delayed. I knew that I would need time following closing to polish up the vacation rental to premium standards, no matter how turnkey ready the vacation rental appears to be. In general, this may be a few days, a few weeks, or worst case, a few months. There were also logistical issues of transferring everything from the old owner, which required additional time as well.

I do not recommend making your VRBO listing public until after you close. It is best to be patient in case a glitch happens, and the property doesn't close as expected or is delayed. VRBO may even have a rule against making your listing public prior to your closing – not sure.

On our most recent vacation rental purchases, I simply switched the listing to 'live,' or made it public, as soon as the ink dried on the closing papers. In one of our units, I had our first booking within hours of the listing going live following our closing.

I remember the day vividly.

My wife and I were on the condo balcony watching the sunset over the Gulf with a glass of celebratory wine, having closed on the condo earlier that afternoon.

It then happened! The VRBO app on my phone first buzzes, then dings, and the text message appears – 'Congrats! You have an Instant Booking!' My wife and I jumped up and down for joy like little kids. Money just went straight into our bank account on our new investment on the same day as closing.

Now that is something to look forward to and celebrate.

RULE: Start building your VRBO listing as soon as the property goes under contract and make it public immediately after you close on the property. Block off the first few days, weeks, or even months following closing to make sure that you have the vacation rental ready in time for the first guest.

Chapter 25

What are the first steps to creating my VRBO listing?

The good news is that it is extremely easy for anyone to create their VRBO listing, regardless of how experienced they are on a computer, a phone, or with technology in general.

The first step is to secure the 50 photos that we discussed earlier, which include the vacation rental itself, resort amenities, and area attractions. They can be provided to you from the previous vacation rental listing. Preferably though, these are photos taken on your smart phone, or emailed to your smart phone. Interior photos need to be taken with a wide-angle lens. All photos should be brightened (again use the 'auto' enhance button available on most smartphones), and all taken with a high-quality digital camera or an updated smart phone.

Second, you need to choose your VRBO subscription. Assuming you plan to aggressively rent your vacation rental on a year-round basis (except for when you are using it), I recommend the flat fee listing, $495 a year (which is about to go up to $595), which does not charge you, as the owner, a commission for each stay, other than credit card processing fees.

You then create a username (which is your email address), a secure password, provide the two-factor authentication for a text message, and at least two security questions.

You will need to secure a credit card that you plan to run only condo expenses through. Call it the 'condo card,' or 'cabin card,' or 'Airbnb card.' Place that initial $495 VRBO subscription as your first legitimate expense on your new condo credit card.

By having one card, you and your accountant or bookkeeper then know that every charge on that card is a legitimate expense. Do not mix condo expenses in with personal or business credit cards. Have one credit card dedicated only to vacation rental expenses. If you have more than one vacation rental, consider having a separate credit card for each separate vacation rental.

While logged onto VRBO through a laptop or desk top computer, you begin building your listing (i.e., simply visit www.vrbo.com and look for 'List your property'). The layout while using the desktop computer is simple and easy to follow.

There is a fair amount of typing and forms to fill out, boxes to fill in, and tabs to work through, and it is a lot easier to do that on a large screen and with a full keyboard rather than through the phone app using your thumbs. You can build from scratch your entire listing on the app, but it is easier to initially set it up on a big screen, laptop, or iPad.

Simply follow the tabs and questions presented by VRBO to build your listing. Most questions are mundane - number of beds, number of baths, is there a kitchen, list of resort amenities, is it on the water or not, etc. You will need to provide a bank account for rental income. There is a multistep process for bank account verification, akin to setting up an account on Venmo or PayPal. This takes time – another reason to start work on your listing sooner than later.

If you have more than one vacation rental, set up a separate bank account for each vacation rental. Do not have one account handling multiple vacation rental properties. Your accountant will later thank you.

For rates, set a season high July 4th rate as your base rate – an outrageously high initial nightly rate. We will talk more about rates later. Other than setting rates, the questions are easy to answer.

Arguably, the hardest part is getting the photos uploaded. But if you can take the photos with your smart phone, and then download the VRBO phone app, uploading the photos to your newly created listing inside the VRBO phone app is a cinch.

The next step after you have started the basic framework of your new vacation rental listing on a desktop or laptop computer, is to download the VRBO app to your smart phone. Do not download the VRBO app with the navy blue VRBO label for a guest looking to book somewhere. Download the VRBO Owner app, with the white VRBO label. They are two totally different apps. Make sure you download the 'owner' app.

Once you have downloaded the correct 'owner' VRBO app, you simply use the same email and password you used while working on your desktop to get your app to link up with the new vacation rental listing you have been working on earlier on your desktop.

Once the app is downloaded, and you have entered your user ID and password, open the VRBO app, and simply upload the 50 photos from your phone directly into your newly created listing, which will be assigned a listing number, usually a 7-digit unique number.

As discussed earlier, photos are the most important part of your VRBO listing. It is the first thing guests look at when they come to your listing. Photos literally will make or break your success, so make sure they are great photos.

RULE: Do not be intimidated. Creating your VRBO listing is easy, even for those who are not technically proficient.

Chapter 26

THE BIG THREE: Primary Photo, Headline, and Description

When building your VRBO listing, you will need to provide a headline, a primary photo, and a description. These three items are extremely important as they are the primary metrics that will affect your listing's position in search results.

We will discuss more on listing positions momentarily. For now, let's discuss each of these topics.

The headline is the ten or twelve words that appear next to your primary photo and appear in search results. The headline needs to grab your prospective guest's attention and let them know the main reason(s) why they should choose your unit.

Here is an example headline from our Splash Resort headline, located in Panama City Beach Florida:

Luxurious, Upscale 9th floor 2/2 Gulf Front Condo w Waterpark, FREE BEACH SERVICE

Here is an example headline from our cabin in Pigeon Forge, Tennessee:

Luxury Cabin at 'The Preserve' w Breathtaking Views, Hot Tub, Game Room, Loft

At this point, stop what you are doing. Do not rely on my title, as every property and vacation rental are unique.

Go into VRBO and pull up your competitor's headlines from the area or resort where your vacation rental is located. Read 10 competitor headlines and write down your favorite headlines, and then create your own perfect headline from the best of them or a combination of them.

Like a Twitter post, or in the old days, a classified ad where every character counts, the title must be no more than a few words and characters – keep it brief but max out all spaces.

Consider emojis if you know how to use them. Consider all caps for emphasis. Like a Twitter post, you can do a lot with just a few characters.

The primary photo is critical as well.

When the search results pop up for your resort, the list shows the primary photo and the headline. The primary photo and headline must capture the prospective guest's attention and impress them. The primary photo should be your <u>best photo</u> that pretty much summarizes the main reason the guest should book your vacation rental, if one photo could possible ever do that.

As an example, we chose for our cabin as the primary photo the picture of the balcony hot tub, on a sunny, blue bird day, that also showed the gorgeous view of the mountains. The main reason guests' book in our resort is for the views, and if there is a hot tub too, that is a bonus. Your primary listing photo needs to capture the main reason that a guest is coming to stay at your resort, if possible.

The description is also extremely important.

The description is your chance to impress the prospective guest and convince them that your vacation rental is the best choice. Think of a job interview and the prospective boss says, "Impress me." You can do this. The description should literally 'close the deal' on the guest's decision to book your property. It also should answer the most asked guest questions, to avoid guests asking the same question repeatedly in endless 'contact owner' inquiries from prospective guests.

You should highlight all the things about the vacation rental that vacationing guests want – epic views, spacious accommodations, updated furnishings, first class amenities, easy booking process, fully automated keyless entry, free beach service, kids' waterpark, lazy river, or whatever is the main draw to your vacation rental. The bulk of the description should be the vacation rental accommodation itself, and the resort amenities.

Your description should include spacing, bullets, lists, and quotes from guests. It should be a comprehensive, easy to follow description of your vacation rental.

Briefly highlight area attractions as well and your proximity to them.

Towards the bottom, you then give a brief overview of the reservation process. If the calendar shows the unit as available, then it is available. You want to get the mundane questions all answered, as you want the guest to book – rather than contact you.

At minimum, tell the guest that the easiest and fastest way to book the vacation rental is to 'Instantly Book.'

At the bottom of the description, you will also want to list some of your most important rules as well – no pets, no smoking, etc.

You will also need to highlight the not so fun stuff, like how parking works, or if a given amenity is closed for renovation, and provide those dates towards the end of your description. Amenity closures are always disclosed, but typically towards the bottom of the description.

The very last thing in your description is to list links to your other vacation rental listings if you have more than one. The guest may be impressed with the overall quality of all your listings, and end up booking with confidence, as you are then perceived as an established owner of multiple vacation rentals.

After you follow the foregoing outline, save what you are doing, and stop. I then want you to go to your competitor's VRBO listings for the same condo or resort and *read at least 10 of your competitor's descriptions.*

You will find in your competitor's descriptions things that you forgot to include, or failed to highlight, and a layout that may be more attractive than what you had initially prepared. Cherry pick from the 10 listings description items or topics that appeal to you, and you then create your own unique version of that for your own description.

Remember, do not create the description in a complete vacuum. Look at competitors' descriptions and keep editing and working on the description until it is perfect. If you are not good at writing, get help. Have someone proofread and spell check your description. It needs to be professional, with no typos, misspellings, or errors.

RULE: Your primary photo, headline, and description are each extremely important. Review your competitors' VRBO listing descriptions and look at the old vacation rental listing of the unit you are buying, if available, for a start on ideas, language, and ordering of topics to follow.

The following is an example title as well as a description for our cabin in Pigeon Forge. For our primary photo, we use the photo of the views from the balcony and hot tub – the same photo that we use on our book cover page.

EXAMPLE TITLE:

Luxury Cabin at 'The Preserve' w Breathtaking Views, Hot Tub, Game Room, Loft

EXAMPLE DESCRIPTION FROM CABIN IN PIGEON FORGE:

Upscale luxury log cabin with BREATHTAKING VIEWS from every window!

This beautifully crafted log cabin, 'Appalachian High,' features all wood craftsmanship, three stories of floor to ceiling glass, cathedral ceilings, a spacious gaming area, a brand new four person private hot tub perched atop its highest deck (installed 2022), third floor loft accessed by log ladder, unique built in kids 'bears den' hideaway play area, lavish all natural wood furnishings, and by far the most astounding views of the surrounding Great Smoky Mountains imaginable.

'Appalachian High' is in The Preserve Resort, a luxury upscale cabin development, and sits at 2,300 feet above sea level, the highest elevation of any resort in the area.

This cabin is the HIGHEST vacation rental unit of its size located at The Preserve - you can't go any higher than this one! The views are simply THE BEST available at The Preserve.

This quality, spacious three story, 2-bedroom cabin has two full baths, and sleeps up to maximum 6 adults / 10 total guests with children spread out on its spacious three floors (King Bed, Queen over Queen bunks, Queen Sleeper Sofa, two Twins in Loft).

GAME ROOM: Guests will love the game room with giant, cathedral style ceilings and epic views, and try their luck at a game of pool, foosball, or enjoy the best gaming experience available on the two Atari stand-alone game systems, including a sit-down race / 3D driving simulator, or play a game of doubles on the table sized Ms. Pacman, Centipede, Galaga or other 1980's favorites!

"A true log cabin experience." - Gunnison H.

FREE HIGH-SPEED WI-FI: Keep in touch with work and school with the in cabin complimentary Xfinity high speed Wi-Fi.

ELECTRIC FIREPLACE: In the winter months the super convenient electric fireplace provides a cozy ambiance.

FORMAL DINING FOR SIX: Prepare a feast in the well-equipped kitchen and dine at the formal dining table for up to six guests. Relax after meals on the balcony in the super comfy polywood rocking chairs or have a picnic outside on the provided polywood picnic table area.

PIGEON FORGE: Located just a short drive from Pigeon Forge, in the quiet Wears Valley area, enjoy all the attractions like Dollywood, Dixie Stampede, The Island, Soaky Mountain, Pirate Voyage, and more while simultaneously enjoying epic views and an authentic log cabin experience!

GSMNP: For those wishing to visit the Great Smoky Mountains National Park, the most visited national park in the country, with its famous hiking trails (we recommend the Appalachian Trail), scenic overlooks (we recommend Clingman's Dome), and soaring waterfalls (we recommend Laurel Falls), as well as the ever-popular Cade's Cove, are all only minutes away - with not a single traffic light in the way!

GATLINBURG: For those wishing to visit Gatlinburg, skip the Pigeon Forge traffic and take the nearby Line Springs Road / Metcalf Bottoms route for a traffic free / quick / back door scenic access directly into Gatlinburg.

'We loved how convenient this cabin was to Pigeon Forge, Gatlinburg and Cade's Cove.' - Jennifer V.

SNOW: Due to the cabin's high elevation, we get snow consistently throughout the winter months. Want to snow ski? Ober Gatlinburg is only minutes away.

BEARS INCLUDED: Bears, jack rabbits, chipmunks, racoons, owls, and more are routinely spotted at The Preserve, especially during the summer.

Some guests check in and simply stay in, and never leave the cabin - enjoying the views, the hot tub, the game room and grilling out together.

ALL PRESERVE RESORT AMENITIES INCLUDED WITH STAY: The Appalachian High cabin is located in The Preserve, a high-end cabin resort community with first class guest amenities. Check out the mountain top huge outdoor pool and jacuzzi tub with amazing views of the Smokys (open approximately from Memorial Day to Labor Day each summer, weather permitting), a fitness center with steam room and sauna (open 24 hours), all of which are perched atop a mountain with incredible blue vistas of the Great Smoky Mountains National Park. The Preserve's guest amenities are complimentary for guests staying at 'Appalachian High.' Simply provide your cabin confirmation at the Hearthside front desk, located adjacent to the pool, for key code access to all resort amenities.

SLEEPING ACCOMMODATIONS:

MAIN FLOOR / LIVING AREA:

Master King Bed with en-suite full bath, walk in shower (comfortably sleeps 2);

Living Room Queen Sleeper Sofa (informally sleeps 2);

SECOND FLOOR:

Queen over Queen bunks (comfortably sleeps 4);

Full Bath with walk in shower, and separate private jetted whirlpool tub

LOFT - THIRD FLOOR:

Two Twin beds (comfortably sleeps 2)

CABIN AMENITIES:

- Plentiful complimentary parking

- No traffic - cabin is at the very top of the mountain and is the highest vacation rental cabin that can be rented at The Preserve Resort

- Keyless code entry - no formal check in required

- Best view in the Smoky Mountains

- Balcony hot tub

- Polywood balcony rocking chairs

- Formal dining for six

- Xfinity cable with complimentary high-speed Wi-Fi on multiple flat screen HDTV's

- Two oversized Lazy Boy recliners

- Electric full simulation fireplace

- Fully equipped kitchen

- Built in 'bears den' play area beneath stairs for a kid's hideout

- 100 % all wood interior

- 100% all wood rustic log cabin style furnishings

- Cathedral style ceilings

- Fully equipped game room with full sized pool table, foosball table, Atari 2-person multicade (Pac-Man, Galaga, Frogger etc.), full size Atari driver simulator

- Loft with two twin beds accessed by real wood ladder, great for kids or agile adults!

- 2nd floor indoor large private jacuzzi tub with views

- Choice of outdoor charcoal grill or outdoor balcony propane grill (cabin equipped for both)

- Outdoor picnic area with polywood picnic table for six

- Upstairs / game room bar style table and chairs, dedicated wine and drink cooler

- Ceiling fans in all rooms, track lighting, bear themed lamps and décor

- Kids can play outside in the woods or snow on the private oversized lot - zero traffic!

UPDATED CALENDAR: If our online calendar shows the cabin is available, then it is. We update the calendar within minutes of a reservation.

NO KEY HASSLE - NO WAITING: No need to stand in line for check in or check out! Entry to the cabin is easy - simply key in the unique custom code we supply you for the electronic keypad at the door. Your reservation confirmation, booking, stay and logistics are all handled by email directly with the owner of the unit in a streamlined and efficient process.

INQUIRIES / QUOTES / AVAILABILITY: To check availability, click on 'view full calendar.' To get an instant quote using our reservation calculator, simply enter your dates of stay, and the reservation calculator will give you an exact quote for your intended stay.

RESERVATIONS: Reservations for the condo are easy! Our preferred method of booking is for you to use the 'BOOK NOW' button on our listing and follow the online instructions to book the unit through the online VRBO credit card payment system. Simply agree to all our rules of stay, and then your reservation will then be finalized within minutes. This preferred payment option is available 24/7 as it is an automated process to book the reservation. No waiting for the owner to 'approve' your stay!

Once paid in full, a confirmation email is sent to you through VRBO. Later, an informational packet on the condo, including the keyless code for entry to the unit, directions to the unit, checkout instructions, and so forth, will then be sent to you by email to you in advance of your intended stay.

REQUIRED ID / AGE RESTRICTION / 3 VEHICLE LIMIT: Renters must be 25 or older - no exceptions. No parties / 3 vehicle limit on premises at any time enforced by 24-hour video surveillance of parking area and RING doorbell video surveillance of entrance (no cameras inside). If you are looking for a place to host a party, or exceed guest capacity, or bring pets, this cabin is NOT for you. Violation of this rule results in forfeiture of stay and damage deposit. This cabin is geared towards couples, retirees, and small families - not large gatherings, college parties or celebrations.

NO SMOKING: This is a strictly non-smoking unit / resort. There will be a $2500 fine, forfeiture of stay, forfeiture of damage deposit, and required reimbursement for all costs of deodorization (which could be thousands of dollars) if smoking occurs in the unit. This rule is closely monitored and strictly enforced. Smokers are not welcome and are prohibited from renting this unit.

GETTING MARRIED? FAMILY REUNION? Feel like getting married? How about a giant wood burning fireplace? There is a beautiful chapel, fireplace, pavilion, and conference room, all with views, available to rent through The Preserve HOA, subject to availability, located two blocks downhill from the cabin. Simply inquire for contact information on rates and availability.

BEACH? Feel like going to the beach instead? Check out our 7th and 9th floor condos with direct Gulf front views located at Splash Resort in Panama City Beach, Florida, with an onsite kids' waterpark, lazy river, and complimentary beach chair and umbrella service included with stay. www.vrbo.com/863722 or www.vrbo.com/873755

LAZY RIVER? Feel like floating down a lazy river in Orange Beach, Alabama? Check out our condo at Phoenix on the Bay in Orange Beach Alabama with gorgeous 5th floor view, and one of Alabama's longest lazy rivers and waterslide. Visit www.vbro.com/513462.

We look forward to your stay with us at any of our properties!

Chapter 27

How do I set rates?

One of the most difficult and time-consuming tasks for a vacation rental owner is setting rates. So how does one do it?

Do not derail an ATM machine.

As you will have researched and secured the annual revenue numbers of your vacation rental before making your Offer of Purchase, you know at this point how much your newly purchased vacation rental can make. If you are happy with those numbers, a 'down and dirty' quick way to get your rates set up on the fly is to simply copy the nightly rates from the previous year as set by the prior owner and or prior management company. It is not a perfect science, but at least you have strong odds that you will meet or beat the previous year's revenue numbers by doing that.

Meet or beat your competition.

If you are starting with your first vacation rental, and the vacation rental that you just purchased does not have prior year occupancy and nightly rates readily available, check your competition, and then meet or (slightly) beat their nightly rate.

You simply go into VRBO or Airbnb, and do a search for your neighborhood, resort, or community for any given date during the next year. You then take the top five search results and write down the nightly rates for any given rental period. You can then average those rates, and then meet, or slightly beat that average.

Meet or beat the largest vacation rental management rates.

Another option is to look at rates as set by the largest vacation rental management company in your resort.

This is a touch less time-consuming than the previous suggestion, as you are then only looking at one set of rates, rather than trying to figure out the rate average of multiple properties.

At Splash Resort, Vacasa is now the largest vacation rental management company at the resort. At Phoenix on the Bay in Orange Beach, and many other Phoenix properties in Orange Beach and Gulf Shores, Brett Robinson is the largest vacation rental management company in each respective resort.

Other areas or communities in the country may have similar large management companies handling a large block of units in any given resort.

First, figure out which vacation rental management company garners the largest share of vacation rentals in your neighborhood, community, or resort.

After you identify the largest player in the resort, go through their listings and match up your unit to their managed units. If you have a one bedroom, then go through their one-bedroom rates for the year. If it's a two bedroom, then go through their two-bedroom rates for the year, etc.

Comparing that, you will quickly learn that every one bedroom that is managed by the large rental management company all have the exact same nightly rate set for the next year. Another words, every one bedroom under their management has the exact same nightly rates for the year. The two-bedroom units – the exact same nightly rates for the year.

Take those comparable rates that match your sized unit and then 'meet or beat' them by pricing $10 per night less. By pricing that way, you will then have 'beat' the two hundred or so listings in the resort, or the largest competitor in the resort, giving you a significant competitive advantage over a large block of competing condos in your neighborhood, resort, or community.

At some point, these larger management companies are going to realize that independents are doing this, and at some point, those future nightly rates may be harder to locate online, but we will see.

Look backwards and continue the upward trajectory.

For those who already have vacation rentals, an effective technique after a year or two of successful operations is to look backwards at your own vacation rental's performance, without looking at the rates of your competitors.

For instance, we had a blockbuster year at all our vacation rentals in the post pandemic recovery year 2021. If we could simply get those sorts of numbers again, or even slightly increase those numbers, it would be miraculous, especially in view of the softening real estate market, higher interest rates, and inflation rates cutting into consumer's discretionary spending.

Since we have so much rental history now behind us at each of our four properties, we see a consistent year on year trend of increasing annual gross rental revenues (except for the pandemic year), and simply follow that system year after year to build or keep that trend heading upwards.

We simply go back to each of the 52 weeks from the prior year. If it is booked, we either set the same nightly rate, or go up slightly 10% during the off season, and 20% higher if in season.

If it did not book, we price the nightly rate lower, a larger discount during off season, and only a slight discount if the unit was vacant during peak season. That's our basic rule of thumb.

Price like the cruise industry

The cruise industry has figured out how to price their cruises to fill their ships, even in the off season. Look at their pricing on an annual basis. Your rates, especially if it is beachfront vacation rental in the Southeast, should ebb and flow in a similar manner based on the time of the year.

Cruise rates are highest during Spring Break, summer, Fall Break, Thanksgiving break, Christmas, and New Year's. Your rates should also be dramatically higher during these times, especially if you have a beach front vacation rental.

Identify your peak season.

It is important to identify your peak season and price accordingly.

As discussed, peak season for beachfront vacation rentals mirror the cruise ship industry's demand for vacationers.

However, this model would not apply to a ski in and ski out vacation rental in the Rocky Mountains. Their peak season is during the ski season – the opposite of the beachfront rental, which is in its off season in January and February.

Similarly, Pigeon Forge's peak season is during the fall for changing leaf colors, and Thanksgiving. This too is a window of time that is not typically busy at the beaches.

By identifying the peak season, you can maximize your nightly rates, as the vacation rental will consistently book during peak season.

Ideally, your peak season rates do not book up way in advance. This may mean you have priced them too low.

Rather, your peak season should book up roughly two weeks or more in advance, or within a month of peak season, indicating that you are not priced too low (which would have booked months in advance), or priced too high (which would mean the unit does not book at all or does not book until last minute when nothing else is available).

With time and experience, you will get better at setting the ideal nightly rate for your vacation rental.

Check the calendar for holidays and events.

Always, always, check the calendar before you finish setting the nightly rates for all major holidays, and make sure that your rental rates reflect a bump or premium for the day before, day of and day after any major holiday during the year. These would include three-day weekends. Martin Luther King, Mardi Gras Break (may be a regional thing in the Southeast), Spring Break, Memorial Day, July 4th, Labor Day, Fall Break, Veterans Day, and Christmas through New Year's Eve.

Check the local calendar for events, concerts, or festivals.

Always, always, check the local calendar for upcoming annual events, and make sure you bump up the nightly rate for the event, festival, air show, or concert.

For instance, Panama City Beach has its annual Beach Jam three-day weekend music festival. In Gulf Shores, there is the annual Hangout Music Festival, drawing 100,000 or more visitors to the area. In Pensacola Beach Florida, the Blue Angels host their annual air show over the beaches on the weekend following July 4th, drawing hundreds of thousands of visitors to the Florida Panhandle.

These are opportunities for you to 'bump up' your nightly rates in response to the anticipated demand. At this point, you may ask yourself, is this legal to do? Should I feel guilty about raising my rates during any given weekend due to an event, festival, or concert.

The answer is no – you should not feel guilty – at all.

If you have ever tried to visit New Orleans for an event or festival, you will quickly learn that the hotel industry literally 'jacks' their nightly rates whenever there is a major festival, concert, or event that draws people to the city, or its historic French Quarter. Known for its Mardi Gras, a travelling guest must book months, if not years in advance to get an affordable place to stay within any proximity to downtown if it is even available.

Price your vacation rental like they do in New Orleans. If there is an event, or festival, major attraction to your area, price your place at a dramatic profit. You want your vacation rental to literally book last minute, or within days of the peak weekend, when everything else is already booked, and you are one of the only ones left, and the guest is desperate to find a place to stay. Think of a local event, festival, or yearly attraction as an opportunity to make some serious money. Price it high and stay strong. It will book, especially when available inventory diminishes.

Price your rates higher and adjust lower later.

You never want a vacationing guest to 'snap up' your place because you failed to adequately price your vacation rental guest. In view of that, price higher than lower, and adjust your rates lower if your vacation rental does not book, during the weeks, and even days, leading up to any given vacancy.

Set a high minimum nightly rate.

Although we mentioned this in an earlier chapter, always set your base rate, before setting specific rates for the following year. The base rate covers the unexpected booking of a date way out in advance where you have not yet set your nightly rates.

For instance, if you set your minimum nightly rate as $100 per night, and you have not yet set your nightly rates for July 4th two years in the future, that nightly rate for a peak holiday will show $100 per night, as you have not set your nightly rates that far in advance yet.

Enter the guest who has a wedding planned for that weekend two years out, who may then try and 'snap up' that stay, when the nightly rates are typically $500 or more per night, not $100 per night. Once the wedding party books it, you are reluctant to cancel it, as that would then negatively affect one of the pillars of your securing strong search result rankings, of never cancelling a guest stay, so you then feel 'stuck' with the reservation.

Don't let that happen.

To prevent that scenario, set your minimum nightly rate, right out of the gate, as the highest nightly rate that you could ever conceivably charge for your vacation rental. In that way if there is an oversight, or hiccup, and you fail to adjust any given nightly rate, either in the short term or long term, the rate will then be too high, rather than too low.

Identify your goals.

Some vacation rental owners want 100% occupancy year-round and are willing to bargain basement discount their nightly rate to get that, especially during the low or off season.

Although the upside on this target may be impressive annual revenues, the downside is wear and tear on the vacation rental, increased likelihood of bed bugs due to increased volume, risk of damage, liability issues, and a lower end guest who wants something for nothing, and their review is reflective of that attitude. The cost and expense (i.e., having to replace furnishings more often, paint more often, etc.) of achieving that type of volume then offsets those impressive revenue numbers.

On the other hand, some vacation rental owners really want their vacation rental to stay in pristine condition. They price their vacation rental extremely high, and do not care that the unit rents only occasionally. If they get one week per month, they are happy. They operate on a break even or on a loss and get to enjoy a pristine high end vacation rental whenever they want, that ends up as a much-needed loss on the tax return.

I tend to land somewhere between these two extremes. We try and price the vacation rental to remain booked 70% of the time or higher on a yearly basis. We make the bulk of our revenues during peak season, major holidays, and events.

When it is slow, such as the winter at the beaches, we do not 'bargain basement' price our rentals, as we do not want low quality guests who tear up the place, expect something for nothing, and tend to leave negative reviews. We would rather our unit sit empty during low season than have that happen and instead focus on making strong returns when demand is higher.

For instance, we have two units rented to snowbirds for the upcoming winter, with two units sitting empty. The two snowbirds were willing to pay the higher end price for their stay, as again, we would rather the unit sit empty than be torn up or be burdened with a volume of low-end renters. This indicates that we are not too high or too low on our vacation rental pricing for snowbirds, with a 50% occupancy rate during low season, an acceptable number for us. Of the two that rented, they are paying a premium to stay, and are a higher end snowbird, who take care of the place, and return year after year.

You as a vacation rental owner need to identify your goals for the unit, and price your nightly rates accordingly.

RULE: If it's your first vacation rental and you have never done this before, consider copying the successful nightly rates from the previous owner's prior year on your newly purchased vacation rental. Alternatively, locate the largest vacation rental operation in your resort or neighborhood, check their rates and slightly beat them. Lastly, for established vacation rentals with strong year on year upward trajectories, forget the competition. If the unit booked the previous year, simply add 10% to the nightly rate during the off season and add a 20% higher nightly rate during season. If the unit did not book the previous year, use a slightly lower nightly rate (10-20% lower) for the next year for that same time.

Chapter 28

Should I approve each booking or allow instant booking?

On VRBO, the host can set their listing to allow for instant booking, meaning that the guest can simply book the unit, without first obtaining the owner's advance permission to book. I strongly recommend setting your unit to being able to be booked instantly, without your having to preapprove.

Let me explain why.

Think back to all the times that you sat down on your device to book a stay somewhere. Once you have found what you wanted, you want to book it and be done and go on down the road. You do not want to have to wait up to 24 hours for the owner to bless or approve your stay.

As such, I feel that listings that have instant booking capability have a dramatic advantage over similar listings without that option.

You may then ask, but what if some unsavory character instantly books my unit. You may feel that you want to be able to screen all guests to make sure that they are a good fit, so the vacation rental does not get torn up. This is an understandable concern.

However, you do not want to get into a situation where you either consciously or unconsciously discriminate against a minority, a funny name, a foreign name, or some other inappropriate basis for a person searching for housing. It is illegal to discriminate against certain classes and categories of people in your vacation rental business. Don't do it.

In addition, your concern that there may be too many guests, or that they smoke, or may exceed capacity, and you 'think' you may catch that bad apple in the approval process versus through the instant booking process, simply isn't going to happen.

I promise you - no guest ever tells you in advance that they are going to willingly violate your rules of stay, guest capacity, or that they plan to have a party at your place. If it is going to happen, it is going to happen. That is why you get a huge damage deposit (money that comes out of the guest's pocket if they violate rules of stay and not some insurance policy covering accidental loss) for every rental, so that you can rest easy. The listing will clearly list the rules of stay and require that the guest agree to those rules prior to booking. That, combined with the hefty damage deposit, should be sufficient to keep the bad guests away.

Indeed, the guests who are most likely to trash the vacation rental will focus nearly all their energy in locating the rental with the smallest damage deposit, the fewest rules, and no video Ring doorbell surveillance – not whether the vacation rental can be instantly booked or first subject to approval.

Finally, the goal of this book and the accompanying online video course is to automate as much as possible your entire vacation rental system. This is just one extra step that you really do not need to go through. Think about it – you are down in Mexico vacationing with your family. You have spotty or limited Internet. A guest requests to book and you do not get to it in time to approve their proposed stay and then boom, you lose it. Don't let that happen. You want your vacation rental booking at all hours of the day and night, especially when you are busy doing something else - sleeping, busy in a meeting, or halfway around the world in some exotic locale. There is nothing more exciting than to come back from a work project, family getaway, trip, or vacation and have multiple instant bookings awaiting your return.

There is an old saying that one doesn't have a business unless the business can operate while the owner is on vacation. Think about it. That is what you want. You are setting up a 'system' for the entire process of renting your vacation rental to work automatically with you doing as little as humanly possible. Allowing instant bookings is a part of that process to make that happen.

RULE: Set your listing to allow instant bookings so that the prospective guest can instantly book your vacation rental without your having to first approve the stay.

Chapter 29

What should I set as the guest minimum night stay?

The 'minimum night stay' refers to the minimum number of nights that a guest must book to stay in your vacation rental.

Generally, if the vacation rental has huge demand during specific seasons, say June and July down on the beaches, or perhaps Thanksgiving and Christmas in the mountains, or January and February at the snow ski resorts, then yes, you can simplify your vacation rentals, and reduce total guest volume through your unit, by doing one-week minimum stays, with a certain check in and checkout day.

The goal would then be to have every single day of the entire peak season calendar completely booked with weekly rentals. In addition, there is less wear and tear, and there is some consistency for your cleaners on cleaning the same day each turn.

However, the downside of this is that the guest may not want to check in on the day you picked, and have only four, five, or six-nights available for travel, or perhaps a shorter stay is all they can afford and cannot do the seven-night minimum you seek.

As a result, the guest may appreciate and book that unit that allows for more flexibility with booking options. Restricting your unit to a given day of check in and for such a lengthy stay, reduces, not increases, the pool of guests that may be able to book - a risky move.

In view of that, I have consistently used a three-night minimum at all of our units over the years. Guests often and do book for four, five, six nights or weekly stays, even though we have a three-night minimum. Our guests get to pick both their check-in day and length of stay depending upon what they can afford, which sets us apart further from the competition that does weekly rentals with a fixed check in day. By having a small nightly minimum, this expands the scope of the potential guests that may book the vacation rental, a competitive advantage over those who require a specific check in day, or those who have a longer nightly minimum.

Indeed, three-night minimums seem to be the common minimum along the beaches for beach stays.

However, up in Pigeon Forge, many vacation rental management companies tend to allow even a shorter nightly minimum, a two-night minimum, or even a one night minimum. At one point I considered lowering my nightly minimum to two nights, to stay competitive with our competition up in Pigeon Forge, but I decided against it.

Nevertheless, I still require a three-night minimum for anyone to book our cabin in Pigeon Forge.

Let me explain why.

I do not want to turn the cabin into a one- or two-night hotel. There is a risk that the guests are just booking the unit for a one-night blowout or a graduation party when you have such a short nightly minimum.

Further, an increase in the volume of guests coming and going tends to cause more wear and tear on the unit (think of suitcases being hauled up and down the stairs in the cabin).

In addition, the odds that a guest will accidentally leave a bed bug increase if you are a revolving door for one- or two-night stays, as opposed to longer higher quality stays.

After I get the reservation, and the guest pays top dollar for their stay well in advance, picks their check in day, and their number of nights, I then always look at any gap between the guest's stay and those either before the booking or after the booking.

Hopefully, the guest has booked up against someone checking out or checking in, for a same day turn, the most efficient type of stay possible.

If there is any gap between guest stays, I can then set my nightly minimum to either two, three, or four nights, to fill that gap between stays, so that there are same day turns and no nights end up being vacant.

If there is a one-night gap between stays, we have a special template email that we send to guests who are already booked, in an effort for them to add on that one night and check in a night earlier, or check out a day later, at a discounted rate, to fill the one-night gap. That technique and the templates used to do that will be discussed shortly. For now, do a three-night minimum.

For naysayers who think that it is impossible to get to 100% occupancy on a three-night minimum, please allow me to explain.

At our Splash unit for June and July this past year, we had every single night of June booked, with all back-to-back same day turns, without a single night of vacancy. We started with a three-night minimum, and most bookings were for four, five or six nights. We had two-night stays only once or twice during that span, and still hit 100% occupancy.

The moral of the story is that even with a three-night minimum, it is possible to get 100% occupancy in any given month. You do not have to have weekly rentals set up for Saturday-to-Saturday stays to accomplish that. If the occasional two-night gap were to happen in a sea of three-night minimums, it is ok to then reduce the nightly minimum to fill that two-night gap when needed.

RULE: Set a three-night minimum for guest stays. If a gap between stays happens, set the nightly minimum to fill that gap so that all nights end up booked. If there is a one-night gap between guest stays, see if your existing guests want to add on an extra night at a discounted rate to fill that single night gap. We will explain how to efficiently fill one-night gaps in a later chapter.

Chapter 30

What should I set as the minimum age

to rent my vacation rental?

As our guests go straight to the condo and enter a code for entry to the vacation rental, there is no formal check in or checking of IDs. This provides an inviting opportunity for a high schooler or college student to try and rent the condo after their parent makes the actual reservation for them with a credit card.

First, make it a rule that no one is allowed to rent the unit unless the person paying is also actually staying in the unit. Be clear that a parent, friend, or other person is not permitted to pay for an underage and unsupervised guest to stay.

Second, get to know the personnel at the HOA front desk. They need to be able to spot a high school or college group without parents around, trying to buy a parking pass, or picking up amenity wrist bands all by themselves. Buy the front desk workers a bottle of wine or two every time you come and stick your phone number on it. That way if they suspect underaged renters checking into your unit, they can report it to you.

Third, place on your vacation rental listing that ID is verified upon check in. We know that means when they buy a parking pass or secure amenity wristbands, but they won't know that unless they book. That statement alone may help ward off underage renters, regardless of whether their IDs are ever checked or not by the personnel at the HOA desk.

Fourth, you may get suspicious that a rental is a group of kids. You first see that they have maxed out capacity, with no children. The guest asks whether it is permissible to have guests over that are not staying in the unit. Further, the guest asks how many people they can get 'on property' each day.

If you start getting red flags like that, simply demand that they email you a copy of their driver license to confirm that they meet your minimum age requirement. Confirm that is not a parent paying for unsupervised kids to stay, and that the person who paid is indeed staying. Some vacation rental owners demand that with every stay, but we do not. Fortunately, we have never had an issue.

Again, the hefty damage deposit (which is required on all stays without exception, even if they opt to get damage insurance), and a statement that their ID will be 'checked' at the vacation rental upon arrival, typically weeds out underage guests.

Fifth, we set age 25 as the minimum age to stay in the vacation rental. This rule helps weed out high school and all college students, which I do not ever recommend.

Let me explain why.

You want families and older adults – not partying college kids that will exceed your capacity by piling in, that may smoke or vape in your unit, and that may destroy your vacation rental. I strongly recommend against ever making the under 25 demographic a focus for your vacation rental. This sounds harsh. I know it does. Is it illegal to have a minimum age requirement for stays in your vacation rental?

No, there is nothing illegal in having a minimum age requirement to stay in your vacation rental.

Should you ever allow exceptions to the minimum age requirement? Yes.

A guest can simply inquire and say that they really love your vacation rental, but noticed the minimum age requirement and wanted to see if an exception could be made. The couple then explains that they are newlyweds and on their honeymoon. Boom. Exception permitted and the underage couple were allowed to book the unit. We have never had an issue with that type of stay or requested exception, even if the guests were below the minimum age requirements.

Finally, be careful of the 'end around.' This is where someone you know, a neighbor, family friend, or perhaps another vacation rental owner tries to talk you into allowing a vacation rental, either on the books or off the books, where the guest(s) are below your minimum age requirement. Don't ever take the bait. That set up always, always yields horrible results. The person vouching for the underage prospective guests have nothing to lose if the rental goes poorly, and further, they are not financially responsible for the kids. You are then left holding the bag. Don't take that bait – ever, regardless of who it is making the recommendation.

The ultimate 'end around' is the one where a neighbor wants their kids to use your unit at a discounted 'off the books' rate. In other words, the kids are so horrible that the neighbor feels compelled to offload the bunch onto you, a few doors down from their own unit. Don't do it.

RULE: Unless you grant an exception, your mandatory minimum age to stay in the vacation rental is 25 years of age. Never deviate from that rule when someone you know 'vouches' for the underage renter – don't take that bait – ever.

Chapter 31

Should I accept a down payment or 'deposit' to hold a reservation?

What cancellation policy should I choose?

Guests will often contact you, via the 'Contact Owner' button on your listing, to ask if you will accept a 'deposit' to hold any given stay.

The short answer is NO.

You simply set your payment policies to require that payment is to be made in full at the time the reservation is made.

Let's think about how reasonable that is.

When you book a hotel room, are you allowed to give the hotel a deposit to 'hold' a room? Are you allowed to finance the cost of hotel stay over one, two or three payments? The answer is no.

I know that cruise lines allow payments. But you are not a cruise line with an accounting department.

You simply require that payment be made in full at the time the reservation is made. You are not a bank or a finance company. You do not have a team of accountants to let you know when each final payment has been made at your various properties so that you can then send check-in instructions. Simply do not accept payments.

The reason is simple.

The system that we have set up is that we immediately provide the guest everything they need to stay, including the keyless entry KABA lock code, immediately after they book. Trying to track four different vacation properties who has finished their payment plans before sending check in instructions can turn into a logistical nightmare.

Keep it simple. Guest books, you then send check in instructions, and you are done.

Some guests will whine and say they cannot afford to pay it all at once and beg for a payment plan. Do not take the bait. You are not a charity. If they cannot pay in full to book the unit, then they cannot afford to stay in your unit.

Every time that we have agreed to allow payments on a given stay, either the guest missed the payment, or ended up cancelling. I typically get poor results whenever a guest is on a payment plan to finance their stay, so require payment in full to book the unit.

On which cancellation policy to use, for the first few years, I went with a 'no refunds' cancellation policy. When COVID hit, that draconian policy hurt bookings, so I went with a more flexible, 30-day cancellation policy. In other words, the guest was able to cancel and get a full refund if they cancelled at least 30 days or more in advance of stay.

The good news is that regardless of which cancellation policy you pick, you are not likely to get a ton of cancellations. We did not get many under the no refunds policy, and even with the more flexible 30-day policy, cancellations are still very rare.

RULE: Require payment in full to book your vacation rental. Do not accept a 'deposit' to hold any given stay. Do not finance the payment for the stay. Keep it simple. The guest pays in full and books, and then you email check in instructions, and you are done. You are not tracking deposits or payment plans, two very time-consuming processes that typically yield poor results.

Chapter 32

How do lodging taxes work?

Do I need a business license?

Lodging taxes are a tricky area for both VRBO and Airbnb.

At some of our properties, VRBO collects and remits all the applicable taxes. Typically, a local, county or state law mandates that the vacation rental service do that for you. I firmly believe that will soon be the rule across the country.

At others, VRBO pays one portion of the taxes, and we pay the other portion. On one property, we collect and pay all lodging taxes.

When we were using VRBO and Airbnb simultaneously, we even had one company that withheld and paid the tax for us, but the other company, in the same location, relied on us to collect and pay the lodging tax.

In sum, the procedure for the withholding and payment of lodging taxes varies depending on the vacation rental location, and which service (VRBO or Airbnb) you are using.

You should, at minimum, research what the applicable tax rate is for your location, and you need to enter that tax rate into the VRBO system. If you are required to remit the taxes, you will then need to log on to the respective tax offices, and electronically pay those lodging taxes when they are due. Yes, you will need to mark your personal calendar to log on and make the remittance monthly. It is typically an electronic payment directly from your vacation rental bank account directly to the taxing authority. Once it is set up, it is easy and quick thereafter, especially because VRBO has monthly lodging revenue summaries readily available for you to use to calculate your remittance.

If VRBO or Airbnb take care of all the lodging taxes for you, then great. You get a break.

Indeed, we have seen recent legislation in some states that requires the vacation rental host (Airbnb and VRBO) to handle the collection and remittance of lodging taxes, instead of relying upon the vacation rental owner to hopefully get it right.

If you happen to fall in a location where VRBO or Airbnb does not remit lodging taxes for you, we have seen services that will charge the vacation rental owner a small fee per month to handle the lodging tax remittances. Hiring a service to handle lodging tax remittances for you will save you time and hassle.

Once you think you have the lodging tax remittance set up correctly (if that burden is yours to do and is not otherwise handled by VRBO and or Airbnb), book an appointment with your accountant, and go over all your tax selections, amounts, and methods to make sure that you have done it correctly. This review is money well spent, and do it sooner, rather than later, as in before you make your listing live and start accepting reservations.

Yes, you need to secure a business license for your vacation rental business before having guests. You want to have that license 'in hand' before your first guest sets foot in your vacation rental.

RULE: If VRBO or Airbnb does not collect and remit your lodging taxes, then you will need to do it. Contact your local taxing authorities to obtain the correct tax table and identify what is taxed. Once it is set, get your accountant to review it to make sure you are correctly remitting lodging taxes. In lieu of you having to calculate and remit the lodging taxes yourself, consider hiring a service to remit your vacation rental lodging taxes for you – money well spent. You must secure a business license for your vacation rental.

Chapter 33

Should I require a refundable damage deposit,

no damage deposit,

or just have the guest purchase damage insurance?

When setting up your vacation rental, VRBO will ask you whether you want your guest to provide a refundable damage deposit, no damage deposit, or require the guest to pay for an insurance policy for damage coverage up to a certain amount (i.e., $59 guest fee for up to $1,500 in property damage coverage for the owner's benefit).

The answer is clear and unequivocal. You should ALWAYS get a significant refundable damage deposit from every guest that stays in your unit, without exception.

For all our units, we require a $1,500 refundable damage deposit. The amount is even higher for the cabin.

The reason for this is that the guest knows that if they have a party, smoke in the unit, exceed capacity, break, tear up or steal something, that I can easily and readily seize their damage deposit with the click of a button. The guest has some 'skin' in the process, meaning they know they have $1500 of their money, out of their pocket, just sitting there ready to be taken by the owner if they do not do right, or fail to follow all rules of stay.

The refundable damage deposit is thus a powerful motivating tool.

In addition, no guest contemplating throwing a party in your vacation rental will like that type of policy, as they know that the cost of stay will increase instantly to the full loss of the damage deposit, so they will try and book elsewhere, somewhere preferably that does not mandate a refundable damage deposit.

What about just making the guest pay $59 to pay for a $1500 insurance policy for the owner's benefit? In other words, if there is damage caused during the guest stay, the owner simply makes a claim for damages caused by the guest with the insurance company, who then pays the owner for the damage or loss up to $1500.

I recommend against that insurance option as your only means of protection.

Please let me explain why.

The guest has no 'skin' in the process. They have zero motivation to not destroy your vacation rental, steal, or obey your rules of stay. They have paid a flat fee for insurance, which they will not get back, and they know that if they trash the place, someone else other than them will pay the owner for the damage. They then feel emboldened to break the rules, as they then feel that they have nothing to lose, as someone other than them pays for anything they destroy. Why bother with rules when one has nothing to lose?

As such, I do not recommend that you allow the guest to use insurance coverage as the sole source of your damage deposit. I firmly believe allowing that encourages the guest to break the rules, as they then have zero motivation to take care of your property, as they may then feel that they have 'nothing to lose.'

Furthermore, if there is an issue with the rental, you would then have to submit your claim to the insurance company, who may or may not approve your damage claim. The burden is on you in the process to produce a qualified claim to be paid. The insurance company may then nickel and dime you on the cost to replace, add depreciation and other shenanigans to pay out as little as possible on the claim as they can.

With a refundable damage deposit, you simply draw upon it, and then provide an explanation to the guest why you seized it, a much easier burden than filing a claim with an insurance company.

If the guest disputes your seizure of their refundable damage deposit, VRBO will let you know and there will be an appeal process. We will discuss the appeal process from a damage deposit forfeiture in a later chapter. As a preview, it is a process that is very fair to you as the vacation rental owner, as you typically always win.

The refundable damage deposit system works, motivates guests to follow the rules, and deters those who may be thinking of having a party or bringing pets to your vacation rental.

RULE: Without exception, require that every guest provide a sizeable refundable damage deposit. We require a $1500 refundable damage deposit at all our beach rentals and even a higher refundable damage deposit for our cabin.

Chapter 34

Should I make my vacation rental pet friendly?

A big decision is whether to make your vacation rental pet friendly or not.

Sometimes that decision is made for you.

At both our Splash Resort condo in Panama City Beach, and at our Phoenix on the Bay condo in Orange Beach, the HOA board at the respective resorts have both passed special covenants prohibiting rental guests from bringing their pets with them. Only owners are permitted to bring pets.

To enforce the rule, there are signs posted and frequent email reminders to owners that each pet on premises must have an HOA issued tag showing that the pet is registered with the HOA, who has investigated and confirmed that the pet is indeed that of an owner and not a rental guest. Further, they require a special super visible sleeve to place on the pet leash that shows that the pet has been duly registered and approved by the HOA.

If a vacation rental guest violates the rule, they will be asked to leave the premises by onsite security. In addition, you as the owner could be fined for guest non-compliance with this strictly enforced rule.

If you have that type of HOA rule for your vacation rental that prohibits vacation rental guests from bringing pets, then you in turn must have a strictly enforced 'no pets' policy as well. Do not go nice or light on the enforcement of the rule. You need to tell the guest that their vacation stay will be cancelled and not refunded if they bring a pet, and that they will forfeit all or a portion of their damage deposit if caught with a pet on premises.

Think about it. Imagine your guest brings a pet, gets caught by HOA security and gets thrown out of the resort. It could happen. Be clear and consistent – no pets are permitted. Period.

You may also explain that pets are also not allowed on the beach, as per local ordinance as well, and list the hefty fines and court costs that are due if caught on the beach with a pet. The reason for the no pets on the beach rule is obvious – one doesn't want pet waste in the sand, so it's primarily a health and safety issue.

There are therefore two very good reasons explaining why you do not allow pets (at least at the beach), if asked by the prospective vacation rental guest.

You may be an animal lover and own pets. Most Americans do. Why do HOA's prohibit rental guests from bringing pets?

Generally, I think the HOAs prohibit rental guests from bringing pets for several reasons. They are perhaps concerned with liability if the pet injures a guest on premises. There is concern with barking or the pet being a nuisance. There is concern with the waste that the rental guest may or may not pick up in or outside of a designated pet walk area.

Another concern is that your cleaning service may have a policy that they do not take on vacation rental properties whose vacation rental guests have a pet friendly policy. This is due to the large amount of time that is required to clean up after a pet is inside a vacation rental.

However, if the HOA does not prohibit a guest from bringing pets, should a homeowner then make their unit 'pet friendly'?

For instance, the Preserve HOA for our vacation rental cabin in Pigeon Forge does not prohibit pets on premises, but rather, allows each owner to decide whether to allow pets or not.

The answer to that question is an emphatic NO. Before you judge me, we are pet owners too and love our animals. We understand a family's need to travel with their pets. We get that.

However, our cleaning crew at the cabin in the mountains have a condition, that they will not accept a property unless it is a 'no pets' vacation rental. This is due to consistent issues dealing with waste inside the cabin, pet hair on the rugs, comforters, couches and chairs, and fleas.

Have you ever tried to get rid of a flea infestation in a vacation rental? It's a nightmare.

There is also the dank odor that accompanies pet waste on rugs and the pad beneath, a smell that is nearly impossible to ever get out. The pet guest is gone for the day enjoying all the attractions of the surrounding area, with their pet locked in your vacation rental. An 'accident' is thus not only possible to happen during this time, but it also then becomes likely to happen.

Further, the pets may cause a flea infestation in your vacation rental. Pet dander may cause your next guest, who is allergic to pets, to breakout in an allergic reaction. The smell of pets and their aftermath in a vacation rental always lingers. Do you really want a review from a guest alerting other prospective guests that your vacation rental smells like a doghouse, or is infested with fleas?

Also, pets may scratch at the door to get out, leaving permanent scratches on exit doorways, or cause other substantial damage. Some pets are known to chew on furnishings, or tear up pillows and cushions, or their claws will rip a hole in your couch or chair cushions.

The list of potential pet malfeasance is endless.

For the foregoing reasons and many more, we do not allow pets. The idea of walking into our cabin in the mountain and smelling dried animal excrement is sufficient reason alone for us to ban guests from having pets (sorry for going there just now). I am a closet germaphobe and the idea of animal excrement in the carpet and pad really makes me nauseous.

Will this policy cause a loss of rental business? I do not believe so. Although you will pick up a lot of guests traveling with pets, you will also lose those guests who will then not want to stay in a pet friendly vacation rental due to the reasons we just discussed, so it is a wash. If it's a wash, just say no.

Do we as owners bring our pets to our vacation rentals?

Yes, we do bring our pets when we visit our vacation rentals and run the risk of all the foregoing issues, which is unfortunate.

Consider it a perk of vacation rental ownership versus being a vacation rental guest – you get to bring your own pets! You can be hypocritical all day long on this issue, as you are the owner, and can do what you want.

When we do stay with our pets, we go to great lengths to not leave any trace that a pet was in the vacation rental, and further, pay an additional cleaning fee to our cleaning crew who must undertake the multiple additional steps following a pet stay in the rental.

As additional consideration, we also typically get the carpets cleaned (only applicable at our cabin since all other units have solid surface flooring), following our departure. Since we only visit the cabin one or two times a year, the carpet cleaning typically needs to be done anyway, so we always schedule professional carpet cleaning immediately following our cabin departures.

We do all of that despite having small, well-trained dogs who never have accidents, and are light on our rental properties.

Check the VRBO options box that you are not a pet friendly vacation rental. You will thank me for it.

What about someone claiming to have a service animal? Technically, you and your resort are both supposed to accommodate service animals under federal law. You cannot even charge them in advance extra to clean – which is ridiculous - but it's the law (you can charge them if the animal damages your unit though). Be careful if that situation pops up and remain in compliance with the law, as some folks sometimes seem to be fishing for litigation if an owner does not handle the service animal request correctly. Fortunately, only one time in ten years at four units did someone inquire about bringing a service animal, and fortunately, they ended up booking elsewhere (thankfully).

RULE: Do not allow pets and strictly enforce the rule. Be very careful if a guest wants to bring a service animal and stay in compliance with federal law on this issue.

Chapter 35

Should I permit smoking in my vacation rental?

You should NOT permit smoking inside your vacation rental.

Allowing smokers to smoke inside your vacation rental would cause the vacation rental to reek of cigarette smoke indefinitely. Further, sticky soot will be deposited on the walls, interior windows, and within the HVAC ventilation system. In addition, there is a risk of fire if the guest fails to snuff out their cigarette, forgets about the cigarette by accident, or falls asleep with it and it catches your vacation rental on fire. Ashes are also a cleanup mess.

Like not being pet friendly, this general rule will reduce or restrict the potential pool of renters interested in staying in your unit.

However, if you went smoke friendly, you would then likely lose 90% of other guests who want to book your unit because it is a smoke free vacation rental. You would then be catering to only a small segment of your potential rental audience (smokers), instead of the largest segment (non-smokers).

Further, no one likes to stay in a hotel room that has been smoked in. One's clothes stink, hair stinks, and it just feels icky. Why would you, as an owner, ever want your own vacation rental to smell like that?

Even if you are a smoker, you are likely to smoke outside to avoid trashing your own home, vehicle, or vacation rental. You may even seek out non-smoking hotel rooms during your travels because you too cannot stand the smell, even though you are a smoker.

Some may ask if it is ok to discriminate against smokers on this issue. The answer is that smokers are not a 'protected class' under discrimination laws. Discrimination in housing based on religion, national origin, sex, race, religion etc. are all considered to be protected classes, and cannot be discriminated against.

Smokers are not a protected class. Therefore, a vacation rental owner may legally ban smokers all day long in their vacation rental, and it is not against the law to discriminate against them.

Your HOA may also have rules that ban smoking in the common areas of the resort. If so, you should also inform your guest of that rule in advance of their stay.

For these reasons and many more, prohibit smoking, vaping and cigar smoking at your vacation rental.

Here is our language from our vacation rental description banning smoking. Do not soft pedal the rule. Be firm and explicit. Ban any type of smoking in your vacation rental.

NO SMOKING: This is a strictly non-smoking unit / resort. There will be a $1500 fine, forfeiture of stay, forfeiture of damage deposit, and required reimbursement for all costs of deodorization (which could be thousands of dollars) if smoking occurs in the unit. This rule is closely monitored and strictly enforced.

We even post a sign on the inside of the unit door that prohibits smoking. Our sign simply says 'Thank you for not smoking' using a light grey font on a black background, with the classic ban symbol over a burning cigarette. The small sign is not as visually distressing as a typical no smoking sign – a toned down directive. Some owners even put out small no smoking placards, which may be excessive.

Make sure your cleaners know also to alert you immediately if they smell smoke following any given guest check out, so that you can make a claim against the guest's damage deposit to deodorize the unit. The cleaner should document the 'smell' in any visible way they can. These steps may include looking at the air condition filters and see if they are blackened. The cleaner may also need to search everywhere for cigarette butts or ashes (and pay the cleaner extra to do so).

Ideally, some type of proof (photos) that smoking occurred is helpful to substantiate your claim against the guest damage deposit. Relying upon just the 'smell of smoke' may be a tough journey through the appeal process if the guest challenges you on your taking their damage deposit. So make sure your cleaner tries to find something objective to show something more than just a mere smell of smoke in order to seize some or all of their damage deposit.

RULE: Ban smoking at your vacation rental. No exceptions.

Chapter 36

Critical things to watch for at closing

As previously discussed, one should work with the seller to divide up closing costs, title insurance and other closing expenses fairly, and to follow guidelines on what is customary in that state or area. These are issues that are addressed in the Offer of Purchase, and are not typically changed while the property is pending. If the property was listed through the MLS, your buyer's agent will help determine what is customary for the buyer and seller to respectively pay at closing. Finally, these same realtors will recommend a closing agent - an authentic real estate agent closing office. That recommendation can be crucial, as you do not want to rely solely on an Internet search for the choice of your closing agent, due to the proliferation of Internet scams.

As also previously discussed, secure a copy of the entire package of proposed closing paperwork in advance of closing, so that you or your realtor or attorney friend can review it in advance. Attempting to make last minute changes in the middle of a frenzied signing at closing is not the best time to do corrections. Make sure you pay particular attention to the proposed deed, to make sure the vacation rental property is being titled correctly (if husband and wife - joint with rights of survivorship; if brother and sister - tenants in common; or if nonfamily members buying together as partners - in an LLC name).

Also, you should make sure you are getting a warranty deed, a deed where the seller is warranting that they have a good and merchantable title, free of encumbrances, liens, or other claims. A red flag should go up if the seller is only signing a 'Quit Claim' deed - which does not warrant that the seller is providing good and merchantable title.

You should always secure and or require title insurance whenever you buy any property. Title insurance is an insurance policy that warrants that you are indeed getting clear and merchantable title, free of liens or encumbrances, at closing. It also guarantees that you are not being scammed by an imposter impersonating the owner. As the purchase of the vacation rental is a sizeable investment of your life's savings, it is critical that you spend the proportionately small amount of money to get title insurance (typically $1500), to protect your investment. It is money well spent.

You should always book a time slot to walk through the vacation rental property within 24 hours of closing. This will help ensure that all listed property in the Offer of Purchase is still there, and that there has not been any new or unexpected loss or damage to the property that may have happened during the time between your inspection and the actual closing.

During the purchase of our Pigeon Forge cabin, we scheduled a time for me to complete a final walkthrough within 24 hours of closing and discovered that one of the seller's vacation rental guests had spilled red wine on the cabin's pool table, ruining it. It wasn't an intentional thing – the seller didn't know it had happened either.

We thereafter entered into a written agreement for the seller to take care of the issue after closing at his expense, saving me $700, a significant repair. I firmly believe that the seller genuinely did not know about the damage, as he never saw his property again after we signed the Offer of Purchase, and he lived a plane ride away from the cabin. It is a lot easier to get the seller to agree to pay for a repair like that before closing, rather than coming back to the seller after the closing, asking for repair expenses.

Unbeknownst to us both as well, some of the seller's action items were not fixed. Again, we took care of this through written agreement for the seller to take care of those issues after closing at his expense.

Be careful with 100% remote closings, where all closing papers are emailed or mailed and overnighted, without appearing around a table in the closing office for everyone's signatures. You need to conduct extensive due diligence to confirm that the closing agent or office is indeed real, has been in business for a sufficient length of time, that their office does exist, that is a legitimate operation, and not some type of scam or made-up business, especially since you are wiring hundreds of thousands of dollars.

You should also be careful with encountering an imposter that may try to impersonate your closing agent. In other words, your closing agent is real, but an imposter comes in and begins impersonating the real closing agent, your real estate agent and or the title company, and you end up wiring your purchase money to the imposter, rather than the real closing agent. Closing agents have seen that happen as well with increasing frequency, so be careful.

Before you wire your money anywhere, conduct an abundance of due diligence.

This should be obvious, but one should always use a reputable closing agent to close any given real estate transaction, and due to the amount of money involved, this is never something that is handled without the use of professionals. You need to use real live people you meet and or talk to in person, not just emails and texts.

The deed that is signed by the seller must be recorded with the local judge of probate to be effective. You should therefore be watching for the recorded signed deed in the mail after closing. Sometimes a mistake occurs, and the signed deed fails to get recorded, which would be a major concern, as there would then be no public record memorializing the transaction.

Remember that there is always a second step or additional step that you must take following closing. You must get the property assessed into your name for property tax purposes. In many states, simply recording the deed does not in turn automatically cause the tax assessor to assess the property for taxes in your name. This is because you often must choose or provide the tax assessor with intel on whether you are buying the property as a primary residence, a second home, or an investment property (as each category may have a different tax category). Typically, there is no charge to get the property assessed in your name.

If you fail to take that necessary step, the property tax bill will then continue to go to the old owner, who in turn will not pay it, as they no longer own the property. If the taxes do not get paid, then the property will get sold for taxes. That sale in turn could then potentially affect your possessory rights to the property. To redeem the property, penalties and interest would have to then be paid. There is an entire cottage industry of businesses that go in and buy up properties which are sold due to nonpayment of taxes. Don't forget that extra step following closing - get that vacation rental property tax assessed in your name.

The seller should also be solely responsible for all HOA dues through the date of closing, and all declared assessments that are not yet due. In this way, you are not buying into a hefty assessment that has been previously declared, but not due until after your closing. When you previously contacted the HOA for their rules and regulations, you should have also confirmed the absence of any declared, but not yet due, assessments. If any assessments were declared, you need to make sure the assessment is paid for by the seller at closing.

RULES: Always get title insurance when purchasing a property. Don't forget to assess the property in your name for tax purposes, a separate step you need to take after the closing. Exercise due diligence before ever separating from your money to confirm that your funds are not diverted to an imposter or a scam.

SECTION III - YOUR FIRST MONTH OF OWNERSHIP

Chapter 37

The Deep Clean

One of the most important attributes of any successful vacation rental is its cleanliness. For just a few hundred dollars, a team of cleaning professionals can clean every inch of your new vacation rental. Everything in the rental needs to be cleaned – the ceilings, walls, floors and all contents.

The deep cleaning may be someone you separately hire just for this task or maybe a service that is also included with the cleaning team you hire to service the unit. We typically do not use our regular cleaning crew for deep cleaning, but rather an independent cleaning company to come in and perform that task. We tend to get better results with an independent cleaning company, and it's more affordable than using our regular cleaning team for that task.

During the offseason, utilize the downturn to schedule a deep clean. At minimum, the vacation rental needs to be deep cleaned when initially purchased (immediately before your guests arrive and after all your improvements have been completed), and on no less than an annual basis each year after that.

Do not deep clean yourself. Deep cleaning your vacation rental takes the joy out of vacation rental ownership. It is a legitimate expense so just spend the money and hire someone to do it. Your job as an owner is administration, not cleaning. Your job is to do owner tasks only - setting rates, adjusting your listing, or deciding upon which piece of artwork you want. Deep cleaning is not one of your job duties.

This general rule applies whether the vacation rental is five minutes from your house or a plane flight away. You may or may not be taking away time from your primary job, so avoid doing things that take away from your primary source of income if the task can instead be efficiently and inexpensively outsourced. Remember, your goal is to get your time down to just an hour a week to manage your vacation rental. Performing labor and time intensive tasks such as deep cleaning or painting is not part of that equation.

RULE: Schedule a deep clean to be completed immediately before your first guest arrives, and after you have completed your initial improvements to your property following closing. Do not do deep cleaning yourself – always hire that task out.

Chapter 38

Painting

At a minimum, paint the vacation rental. Even if it is a color scheme you like, it will likely need to be freshened up.

A fresh paint job with the latest colors and styles will really make your vacation rental pop. Do not skip the baseboards, bead board, chair rails, doors, windowsills, and crown molding. It all needs to be painted too.

Sometimes cabinetry can be updated by simply painting it as well. Cabinets can be sanded, primed, and painted, instead of being completely replaced, and simply change out the hardware on the doors for a more updated look.

If you are not good at coordinating colors, furnishings, wall paint and décor, consult an interior decorator for assistance. Identify and map out the theme for your vacation rental, whether it's a bear theme in Gatlinburg, an Aspen tree theme in Vail, or Southwestern style in New Mexico, know that that theme is and make sure the paint colors are consistent with that theme.

Always choose eggshell finish. You may not like the sheen as much as semigloss or satin, or even flat, but you really need to do eggshell. The reason is simple – eggshell sheen can be washed with soap and water and get out marks and blemishes, without having to touch up paint.

You should also make sure your painting crew leaves behind any unused paint. The unused paint cans will then provide years of touch up paint to blemishes on the wall that cannot be washed off with soap and water. Simply store the spare paint in your owner's closet, and always keep spare disposable paint brushes. When you visit the unit, you won't be able to resist the temptation to take a few minutes and touch up the paint in the unit – so that the walls are perfect. As an owner, you can spend a few minutes during your stay touching up walls as needed – that's fair.

However, do not tackle the entire paint job yourself. Hiring a professional painting team is a legitimate business expense, they will do it right, and it will look professionally done. They will also do it quickly, which allows you to get your property ready for the first guest sooner.

You likely have a primary job that you have previously relied upon as your primary income source, and you need to focus on that. You have a family and a life to live. You are not a skilled painter. You should hire that task out. Save your finite resources for owner only tasks, or enjoying yourself, not completing labor intensive and time-consuming tasks that you can easily hire out.

Again, you want your vacation rental to be updated, and with the latest fashionable paint colors and or look that is consistent with the theme of your vacation rental.

RULE: Have a professional painting service paint your vacation rental with the latest style colors to fit the overall theme of your vacation rental.

Chapter 39

Replace dated light fixtures and ceiling fans

For a small amount of money, replace any dated ceiling fans or light fixtures. Light fixtures and ceiling fans are relatively inexpensive. Gather the group of them while you await closing. Then, hire an electrician to have all the fixtures installed in one visit. This will take planning for you to order all the fixtures in advance, assemble them for delivery, and then book the day for the electrician to install the replacement fixtures.

If the ceiling fans do not look dated, or fit your theme, still replace them if they are wobbling or make noise. Your ceiling fans must be fully functional and quiet.

RULE: Order replacement ceiling fans and fixtures that fit the theme of your vacation rental, and have an electrician install all of them in one day.

Chapter 40

Choose your theme / décor selection

early on and stick to it

For your vacation rental, choose a theme or a décor selection that is appropriate for its location.

Themed resort stays are the new frontier. Lodging resorts are now moving in the direction of an all-encompassing experience for their guests. An example of this trend is Great Wolf Lodge. There is the anchor attraction of an indoor heated waterpark, with themed log cabin style rooms, a gem mining operation, a magic wand treasure hunt, storybook 'pajama' sessions, and multiple other activities, all in one location.

The main point is that the resort, and its accompanying guest rooms, have a theme.

Another example is Disney World, which has themed resort locations. These range from The Grand Floridian, Polynesian Village, and the Contemporary Resort. Each one is a themed lodging resort within Disney World where the theme in each room matches the resort theme.

For a beach condo, a nautical or seaside theme with light colors may be something to consider.

For a cabin in the mountains, exposed wood walls, darker furnishings, and a more rustic log cabin feel may be in order.

Before deciding on the décor and theme that you want, look at your competition on VRBO and Airbnb for ideas. Once you get the theme and décor, you will have a plan in mind as you pick out your paint color, fixtures, furnishings, artwork, and accents so the feel of the vacation rental is consistent throughout.

Be careful with choosing a theme that may not fit for your location.

For example, you may have loved the 'over the water' bungalows in Tahiti. Even so, do not try and make your Panama City Beach condo into a Tahitian hut.

Similarly, do not jam your love for a New York style modern minimalist look into your Colorado mountain cabin. Rather, embrace the area and the décor that is there. Use local furnishings that source materials locally, seek out local artwork, and embrace interior styles that are customary for the area.

People want to experience an area, so embrace it. I never thought in a million years I would have a cabin with rustic, mountain themed décor, complete with bears and deer. After buying our cabin, that is exactly what we did, as that was the décor that vacationing guests wanted in a Tennessee mountain cabin. Never say never.

RULE: Embrace the area and incorporate it into the theme and décor of your vacation rental.

Chapter 41

Update all appliances.

If the appliances are dated, simply have Lowe's or Home Depot come out during that first month and update all your appliances. Use the finish that is the latest style, whether it is stainless or a smoke color or something else. You need new appliances, so it makes the kitchen pop. Guests rent vacation rentals often to stay in and cook and is one of the main benefits that a vacation rental will have over a traditional hotel room. A beautiful kitchen with new appliances and freshly painted cabinetry will go a long way in convincing a guest that this is where they want to prepare meals for their family.

Also, many of your guests will likely be accustomed to having a nice kitchen in their home. We also need the appliances to consistently work. Starting off with new appliances helps reduce the risk of a breakdown during their stay. The automatic ice dispenser on an old refrigerator is more likely to break down. Older dishwashers tend to be noisy. The older microwave may have blemishes due to age that makes it hard to appear clean.

Doing this will also dollar for dollar increase the fair market value of your vacation rental (an understatement) so it is money well spent. Studies have shown that improvements in the kitchen and bathrooms result in a several times increase in value to a property, more than paying for itself in the long run.

You must get a quality washer and dryer. Guests will use them. Your cleaner will use them to wash bed protectors, blankets, and other soiled items on the fly. Do not skimp on the expense for these two appliances.

Finally, breakdowns will cost you dearly, so do everything you can early, before guests arrive. Replace anything that may be on its last leg, or is dated, or needing to be replaced, is missing parts, or is not fully functioning. You want to avoid that negative review, or crisis mode fix.

Finally, some guests get prickly about it and ask for a refund when something breaks down, so try and avoid all of that by simply going in with new appliances.

RULE: Hire Lowe's or Home Depot to come in and replace all the appliances in the unit. It's money well spent and will increase the value of the vacation rental in the long run.

Chapter 42

Should I replace all light bulbs?

After you do your inventory of the vacation rental's light bulbs, order a complete replacement set, and replace every single light bulb in the vacation rental with the highest quality bulb you can afford, and that match the color of all the other bulbs in the rental.

You should then have a batch of extra matching bulbs on hand in your owner's closet to use if one goes out.

By going in with high quality (LED) bulbs, they last longer, and then become less likely to burn out during any given guest stay. In addition, the newer LED bulbs use less energy, and run a lot cooler than hot incandescent bulbs, which saves you energy, especially in the summer.

In addition, you may be able to skip having a bulb maintenance plan with a maintenance team or maintenance person. Simply let your cleaner know that there are extra bulbs in the owner's closet, and if they see a bulb burned out, they simply replace it. If you make it easy for the cleaner to replace a bulb, and they are on hand, they match, are easy to get to, the cleaners are usually more than happy to replace a bulb as needed, especially if it rarely happens with a higher end bulb. Perhaps provide a small step ladder as well. Pay the cleaner a little extra each time they do it so that they are sufficiently motivated to do this task which is above and beyond simply cleaning. If replacing the bulb is simple and quick, and you are willing to pay extra for the service, the bulbs will get replaced. Otherwise, they won't.

When we purchased our vacation rental cabin, there were no less than three different sized bulbs in the track lighting, and some of the bulbs were daylight, while some were warm white, and others were soft white. Their color and size did not match at all. All were dusty. Some had paint splatter. Others were half burned out and black.

You want the same size and quality bulbs, and for them to all be the same color. There are exceptions – you may want a white light for inside the fridge, or perhaps a white light over a shower stall, but soft white everywhere else, and that is fine. Use your discretion.

Generally, you want your vacation rental to be bright, not dark, and cavernous. You need plenty of light to showcase the beautifully painted walls, the cleanliness of the vacation rental, and updated appliances, fixtures, and furnishings. Every room should have sufficient lighting capacity, even if all of it isn't used all the time.

Yes, you can certainly add a dimmer switch for appropriate mood lighting, and that is a great idea. You can perhaps have a small lamp with a 40-watt bulb but allow for higher wattage on the bulbs in the ceiling fan. Use your discretion.

Remember - there is nothing that screams cheap than having a room that is dimly lit. The kitchen and bathroom must have plenty of lighting, especially over the sink – at minimum. This is a first world accommodation, not a third world accommodation, so make sure your rooms are sufficiently lit.

RULE: Replace all bulbs in the vacation rental with matching color LED bulbs and have labeled and plentiful matching spares on hand in the owner's closet.

Chapter 43

Should I replace the HVAC?

Your heating, air conditioning and ventilation system (HVAC), is the single most important product of your vacation rental. It is the only appliance that if it quits working, that a guest may not be able to stay in the vacation rental. It absolutely cannot break down at any point and must be easy to use and adjust. If the microwave goes down, guests can adjust. If the HVAC breaks, it can be a huge deal, depending upon what time of year it goes down.

Unless it is relatively new, or still under warranty, I tend to just go ahead and replace an HVAC right at the beginning.

If you are reluctant to do it, at minimum, get a formal inspection which includes photos of the entire system and get an HVAC person to estimate the remaining life of the system. With photos of the HVAC and remaining life span in hand, you may then be more likely to replace it.

There was a time that I thought our HVAC at Splash was in good shape. Once I was shown photos of a completely rusted out condenser on one of our units, I was shocked that the system was still operating. The salt air rusts out outdoor condensing units at the beach, so just because they are allegedly new does not mean that they are not deteriorating.

Yes, it would seem to be an expensive replacement, but in the long run, it will pay you dividends to go ahead and get new HVACs from the beginning. Be proactive on this one – don't wait until it quits working. Replace it well before you get anywhere near the point that it may possibly break down.

This is what we do not want to happen.

You have booked your beachfront condo for the Fourth of July holiday weekend at the highest rate of the year, $800 per night for peak season at the beach. No one can find a beach condo, everything is sold out, and people will pay anything for a place to stay. Boom, your air conditioning goes out. It is 95 degrees during the day, and simply too hot and humid to spend the night. Your guests are angry. They have nowhere to go as everything is booked up. They can't stay as its too hot. You must refund their stay.

After a week spending thousands of dollars to replace the HVAC on an emergency basis, you then refund the most lucrative stay of the year, nearly doubling the total loss. The lost rental and refunded stay cost more than what it cost to replace the HVAC.

That is not what we want to happen.

You have your cabin booked for Christmas. Guests will pay any amount as everything is booked up, and they want a white Christmas. Boom. The heat goes out (not the power – your heating system). It is 10 degrees at night. They won't stay.

Just like the former example, the guests have nowhere to go as everything is booked up for Christmas. The guests are livid and are forced to drive or fly home. You must refund their money, and then endure the wrath of a horrific review.

Like the foregoing example, you lose more in lost rental income than what it ended up costing to replace the system. In addition, future rentals may be affected by the negative review as well.

We will talk about refunds more later.

The rule is that if your HVAC breaks down, and the guest is then not able to stay in the vacation rental due to it not being habitable (due to extreme heat or extreme cold), you must refund their money.

Don't set yourself up for that – replace the HVAC sooner than later and avoid that type of breakdown, as it gets super expensive when you factor in how much rental revenue potentially is lost if it breaks down during peak season.

Although we will talk about this in the next chapter, go ahead and get a Nest thermostat system when the HVAC system is installed. Also, if you are on the coast or on water, see if you can locate a HVAC system designed to withstand a saltwater environment, or incorporates anti-corrosion construction.

On maintenance of your new system, remember to purchase a couple bottles of bleach and a funnel, and schedule your cleaner or maintenance person to pour some bleach in the AC drain lines to prevent a backup.

Keep the bleach and funnel supply in the owner's closet. If there is no owner's closet, simply store the items above the refrigerator. If the supplies to bleach the AC drain are readily available, then it is more likely to get done. Again, motivate the cleaner to do this routinely by paying them extra for this service.

On our visits to the vacation property, it's also a 30 second owner 'honey do' – no big deal. By being preventative, this too will help prevent a breakdown. Every time we stay at a vacation rental, it's a 30 second per unit task if you have the supplies on site.

If you are not regularly visiting your vacation rental, schedule a maintenance person to do it every few months, or pay your cleaning service to do it. Otherwise, the drain will clog up and shut your system down, or the drain overflow may damage your unit.

RULE: Unless it is a brand-new system, replace the HVAC. Otherwise, it may go out at the most inconvenient of times, and the resulting refund to a guest may cost you more than the cost to replace the HVAC.

Chapter 44

Should I get a Nest thermostat?

I highly recommend that when you replace the HVAC system, that you have installed professionally, a Nest thermostat, or whatever is the latest app controlled remote thermostat. This will allow you to adjust the vacation rental temperature from the Nest app on your smart phone when the vacation rental is empty.

For example, our cleaning crew came in to clean the cabin during the middle of summer, and they cranked the air down to 60 as they are hot and are working hard. I am fine with that and understand.

However, when they were done, the cleaners forgot to turn the air back up to 76 degrees, the temperature we recommend between guest stays. Imagine the utility bill after ten days of 60 degrees on the air conditioner with 90-degree temperatures outside. We never would have known that was going on if we did not have the Nest app.

Similarly, during the winter, and when the cabin is vacant for a week or two, I can remotely turn the heat to 55 or 60, so that we are not unnecessarily heating the cabin when it is vacant. During long absences, you can also remotely turn on the fan to keep the air moving around to help combat mold.

Our guests have had no issues using the thermostat and have figured out how to adjust it while they are there, and it is simple enough to use from that perspective, which is good.

Another perk of the Nest thermostat is that you can use your Nest app to cool the cabin off immediately before the guests check in at 4pm, and during the winter, warm the cabin up right before the guests arrive. In that way, the vacation rental is already set to a comfortable temperature and the guest is not entering a hot vacation rental in the summer, or a freezing cold vacation rental in the winter.

If you do not use a Nest thermostat, you should then go with the simplest, easiest to use and understand thermostat that even the most unsophisticated of guests will know how to use and understand. The simpler the better when it comes to choosing which thermostat to use. It needs to literally be dummy proof.

RULE: Get a Nest thermostat.

Chapter 45

The Coastal Green Air system

Guests often arrive at their Gulf front vacation rental, and in the middle of the summer, leave the balcony doors open for hours on end, so that the kids and parents could both run in and out, with the air conditioning running non-stop trying to cool the unit.

At night, guests often leave the balcony doors open so they can hear the waves crashing at night while they sleep - a soothing sound.

The convenience of leaving the balcony door open, and the temptation of hearing the waves crashing at night, have both drowned out any guest thoughts of saving energy.

The convenience is at the expense of the air conditioning system, that runs continuously while the balcony doors are open. The air conditioning system will condensate heavily due to the high humidity passing through its system, swamping the drain line with more than ten times the volume of drainage than usual, resulting in the need to bleach or blow out the drain line on a more frequent basis.

This situation also in turn leads to outrageously high utility bills during the summer for the vacation rental owner.

During the winter, when the same vacation rental sits empty for weeks on end, the hot water heater keeps running, heating water although it is not needed.

To fix these utility waste issues, a man from Gulf Shores Alabama formed a company called 'Coastal Green Air.' He designed a sensor system that would cause the air conditioning system to turn off if either the condo front door or balcony doors remained open for more than a few minutes.

This, in turn, forces guests to close the doors as the air conditioning system does not otherwise run.

He also installed a motion detector in the unit. If no motion was detected for a day or so, the sensor turns off the hot water heater. As soon as motion is again detected inside the vacation rental, the hot water heater turns back on.

The company also has before and after records of typical utility use of any given condo, that show the dramatic savings of having that system installed at your vacation rental. The idea is that the utility savings will quickly pay for the system. As the system costs around $1500 - $2500, which includes installation, it does take a few years for the system to be cost-effective.

In the welcome instructions that you send your guests, with the keycode to get into the vacation rental, you will explain to the guests that the unit utilizes the Coastal Green Air system, and that the air conditioning and heat will turn off if the doors are left open for more than a few minutes. You also tell them that it may take up to 20 minutes upon arrival before there is hot water.

You then explain that by keeping utility rates low, it is good for the planet, and saves them, the guest, money with lower rates due to lower expenses – something along those lines.

Here is the sample language from our check in instruction email:

Air Condition / Hot Water: To conserve energy, this unit is installed with sensors which will shut the A/C system off if the balcony door or front door is left open for more than 90 seconds. Once both doors are securely closed for a few minutes, the A/C will ultimately resume. For any additional issues with the AC, please review the 'Coastal Green Air' placards in the unit and follow its instructions.

If by chance the thermostat is completely blank, the thermostat battery may need replacement, or the float switch is triggering a shutdown. Both issues typically can be remedied very quickly, as the AC system is new. If there is an AC issue, please contact maintenance personnel listed on the top of this sheet.

Hot water will be available typically within 20 minutes of entry into the unit, following a vacancy or extended absence. Thereafter, the hot water will be at a very high temperature in order to avoid running out of hot water for guests. **Please be mindful of children, the elderly or other special needs guests to avoid scalding.**

Dryer lint screen must be emptied with each use. To prevent rust or damage to the dryer, please do not put wet saltwater items in the dryer such as salty or sandy bathing suits, or salty or sandy beach towels.

A downside to this system is that you must use the Coastal Green Air thermostat, which is not adjustable remotely like a Nest thermostat, or at least wasn't available when the system was initially installed.

With no Coastal Green Air app telling you what the temperature is in the unit between guest stays, or during those long winter off-season months, you remain wondering what the thermostat is set to when the unit is vacant. Perhaps Coastal Green Air will soon have an app that allows that, and when and if it does, that would be a dramatic game changer.

Another downside is that the balcony and unit door sensor batteries must be periodically changed, a service hassle.

Finally, after installing the Nest thermostat at the cabin in Pigeon Forge, I have grown addicted to that system, as there is nothing better than being able to shut down the HVAC on the phone app when the unit is empty between guest stays. I can then return it to a comfortable temperature just before a guest check in, all from the app. The ability to do that feels empowering.

Perhaps the Nest system will someday also include the ability to turn off the hot water heater during vacancies. Perhaps the Coastal Green Air system will someday include an app where the owner can adjust the vacation rental temperature remotely. We will see.

At this point, this continues to be a debatable situation on the pros and cons of the two respective systems. The goal of both is to save energy, so pick your poison, and check and see if either or both have updated their products.

RULE: At minimum, install a Nest thermostat system so that you can adjust your vacation rental temperature through the app when the vacation rental is vacant for an extended length of time. Consider the Coastal Green Air system as an alternative as well, especially if you have a beachfront vacation rental.

Chapter 46

Should I Install security cameras and/or an alarm?

At most typical Gulf front condo resorts, the Homeowners Association (HOA) will have security cameras set up around the resort or will maintain a security presence for the premises. In those situations, security cameras or Ring doorbell cameras may not only be unnecessary, but the HOA may also not permit them in the common areas outside the unit.

On a standalone vacation rental, such as a house or cabin, exterior security cameras are an absolute must. You will want to see how the weather looks, whether the roads are clear of snow, and you will just want that peace of mind confirming that all is well at your rental. Remember the previous chapter where I could see from our cabin the forest fire in the distance on our surveillance cameras – having them at that moment was a priceless thing. I always say not knowing is worse than knowing – especially in a circumstance like that.

For instance, if the security system is up and running, this would indicate that the cabin has power – a good thing. This is important to know perhaps after a major storm came through and you live far away from your vacation rental.

Most importantly though, you will want to check in on occasion to make sure that your guests have not exceeded their parking capacity for the vacation rental. Ideally, the security camera can be linked to an app on your phone, where it is simple and easy to check in on occasion, even at random times.

Realistically, however, you are not going to have the time to check in on every guest, or to sit there and make sure a guest is not bringing in a pet or hauling off your TV's.

Informing the guest in your listing in advance, and in your welcome instructions, sends a message to the guest that the rules will be enforced, and that you have eyes on the property, which will motivate the guest to stay in compliance with your rules. Having the cameras are essentially *a deterrence mechanism*, as the odds of you needing the footage are very small.

Yes, some apps may keep a recording for a certain length of time, and if that is not cost prohibitive, may be a good idea. Damages or theft is typically reported immediately by your cleaning crew, and the damage deposit can be forfeited for up to two weeks following departure, so it would not make sense to keep outside security footage for longer than two weeks or so.

As an example, let's change perspective from thinking like an owner to thinking like a prospective guest for a minute.

Let's say that a prospective guest owns a small dog and is shopping the vacation rentals for their upcoming stay. The prospective guest narrows it down to a couple of rentals, and in the end, chooses the one that does not have in their listing that they utilize security cameras, in the hopes that they can violate the no pet rule and not get busted.

In other words, the vacation rental that had the security cameras, or even said they had the security cameras (whether they did or not), resulted in deterring away from that rental a guest with intentions on breaking their no pet policy. This is a good thing.

The same thing would apply to a prospective guest considering a party in the vacation rental, or an entire fraternity house piling in one night for a party. The guest would immediately discard those vacation rentals that use security cameras.

The pet owners and party crowds are the type of guests that you do not want in your vacation rental, so the listing stating that there is exterior video monitoring, with photos showing the exterior cameras, is a good thing, and will help deter rule breaking guests from booking your unit.

Your vacation rental may also be in a remote area, with a limited municipal police presence. If a thief has a choice between two empty vacation rental cabins, and one has security cameras, but the other doesn't, the thief will likely choose the one with no security cameras, so yet another reason to have them.

Obviously, one can never have any type of camera or device that records either video or audio of your vacation rental guests, while they are inside the vacation rental. Doing so could result in criminal and civil liability. Cameras should never in any way be able to see what is going on inside the vacation rental.

In an abundance of prudence, I would even recommend against them being used outside around the hot tub, or a shared swing or any other situation where any given guest may have a reasonable expectation of privacy.

For example, no guest would ever have any reasonable expectation of privacy for a camera to be monitoring all parking areas at the vacation rental. It is reasonable to video surveil parking areas.

For exterior video surveillance, post a sign that states that video surveillance is on property, and fully disclose it in your check in instructions. Again, deterrence is the key here. Here is our video surveillance disclosure paragraph from our cabin check in instructions, where exterior video cameras are utilized:

RING Doorbell / Cameras: This cabin is equipped with a Ring Doorbell mounted at the front door that records both audio and video. There are additional cameras mounted around the cabin that monitor the parking area and the areas around the cabin. By renting this cabin, you consent to both audio and video surveillance (a sign to that effect is also posted outside the cabin). There are no cameras located inside the cabin. All exterior cameras are pointed in a direction away from the interior of the cabin and are primarily set to monitor the parking areas of the cabin.

The next question is whether an alarm may be necessary for your vacation rental. We have found that alarms generally end up being more trouble than they are worth, and do not use them. Instead, we rely upon keeping the vacation rental booked (i.e., constantly occupied), and keeping the exterior security cameras operable. 99.9% of alarm issues are caused by a guest simply trying to access and or use your vacation rental. It turns quickly into a crisis mode phone-call from a guest or the alarm monitoring company. Do not set up a system that will result in crisis level phone calls in the middle of the night.

There may be some exceptions on high-end vacation rentals in remote locations, and an alarm may be necessary. Presumably you would simply give your guest the code to disarm the alarm upon entry, as part of your check-in instructions.

When we bought our cabin up in Pigeon Forge, the previous owner had at one time a functioning alarm system, with posted signs and stickers. He joked with me that he hoped that the presence of the signs and stickers would themselves possibly deter a burglar, as the alarm system was disconnected years earlier due to constant problems with the guests understanding how to disarm it.

Rather than the alarm system, I would focus on beefing up the amount of your refundable damage deposit, investing in a Ring doorbell camera and an exterior surveillance system (with extensive posted signage), and securing comprehensive contents insurance. In that way, your property is protected without you having to worry about constantly changing out an alarm code.

I firmly believe that if someone is going to burglarize your home, it will be someone other than a guest legitimately staying in the vacation rental. Keep your vacation rental booked, if anything, for the presence of a visiting guest be the deterrence that keeps a burglar away from a vacation rental. The vacation rental guest is your ally – by keeping the vacation rental occupied- it is then less likely to be burglarized.

After owning and renting six different vacation rentals in three states for more than ten years, we have never had anything of significant value stolen from our vacation rentals. If you follow all the rules in this book, you too should have a similar experience.

RULE: If you have a standalone vacation rental (not a condo in HOA controlled resort), install a Ring Doorbell camera and exterior surveillance cameras of the parking area, that are both tied to an app on your smart phone. Avoid using a home security alarm if you are actively renting out your vacation rental. If exterior alarm signs and placards are already up when you buy your vacation rental, do not take them down.

Chapter 47

Should I install a Ring Doorbell?

Ring Doorbells have become extremely common and popular across the United States. They are a terrific, new, affordable invention, that one should try to incorporate into their vacation rental, if possible. They are a convenient way to monitor who comes to the door, and who is coming in and out of the vacation rental, all from the convenience of a phone app.

One of the most valuable benefits of having the Ring Doorbell is knowing when someone comes to your vacation rental, when it is empty, or it is between guest stays. This is where you really get your money's worth.

For instance, let's just say your cleaning team uses a lot of different cleaners, and so they have kept the owner code to get into the cabin or condo or vacation rental. They then know from your website listing and or through the software you use for scheduling cleanings, that the vacation rental is open for a certain length of time.

Let's say your own children, or your friends, or other family members who have used the condo in the past, have the owner KABA door lock code too, and know how to check the vacation rental condo calendar to see if it is empty or not, and so they may know exactly when the unit is not being used as well.

When I was in college, if I knew a condo at the beach was open, or a cabin on a remote mountaintop was open, and I could *get away with* using the facilities for me and my buddies or me and my girlfriend, and I am embarrassed to say this, but I would have been very tempted back then.

How many of us teenagers had a party at our house when our parents went out of town?

Well, the Ring Doorbell can help prevent or provide needed deterrence from something like that.

The cleaner will know that they will get caught if they come and go to the cabin between guest stays.

The friend or family member will know that they will get caught if they come and go to the cabin between guest stays.

I am not saying that this has ever happened, or would happen, but it is certainly possible.

You would be surprised on how often you give someone access to your vacation rental, whether to deliver an appliance, to give an estimate for a cleaning, or to decorate, or to fix something (we will talk more about door lock codes in a later chapter), and then that code is again used inappropriately.

All it takes is one 'bad apple' to abuse the key code privilege and keep that door code you gave them. They can make your vacation rental their own private love shack. Get the Ring Doorbell and it will help prevent something like that from happening between guest stays. Peace of mind is indeed priceless.

Another interesting development is that one can then tell how long your cleaner stays in your unit to clean, as the Ring camera monitors their arrival and departure times. If only one cleaner cleans, and they clean in less than thirty minutes, this may be a genuine concern to address.

In other situations, the Ring Doorbell camera can pick up something cool, like a bear walking by. One time our cleaners were at the cabin and a bear came walking by. They told me about it, and we secured the Ring footage of it and posted it to our cabin Facebook page for publicity, which led to more rentals. Pretty cool.

If your cleaners alert you that they found pet hair in the vacation rental, you could then pull the footage to see if the guest brought in or out a pet, in violation of your no pets policy. Again, the Ring video may prove instrumental in a claim against the guest damage deposit.

The doorbell also allows two-way conversations, so that you can talk to and see someone standing at your front door (you hear each other, but only you see them, they do not see you).

Sometimes, a guest will push the doorbell, not to communicate with you as the owner, but to alert someone inside the vacation rental that they are standing at the door. For that reason, I recommend getting the chime accessory that can be installed with the Ring system that chimes or rings like an old school doorbell, if someone pushes the doorbell at the entrance. This then alerts occupants that someone is at the door. For a small subscription, the app also records and keeps the video of who is coming and going for a certain length of time as well.

However, you will receive a notification every time someone comes up to the door, and that may be overkill with your vacation rental, so it may be best to turn off notifications. For instance, you may not want to be getting 2 and 3 am notifications that guests are coming and going at all hours of the night for their late night out on the town, so turn notifications off.

The doorbell itself is relatively inexpensive, typically under $200. The camera is high definition, and one can zoom in and zoom out. There is an audio link so that someone at the door can talk to you the owner, as if on an intercom.

If you do not have an actual doorbell on your vacation rental, then you will simply purchase a power adapter, in addition to the Ring Doorbell, that needs to connect to the nearest outlet. Otherwise, if the Ring Doorbell is not plugged in, it will have to be charged back up on occasion, a real hassle, especially if you live a fair distance away from your vacation rental. So, you will need one that stays plugged in.

If you do have a doorbell, you will need to hire someone that is electrically savvy to hardwire the Ring Doorbell into the existing doorbell. There are instructions, but with electrical wires, it is best to simply hire that out to someone who knows how to do it. Don't risk hurting yourself or burning down your place!

Once it is set up, you or the installer will connect the doorbell to your unit's Wi-Fi and then you can access the doorbell camera through your Ring app on your smart phone. It's a lot easier than it sounds. The Ring app has made it incredibly simple.

Again, secure the Ring subscription, so that the video is preserved for a certain length of time in case there is an issue. The cost of the device, installation, and subscription are legitimate expenses of your vacation rental, and should be tagged as such in your accounting.

You will need to disclose on your listing that you have the Ring Doorbell and disclose it in your welcome instructions.

Like security cameras, the mere presence of the device will deter guests from breaking the rules, such as bringing pets that are not allowed, having a large party, or scaring away thieves that may be interested in breaking into your vacation rental.

RULE: Get a Ring Doorbell unless prohibited by the HOA.

Chapter 48

Should I keep the seller's knick knacks?

Can I put out family photos?

The first thing you do after you buy the vacation rental is toss out all clutter, fake plants, fake greenery, and cheesy décor. You should also remove all personal items and personal photos from the previous owners. People want a clean, tidy, and I know this sounds off - but a slightly impersonal place to stay.

Allow me to explain. When you go and stay in a hotel room, is there a photo of the hotel owner in the room? A photo of the hotel owner's cute kids? Absolutely not. Like a hotel, you do not want your personal photos in the vacation rental. Regional artwork, yes. Personal photos of children, no. You may add one small family photo somewhere inconspicuous (not the bedroom or bath), but that's about it. Perhaps a small inconspicuously placed photo of the family skiing if it is a ski vacation rental – but that's about it.

Throw away the stained placemats. Throw away the stained oven mitts. Throw away the soiled dish-mat. Toss out the cheap knickknacks hanging on the wall. Toss out that plastic cup collection that the owner collected from various local bars. Think of a hotel room. It is simple, it is clean. There is usually one piece of general artwork. Everything in the room has a functioning purpose. Approach the cleanout of the vacation rental from that perspective. Does this item serve a useful, functioning purpose? If not, is it an essential or tasteful addition to the décor or theme that you are attempting to establish? Finally, is the item in new or near mint condition? If not, consider tossing it out.

For example, when we bought our cabin in the mountains, the previous owner had fake greenery, old whisky bottles, and old kitchen utensils across the top of the kitchen cabinets. The idea was presumably to present a cozy, country cabin, sort of like a Cracker Barrel feel. The decorations absolutely did not have a useful purpose. It also did not fit in with the upscale mountain look we were seeking.

Finally, and this was nail in the coffin, the greenery was faded, covered in spider webs and dust, and had this sticky greasy texture from the kitchen air when people cooked bacon. As we were seeking an immaculately clean, upscale, more sophisticated cabin look, the dusty and fake country greenery was tossed. It was so bad it didn't even get donated.

RULE: If the item is not functional, does not fit your theme or décor, or is old, broken, damaged or dated – toss it. Eliminate personal items and clutter as much as humanly possible. Ask yourself the question constantly – would something like this ever be in a hotel room?

Chapter 49

Should I use carpet or solid surface flooring?

In the rare instance that your vacation rental does not have stained carpets, you may be able to squeak by the first year before having to replace them. After that, carpets are a magnet for guest complaints about stains and or wear. At the beach, the carpets collect sand, which is nearly impossible to get out, no matter how much vacuuming your cleaning team does.

In addition, with the updated paint on the walls, and your redone kitchen cabinetry, the odds are slim that the carpet color will fit with your new theme and décor for the overall look of the vacation rental.

Even if it does, do you really think a white or very light carpet in a vacation rental is a good idea? If the carpet is dark, this is good to hide stains, but then defeats our overall goal of having a bright and clean-looking room, not a dark cavern. Either way, carpet is a bust.

A simple fix is to remove the carpet and come in with solid surface flooring for the entire vacation rental. You then purchase smaller area rugs that you can easily replace on a yearly basis. These same area rugs are also easy to take outside and shake out between cleanings, machine wash on occasion, and clean beneath.

You may consider coming in with solid plank or solid tile flooring, but remember that if there is any grout, it will turn black with time, and that is nasty. If you nevertheless want to use that option for flooring, keep the grout as thin as possible.

Another inexpensive option, which we suggest, especially for a beach condo, is to consider luxury vinyl plank (LVT).

After the carpet is pulled out, the vinyl comes in strips that click together in a pretty design across all rooms. It is waterproof, and if you go with higher, thicker quality LVT, it is virtually impossible to scratch. The flooring looks like real wood, or real stone, or real stone plank, but is smooth vinyl flooring. The flooring color will match your new wall color and kitchen colors, and really make the vacation rental pop in photos and give it that wow factor in pictures. The pictures are what matter, not the overall perspective that they may feel slightly different under feet than real plank tile.

Yes, the vinyl flooring doesn't feel the same under the feet as tile or real plank. However, the convenience and affordability of the option far outweighs that consideration. It also is inexpensive to remove and go in with a different color or look as styles and colors change over time, as you update your theme or décor.

Often the vacation rental may have carpet in the bedrooms and solid surface tile with the nasty grout in the living areas. How do you lay LVT across multilevel surfaces without a guest tripping at the threshold where the elevation change occurs? Obviously, ripping out concrete tile will make a dusty mess, and is expensive, but that would certainly even out all the flooring. Let's try and avoid that.

Consider purchasing a large roll of cork, that can be cut up and adhered to the floor, to raise the level of the lower floor. The LVT is then installed on top of that cork. We did this in several of our units and it worked great, without us having to go in and chisel out floor tile to get the floors even between the various rooms.

RULE: Whether now or down the road, ditch the wall-to-wall carpet, and move towards solid surface easy to clean flooring in your vacation rental, and use area rugs that are easy to clean and replace throughout the unit.

Chapter 50

Should I replace outdated, broken or worn furnishings?

The odds of the sleeper sofa couch matching your new color scheme and décor are very remote. The couch will likely be worn, the sleeper portion inoperable, or the mattress is covered in stains. We pretty much just assume that we must replace the sleeper sofa every year and a half or so. Guests are hard on them, and the sleeper mechanism routinely gets bent and fails. It is simply cheaper to replace the whole thing.

We went through a phase where we tried to focus on having solid surface furnishings (as opposed to cloth furnishings), thinking that it would be easier to clean. For instance, we had wooden bar stools, a leather couch, and leather chairs.

Unfortunately, the solid surface furnishings were uncomfortable, and inevitably, sunscreen or wet bathing suits stained the leather furnishings. Do not use real leather – that was a hard lesson.

That consensus opinion was backed up during a recent discussion with a carpet cleaning company that I had hired to try and clean our furniture. The takeaway – don't buy leather and limit your expense as there is only so much that he can do.

We have since just given up and now go in with a tight weaved fabric furnishing that has a special stain resistant heavier fabric called Sunbrella that is supposed to be impervious to stains and is covered in Scotchguard.

Surprisingly, the lighter colored cloth furnishings fared better over time for us than the solid surface, pleather, vinyl, and leather furnishings.

Make sure you spray down the fabric with several coats of Scotchguard on no less than an annual basis. Ideally, the cushions have zippers where the cover can be laundered as needed, and air dried. Once back on the sofa, Scotchguard them again.

Ideally, you can machine wash most of the stains, except for the arm rests.

For the arm rests, purchase a carpet cleaning aerosol can with the bristle brush on the top. Keep a couple cans in the owner's closet. If the cleaning spray is handy, and your cleaner sees a spot on the arm rest, they can spray it, brush it, and then dab it off with a paper towel. Include a can of Scotchguard too for the final step.

By having machine washable cushion covers and using the carpet cleaner with brush on the arm rests, our sofas seem to have a longer life span, which is good.

There are exceptions though.

At our cabin, we replaced the sleeper sofa with a leather look alike (pleather), and it has held up wonderfully, is super easy to clean, and does not discolor like real leather can. It is also hard to tell whether it is leather or not which is cool. Since we have dark hues and it's a cabin, we can get away with a dark colored couch, as it fits the mountain top theme we have.

For the beach units, where we use the cloth-based furnishings, we place a small placard in our units, which encourages guests to not put their dirty feet, wet bathing suits, and sunscreen on the furnishings, to hopefully cut down on accidental spills. I doubt that any guest heeds the warning, but surprisingly, the fabric couches have held up a lot better than I ever would have imagined.

Replace any other furnishings in the vacation rental that are either outdated, out of style, broken, worn or lacking functionality. Again, ask yourself, would you see this accessory typically in a hotel room? How much would someone pay for this accessory or piece of furniture at a yard sale? If it is worthless, throw it out.

No, do not go out and purchase all new furniture right out of the gate. Over time, you can replace furniture that fits your décor and theme.

No, do not immediately go out and replace all the mattresses. If they are functional and still reasonably comfortable, wait on that. I will explain why later.

RULE: Replace any outdated, worn, or non-functioning furniture that does not fit your theme and décor.

Chapter 51

Always replace dishware, glassware, pots, and pans

On the day after closing, box up all dishware, silverware, glassware, and pots and pans, and donate all of it to Goodwill. I kid you not. Every time we purchase a vacation rental, the quality of the dishware, glassware, and pots and pans, is horrific.

At our cabin, we found a pizza pan in our cabin that I think someone must have used to sled down a snowy road. The pan was that scratched up.

At our beach condo, the plates were made of plastic, with knife cuts through them that the guests from overuse. I mean, really? Let's think about this for a minute.

If you are going to command top dollar for your vacation rental for July 4th, peak ski season, or the mountain leaves turning colors in the fall, you are going to have a higher end guest in there who can afford those super high rental rates.

As such, you do not need to have dishware, silverware, cookware, and glassware that is dramatically inferior to what this guest is accustomed to. Spend the money and replace all of it. It doesn't have to be the most expensive stuff, just new. We typically throw away the pots and pans every year anyway due to overuse, so again, don't go overboard as it all has to be periodically replaced. The main thing is that it is of reasonable quality, and is at minimum, new.

Remember that on silverware, spend the money and get the good stuff so that forks don't bend, and the sheen doesn't discolor or fade. Discerning guests do not dine on rusty silverware, bent silverware or blemished cutlery. Do not go cheap in this department.

Also, purchase an extra set for the owner's closet, and when you return to stay, replenish missing forks, spoons etc., as needed to keep a complete set. I would recommend a complete set of 12 of everything.

Yes, forks and spoons will disappear during any given rental year, and you want the silverware set to match, so plan to have extras to replenish the missing items as you go. Otherwise, you will end up with mismatched set and that will be noticed by your higher end guest. You cannot have seven different sets of silverware all combining to make one complete set.

Also, if you empower your cleaning crew with the knowledge that a readily available replacement silverware set is sitting in the vacation rental owner closet, they will update that for you as they proceed, if it is available. This is quick and simple and easy for them to do on the fly.

RULE: Throw away or donate all dishware, glassware, silverware and bakeware, pots, and pans. Start with a new inexpensive set, and make sure the plates are microwave safe. Spend extra on the silverware for quality and purchase an extra set for the owner's closet for spares.

Chapter 52

Replace the small appliances and update coffee maker(s)

On your first day following closing, box up the coffee maker, toaster, can opener, and blender and donate all of it to Goodwill. The odds of those smaller appliances being in good to new condition are very small.

Go down to Walmart and purchase affordable replacements. By then, you may know what the finish of your major appliances will be, so ideally you can buy smaller appliances that match.

These days it is a good idea to have both a standard coffee maker and a Keurig available for guests to use, so that they won't have to haul their own machine from home. Coffee drinking guests are particular about their coffee so be prepared to have available both types of machines.

RULE: Replace all smaller appliances (toaster, blender, can opener etc.) with new ones that match your major appliances. Purchase both a standard coffee maker and a Keurig for your unit, so that both types of coffee production are available for your guest to use.

Chapter 53

Should I buy a smart TV or not?

Should we provide DVD players?

How do I keep a guest from calling me, the owner, for assistance with getting the TV to work?

TV's can be one of the most frustrating aspects of self-managing a vacation rental. Guests come in to stay and they cannot get the TV to work. Unhappy, the guest calls you for assistance. To avoid this scenario, please follow my advice, so that you can dramatically reduce the number of issues, calls, and receipt of a poor review on this issue.

If you get lucky, your vacation rental will come equipped with flat screen smart televisions in the living room and all bedrooms, with one programmed remote for each TV. Otherwise, if you have box TV's or 'non-smart' TV's, you will need to secure flat screen smart televisions for your vacation rental.

For the living room, go for the biggest, cost effective flatscreen that will fit in the space. Guests coming into your vacation rental to watch the Super Bowl will appreciate the 65" flat screen smart TV (or larger) in the living room, so go big on that main TV. Believe it or not, a lot of guests watch TV on vacation, and they will check the size and quality of the TVs of the rental before booking.

This advice assumes that you have high speed Wi-Fi available in the vacation rental (which is a must have). If you do not have Wi-Fi, a traditional non-smart flatscreen TV will suffice, but is only an absolute last resort. We will talk more about Wi-Fi in the next chapter.

If you are replacing TV's, I do not recommend 'mounting' the TV's. A lot of guests bring gaming devices, and they need access to the HDMI inputs behind the television.

Rather, simply have each television sit on top of something, a tall dresser in the bedroom, or a console table in the living area, so that guests can have access to the inputs located on the back of the television. It is also a lot easier to confirm that the TV is indeed plugged in, that the cable from the wall is plugged into the back of the TV, and all necessary connections are made, rather than it being all crammed up behind a wall mounted TV, when and if the guest has a technical difficulty. The free-standing TV is also significantly easier to replace.

Our guests have moved away from DVD players, as most guests now have their own Netflix, Amazon Prime, or YouTube TV accounts for access to movies. By having a smart TV, your guest can log into their account while staying at your vacation rental and enjoy their favorite programming. DVD players are now a thing of the past.

For example, families with small children may have a favorite cartoon their child likes to watch. By having a smart TV, they can log into their subscription service and their child will feel right at home.

The other beauty of the smart TV is that on the welcome screen it shows the guest the various inputs to select from, including the first choice, 'Live TV,' which is what is typically provided through cable to your vacation rental. Other options, such as the subscription services that any given guest may have, are all then lined up across the screen.

When you first set up your smart TV, you can even customize the welcome screen to eliminate unused inputs, or options, to make it even simpler, or 'dummy proof' for the most untechy of guests.

On traditional 'non-smart' TVs, if the input was left on a game console that had been plugged in for example, the guest would get a blank screen that said, 'No Signal.' The guest would then be clueless on how to get off that old input and over to the input where the programming was located. It is as simple as pressing 'input' on the remote, and scrolling through the various input options until the programming appears, but for some reason, our less than techy guests can never seem to figure that out, even with instructions.

For this reason, to save yourself the headache of a lot of calls from guests who are having problems operating any given TV and go ahead and get all smart TVs, as that will dramatically reduce the number of television issues for each guest.

Again, this recommendation assumes that you have high speed Wi-Fi in your vacation rental, and some type of cable or satellite programming piped in through a wire into each room. This way the guest can access the free TV programming that you have provided and access their own subscription services through the Wi-Fi connection, on the preloaded apps on the smart TV.

After you get all your smart TVs set up in your vacation rental, so the guest can either choose the programming that you provide (i.e., cable or satellite), or their own subscription service through a smart TV app, you will then need to label each remote, and label a second identical remote as a spare to keep in the owner's closet.

With a smart TV, you hopefully will only have one remote to work with - hopefully. By having the spare remote, you can quickly replace a damaged remote on the fly that has been dropped or used as a play toy by a toddler staying in the unit, or which accidentally went home in the suitcase. We also keep extra universal remotes and batteries above the fridge as well, just in case our two primary remotes quit working.

It is so clutch to have a spare universal remote handy just in case your primary and back up remotes go down for any given TV. Buy one or two and keep them above the fridge as a backup.

Once we had a tech savvy guest who narrowed down the TV issue to an inoperable remote and contacted me for assistance (the remote literally rattled when he shook it so we narrowed the issue down to the remote). I simply directed him to the location where we had a spare universal remote (typically in the cabinet above the fridge) and he then programmed the new remote by following the instructions that came with how to set up the remote. Boom! Issue fixed and happy guest. So yes, keep spare universal remotes and batteries on site and accessible to the guest, but also keep some in an inconspicuous place so they don't disappear.

On another occasion, our maintenance person narrowed down the issue to a broken remote, and with the knowledge that we had a spare universal remote stored in the unit, he secured it, followed the directions, and got the remote and TV working again, without having to take a trip back and forth to Wal-Mart for a replacement remote.

At this point, you then need to prepare a step-by-step guide on how the guest can access the free television programming under Live TV and how to access their own subscription movie service.

Prepare the instructions for every possible contingency you can think of, from the cable not being connected to the TV, to the TV not getting power. Then laminate the detailed step by step instructions on how to work each TV and place the laminated instruction sheet under the remote in each room. Keep an extra laminated copy in the owner's closet in case it gets soiled or lost.

Similarly, you should attach the television instructions to your check-in email as well.

What you don't want to happen is a phone call at 10 pm from a guest who cannot figure out how to operate the television. Hopefully, your instructions will guide them through how to do it.

As an additional precaution, conclude each instruction listing with the toll-free number to the customer service department for your television service provider at the vacation rental. In other words, direct the guest to call someone other than you, if possible, to get assistance with understanding how to properly work the television.

Sometimes a resort will have an annual maintenance contract that may cover replacing batteries in remotes or assisting the guest with getting the TV to work. *This service is priceless if it is available and is money well spent.* Include that telephone number as well on the laminated instruction sheet, again, to try and avoid that late night telephone call from a guest on an issue with any given TV.

Try and outsource technical assistance with the televisions if the guest instructions are followed and the technical difficulties persist. I add at the very bottom of the TV instructions the following language (or similar):

"If you are unable to operate the television despite carefully following all these instructions, we encourage you to contact customer service at (phone number). Onsite maintenance can also assist with television issues and may be reached at (phone / email). Unfortunately, the owner is not able to provide any additional technical assistance beyond the provided instructions. Please contact the owner only as a last resort (email). Please do not contact the owner for technical assistance that can otherwise be provided by either the cable provider and/or onsite maintenance."

A couple of final tips - make sure your guests cannot order movies from your TV. Program a passcode that only you know to prevent that. One time we did not have a password set up for purchases on one of our TV's and a young child ordered a $40 cartoon. The bill showed up weeks after the guest had already checked out and their refundable damage deposit returned, so we were stuck with it. Don't let something like that happen to you.

Make sure also to include on the TV instructions a reminder for the guest to log out of their own subscription service before departing.

One time I found multiple TVs logged in at our cabin to no less than three or four different subscription services. If another incoming guest ordered a movie on the departing guest's TV subscription account, the departing guest would then have to pay for that movie or contest the unauthorized charge – a real pain.

You should also train your cleaning crew to check for that oversight as well, and always log the departing guest out of their TV subscription accounts, if they forget to do it themselves.

RULE: Purchase flatscreen smart TVs for your vacation rental. Have spare remotes and spare universal remotes. Prepare detailed step by step instructions to the guest on how to operate the TVs. Outsource technical assistance with use of the TVs.

SAMPLE TV INSTRUCTIONS EMAILED TO GUEST WITH CHECKIN INSTRUCTIONS:

Splash Resort, Unit 902 West

TV / WOW Cable FAQ's, Troubleshooting

We want you to have a wonderful stay and enjoy the free WOW cable programming on all three TVs in the unit. Sometimes guests cannot figure out how to operate our equipment. This guide is here to help.

Most TV / cable issues can be remedied simply by confirming that the TV is on, and the TV is hooked to the cable outlet on the wall. If the remote does not work, the batteries may need changing. If the TV screen says, 'no input,' simply press the source / input button on the remote, and scroll through the options to select 'TV' This step is necessary if the TV was previously using a different input source such as a DVD or PS4 and was not switched back to TV when they were done, or the TV accidentally had its source switched from TV to another input.

If using a DVD player, PS4 or Xbox, please make sure that you return the TV input back to the correct input source for the next guest following your departure (return the source to 'TV') and make sure programming is up and running before departing.

Please be considerate of the owner / and other guests - do not steal or switch out our remote batteries. This causes havoc to the guest checking in following your departure.

Please do not let kids play with the remotes, or remove them from the room they are in. They should be stored and kept visible directly beneath the TV for inventory following departure.

Missing / Damaged remotes are billed against the security deposit.

LIVING ROOM HDTV

1 Locate the Living Room Remote;

2 Press power button; Programming should come on; If TV won't come on, the remote batteries may need replacing; If that is the case, use the Power button on the back / side of TV. If the TV still won't come on, check, and make sure the TV is plugged into a live outlet (as some outlets are wall switch activated);

3 If TV comes on but programming does not come on, hit 'Input' repeatedly, and or scroll / use the arrows to select the 'TV' option. Wait or hit Ok / Enter. Programming should come on. If not, double check that the TV is connected to the cable outlet in the wall.

MASTER BEDROOM HDTV:

1 Locate the Master Bedroom Remote;

2 Press power button; Programming options should come on; If TV won't come on, the remote batteries may need replacing; If that is the case, use the Power button on the back / side of TV. If the TV still

won't come on, check, and make sure the TV is plugged into a live outlet (as some outlets are wall switch activated);

3 If TV comes on but programming options do not come on, hit 'Input' repeatedly, and or scroll / use the arrows to select the 'TV' option. Wait or hit Ok / Enter. Programming should come on. If not, double check that the TV is connected to the cable outlet in the wall.

GUEST BEDROOM HDTV:

1 Locate the Guest Bedroom Remote;

2 Press power button; Programming options should come on; If TV won't come on, the remote batteries may need replacing; If that is the case, use the Power button on the back / side of TV. If the TV still won't come on, check and make sure the TV is plugged into a live outlet (as some outlets are wall switch activated);

3 If TV comes on but programming options do not come on, hit 'Input' repeatedly, and or scroll / use the arrows to select the 'TV' option. Wait or hit Ok / Enter. Programming should come on. If not, double check that the TV is connected to the cable outlet in the wall.

TECHNICAL ASSISTANCE

Yes, we can send a maintenance person out to assist you with one or more of your television issues, upon request, and / or to replace remote batteries. Please simply contact the owner through the VRBO app, or email the owner at jamesrdorgan@gmail.com

Maintenance assistance at night and on weekends for TV programming issues may or may not be available until the next business day. It's not instant assistance, but at the same time, rarely takes more than 24 hours before the TV issue is resolved. **This is why it is important for you to first try the foregoing directions first before emailing for assistance.**

Unfortunately, we do not offer 'over the phone' TV troubleshooting / assistance. This is because over the phone assistance would be futile if you have already followed all the foregoing steps without success. The best way to ask for TV assistance at any hour is to simply **email the owner,** who will then coordinate with maintenance for onsite unit assistance.

As we do not refund for inclement weather, or any given resort amenity not being available, we also do not provide credits, discounts, or refunds for not being able to figure out how to use our TV / Smart TV options, or if the WOW service or Wi-Fi service becomes temporarily unavailable.

Chapter 54

Who provides Wi-Fi for guests to use?

If the HOA does not provide Wi-Fi, should I provide it?

In today's rental environment, you absolutely must provide free, high speed quality Wi-Fi for your vacation rental guests. It is an absolute must have and is not an expense to skimp on. Guests expect it, and do confirm its availability, prior to booking. Many guests rely on the connection for their work, or to homeschool their kids, access their favorite TV programming through your Smart TV, and many other reasons.

You also need the Wi-Fi for your Nest thermostat, Ring doorbell camera, and video security system to operate correctly in connection with your smart phone. At our cabin, I counted one time no less than 8 guests logged on, along with the thermostats, cameras and so forth – all pulling some serious bandwidth. You need to be able to meet that bandwidth demand.

In your property listing description, make sure you state that free high-speed Wi-Fi is available. Buck up and get some serious bandwidth and advertise it. The additional cost will more than pay for itself over the long run to lure bookings.

Hopefully your HOA provides a high bandwidth broadcast in or near your unit. If the HOA doesn't provide that service (like at our cabin), we simply pay Xfinity for both cable programming and high-speed Wi-Fi.

Attach to your welcome email the Wi-Fi username and password to access the service. Also, post inside the vacation rental on either a placard, sign, or laminated sheet, the username and password information. Post this information in multiple areas throughout the vacation rental, as each guest will be looking for that information immediately following their check in.

For instance, the guest that booked the unit may have read the check in instructions and know the Wi-Fi username and password. However, their kids may not have read those instructions, so the kids will be looking for that Wi-Fi password within minutes of arrival, so post that Wi-Fi user and password throughout your vacation rental.

RULE: Free super quality high speed Wi-Fi for guests is an absolute must have. If your HOA does not provide it, you should. You also need that same Wi-Fi to run your Ring Doorbell camera, Nest thermostats, and/or security cameras so it is money well spent. Provide the Wi-Fi username and password to the guests in both the keycode welcome email and post it on signs and placards throughout the unit.

Chapter 55

Quality mattresses / bed bug protectors / mattress protectors

Inspect every mattress, sleeper sofa, and sleeper chair for bed bugs or evidence of bed bugs. There are tutorials on YouTube and information on the Internet on how to do that. If you find an issue, you will need to dispose of all bedding, linens, and blankets, and have a <u>professional</u> pest control service (do not try and do this yourself) exterminate the vacation rental.

Assuming there is no evidence of bed bugs, the next step is to check for defects, odors, holes, stains, or tears in any of the mattresses. If it's questionable, replace them.

You should also set up a schedule for your cleaning team or maintenance team to turn or spin or flip the mattresses periodically to extend the life of the mattress. If not turned, the bed will develop sunken areas where guests typically sleep.

Assuming you have a high-quality set of mattresses, and a bed bug professional has already confirmed the absence of bed bugs, you then need to purchase a fully zipped bed bug protector. This bed protector is both waterproof but soft on top of the bed, and then fully zips, akin to a pillowcase protective cover, which seals the entire bed.

The sealed, fully encased, and zipped bed protector is designed to do two things – to eliminate seams and places for bed bugs to hide so they are easier to spot, and to provide a waterproof layer.

You must assume that there will be a child that may have a nighttime accident and you do not want to have to replace the entire mattress or have the cleaning delayed while trying to air out a saturated mattress in time for the next guest. These protectors are expensive, difficult to put on as they fully encase the mattresses or box spring but are so worth it.

As there is a good bit of work getting the mattress inside and out of the fully zipped bed bug protector, you still need a bed protector to go on top of the encasement bed protector that can be easily and quickly removed and laundered when needed. The easy to remove bed protector becomes the first line of defense, and the encasement is the final waterproof line of defense against guest accidents.

Simply purchase an inexpensive washable bed protector to go over the top of the bed bug protector, that can be pulled off and washed when soiled. Typically, most vacation rentals have an onsite washer and dryer, and offer your cleaner extra compensation to wash a bed protector while they clean, to motivate them to watch for bed protector stains and get them cleaned.

Encourage the cleaning crew to also inspect for bed bugs as well, every time. Having the mattresses and box springs encased should make it easier to spot them if they happen to arrive in your vacation rental.

Another option, if it is available, is to formally pay a pest control service to preventatively inspect for bed bugs on a quarterly basis and preventatively apply pesticide (such as Apprehend) if that option is available.

It is my firm belief that the absolute worst thing that could happen is for your vacation rental guest to be bitten by bed bugs in your vacation rental, and then subsequently leave a review that indicates that your vacation rental had bed bugs. This could irreparably tarnish your unit for years. Some 92% of prospective guests read the reviews, so do everything you can to preventatively check for and preventatively treat bed bugs on a routine basis.

If bitten by bed bugs, the guest may also pursue a civil claim through an attorney for being bitten, and other damages.

If that ever happens, you need to turn the guest claim over to your insurance company for resolution. We will discuss more on how to handle a bed bug issue, if that were ever to happen, in a later chapter.

RULE: Replace worn or defective mattresses, encase your mattresses, and box spring, and have both your cleaning crew and a professional bed bug inspection team routinely inspect for bed bugs.

Chapter 56

Should I focus on hiring a large commercial cleaning team or focus on a smaller 'Mom and Pop' cleaning team?

The #1 key to a successful and stress-free vacation rental is having a thorough and reliable cleaning service in place for your cleaning services.

During the first week following your closing, meet with the prospective cleaning team at the vacation rental, walk around the vacation rental and its exterior, and go over every single expectation that you have on any given service between guests.

Discuss whether the cleaning service utilizes the Resort Cleaning app for scheduling (which we highly recommend), or whether you must email or text the cleaner all checkout and turn dates (turn dates are dates where a guest checks out and an incoming guest checks in on the same day).

Discuss who provides 'starter supplies' for guests. If they provide supplies, what specifically do they supply?

We also require that the cleaning service launder the bed protectors, blankets, and quilts on a routine basis, and always, always when visibly soiled. The price charged by any given cleaning service for that task may greatly differ from one another on this 'bonus' task, so find out sooner rather than later whether they can perform that service, and what they charge.

For special circumstances, such an indoor pool or hot tub, this requires special attention and specialized knowledge on how to service, maintain and clean - above and beyond what a typical cleaning service may know how to do.

Similarly, if you have some other special, unique amenity that requires special training, you will need to figure out whether it is something the cleaning service will handle or if you need to separately hire that task out, apart from the standard cleaning service.

You also need to make sure the cleaning service has a complimentary, 24/7 'call back' service if there is a cleaning oversight. You will want to be able to list the cleaner's direct line or telephone number that if a cleaning oversight occurs, or the starter supplies are missing, that the cleaner will return on a complimentary basis and take care of the cleaning or starter supply oversight.

Proximity to the vacation rental then becomes important as well, as call backs do occasionally happen, even with the best of cleaners.

This is because some guests are just impossible to please, and they will always find something somewhere to complain about. I kid you not, one time a guest took a zoomed in photo of dust on the baseboard behind our refrigerator and complained about it.

The best policy is to simply place the guest in touch with the cleaning team for the return visit and stay out of that process.

Some vacation rental guests are versed at 'working the system' and pull complaints like that in the hope of finding an owner that will just knee jerk and give them a refund, even if the most absurd oversight is found. When they find out no refund is coming, suddenly it is an oversight that the guest can live with.

In view of that issue, you need to make it crystal clear in your check-in instructions that *there is never a refund for a cleaning oversight.* Otherwise, you will get a cleaning complaint with every single guest you have, no matter how super awesome your crew may be. When one is looking for an excuse, any excuse will do. Simply state that if a cleaning oversight occurs, the cleaning team will return and take care of the oversight as soon as possible. Leave it at that.

You also need to restrict complaints for cleaning oversights to the first few minutes of stay. Otherwise, the checking in guest will call to complain about their own messes one or two days into the stay.

I recommend interviewing not only larger cleaning services, but also smaller, 'Mom and Pop' cleaning services in the area. I then recommend joining on Facebook any group pages where cleaners may have joined together to share ideas, market their work, and so forth. You could then post on there that you are accepting applications and doing interviews as well. The more options and choices you have typically, the better the results.

The final option is to continue using the same cleaning crew the previous owner had, assuming they were happy with them. They will already be familiar with the unit and will have already been tried and tested. The idea is to not fix something that isn't broken. That is an additional option.

There is no set success story on whether the big cleaning services work best or whether a smaller 'Mom and Pop' crew work best, as we have used and continue to use both types of services at our various vacation rentals. There is no definitive 'this way is better than the other way' answer on this decision.

For our two vacation rental condos in Panama City Beach, we use a small 'Mom and Pop' team that is just one worker. We are the cleaner's only source of income, as the two units at Splash Resort put together, keep her sufficiently busy.

Our cleaner is always the one who cleans the vacation rentals every time. She takes tremendous pride in her work, and typically, she cleans beautifully. She will readily notice something broken or missing, as she literally was there both before and after any guest stay and could provide key testimony in the event of a dispute over property damage, loss or theft.

Even though guest damage is rare, having the same cleaner every time helps to pinpoint before and after damages following any guest stay.

With a smaller 'Mom and Pop' type crew, the owner typically provides and pays for the three to four sets of laundry used in the operation. Purchasing that many linens right out of gate can get expensive.

The biggest downside of the smaller cleaning crew is that on rare occasions, the small crew simply isn't available for any given turn. They are either out of town, or their car breaks down, or they get sick. You therefore must either rely on them to find a suitable substitute, or in a worst-case scenario, try and cover for them on the fly.

In addition, the smaller cleaning crew or team may or may not be versed in how to use Resort Cleaning, an app that larger cleaning teams typically use for automated scheduling of cleaning appointments each time a reservation is made.

With the 'Mom and Pop' cleaning crew that typically doesn't have Resort Cleaning, providing them with the cleaning dates becomes a challenge. One literally has to periodically 'screen shot' their calendar of bookings, and then text it to the cleaner, so they know when to clean. This hassle factor is a significant downside, especially when all your other cleaning services for other vacation rentals are on Resort Cleaning, where all cleaning appointments are booked automatically with each guest reservation. Automation is the way to go, especially if your goal is to manage your vacation rental on only one hour per week.

The larger cleaning services also have pros and cons. We use them at our Phoenix on the Bay vacation rental in Orange Beach, Alabama, and at our Appalachian High vacation rental in Pigeon Forge, Tennessee.

The large cleaning services typically provide the linens, which may or may not include a start-up 'linen fee' and an annual linen fee. Some require both fees, and some require neither fee. Each of our commercial cleaning services approaches linens, start-up linens, and replenishment linens uniquely.

Some of the bigger start-up operations provide all the needed 'start up' supplies (soap, shampoo, dish detergent, laundry detergent, trash liners, etc.,), while others, the owner must purchase starter supplies and have them stored in the owner's closet. The cleaner then accesses the owner's closet and puts the supplies out with each incoming guest.

One of the most significant advantages of a commercial cleaning operation is that they are typically set up on Resort Cleaning, a cleaning scheduling program and or app, that completely automates notifications of when a cleaning service needs to clean. This is a real perk. When the owner gets a reservation, the Resort Cleaning app automatically books the cleaning appointment with the cleaning service to clean the unit – a huge advantage.

The downside of the larger, commercial cleaning service is that they may or may not have the same cleaner assigned to your vacation rental every time, and it is literally a revolving door on who cleans the unit. Brooms and vacuums tend to disappear, and sometimes, the quality and or breadth of the cleaning slips. The larger service also relies upon a team of inspectors to check behind the cleaning crews, but they sometimes run behind or fail to inspect during peak times, so sometimes quality suffers. It is rare that the same cleaner cleans both before and after any given guest stay, so it is difficult to pinpoint when any given vacation rental damage happened.

On the bright side though, the larger cleaning operations <u>never</u> ever miss a cleaning appointment or call you with an issue of a cleaner's car breaking down or someone being out of town. They handle covering the cleaning and it is not your issue to address. You then relax knowing that they have got it covered, regardless of whether any given employee has car trouble, fails to show up, or has any other issues. You will remain blissfully ignorant of any challenges that the service endures in trying to get someone to cover any given cleaning – a real perk.

As with most services, always pay as you go, and never in advance, regardless of the size of the service. No exceptions.

RULE: The most important factor in a successful vacation rental is a dependable, and quality cleaning team. Personally interview as many as you can and go with the best that works for you. If the cleaning service misses a cleaning, or gets complaints, cut the cord, and hire the 2nd place cleaner on your list. Always, always have a list of cleaning team backups on go, as you never know if your first choice for cleaning service will work out or not.

SAMPLE LANGUAGE IN CHECK IN EMAIL DISCLAIMING REFUNDS IF A CLEANING OVERSIGHT IS FOUND:

Housekeeping and / or Maintenance Issue:

If the unit has not yet been serviced at all when you arrive, please contact the owner directly and do not enter the unit until after the unit has been serviced.

Although extremely rare, please report any cleaning oversights immediately upon arrival for a return visit, as refunds are not allowed.

If you have any questions or concerns, or if you need a cleaning oversight remedied, please call us at **251-928-0192** (during regular business hours), or call or text **251-209-9299** (after hours, weekends or emergencies), or by email jamesrdorgan@gmail.com.

Due to the cabin's remote location, please allow up to 24 hours for any given cleaning oversight to be corrected by our cleaning crew.

Chapter 57

What additional, specific questions should I ask the cleaners?

What clues are indicative of a great cleaner?

Let me repeat. Take the time out of your busy schedule and meet the prospective person or cleaning service in person, at the vacation rental. This is such an important decision that you do not want to rely on a website listing alone.

Having a reliable, solid cleaning team will ensure that your vacation rental is always ship shape and ready for each incoming guest, without you having to lift a finger.

I recommend trying to arrange at least five interviews one morning or afternoon, all back-to-back. This series of meetings would be set after closing, but well before your first guest.

Take note of how easy or difficult it is to set up the meeting with the service. Observe whether the cleaning team shows up on time. Some appointments will be easy to set up, while others not so much. Some will arrive on time, some not, and some not at all.

When the cleaners arrive, look at their mode of transportation. Will this vehicle be able to consistently make it up the mountain roads to your cabin – especially in inclement weather? How will they haul away each turn the four potential cans of garbage needing to be removed. Is the vehicle literally a step away from breaking down or does it appear reliable?

Once you meet the cleaning team, or owner, walk them through the vacation rental, and see if they are familiar or not with a keyless entry system.

Observe whether they take notes or not and whether those notes are electronically preserved or written down. The cleaners that write down everything, understand that your time is valuable, and that this meeting may be the only chance to ever meet you, the owner, in person, speaks volumes. The cleaner that writes down what you want, is a loud message that they want to do it your way, not their way, and that is huge.

Determine whether the cleaner will have the physical ability to get up on a chair or ladder and be able to physically clean ceiling fans or ceiling vents. Cleaning vacation rentals is a physically demanding and labor-intensive task.

Most importantly, listen to what they say as they walk through your vacation rental – do they spot or suggest things that are within or beyond your cleaning expectations?

Ask a million obvious, but simple questions.

How long have you been in business? How many properties do you service? Ideally, you want an established operation, not one just starting out, as that poses risk.

Who does the owner call or email if there is an emergency or a cleaning oversight? The answer should come quickly and with confidence that in an emergency the issue will be immediately addressed.

Will the same cleaner be cleaning each time? You want the same cleaner each time if possible. How long have each of your cleaners worked for you? You want stability, not a continuous revolving door of employees or subcontractors.

What bath, kitchen, or laundry supplies do you supply, if any? Ask them to show you what they place out for each guest. They should have a sample supply in their vehicle.

Perhaps ask them to bring what they use for supplies for each guest turn to the meeting in advance. The time to secure higher end shampoos, soaps, hand soaps, detergent, dish detergent and so forth is when hired, not later. The cleaners want your business, and they will be trying to impress, so lock in quality disposable items from the get-go, and confirm the types and quality of supplies that you want your guests to have. Evaluate selection, quality, and cost.

If they supply linens, ask them the color, quality and or see if they can bring a sample of the linens. Evaluate selection, quality, and cost.

Ask them whether they are comfortable with changing air filters, batteries, and bulbs, especially if your owner's closet is stocked with a year's worth of supplies. If the owner's closet is stocked (which is the owner's job to keep stocked annually), it should be quick and simple for your cleaning crew to keep up with bulbs, batteries, and filters. The service may or may not charge an additional fee to do those extra steps. If they won't do it, that is fine, and you will need to have your maintenance person do it. If the cleaning team will do it, factor that cost savings into the equation.

Yes, compensate the cleaners accordingly to replace bulbs, filters, and batteries. Say it once, say it a thousand times to your cleaning crew. Tell them 'I do not expect anything for free. I will pay you for your service, whatever it is.' You want your cleaners to aggressively monitor for dead remotes, burned out bulbs, and taxed air filters. Pay them.

On stand-alone properties, there may be the need for cleaning the outside, or exterior areas.

At the beach, exterior areas needing cleaning may include sweeping the balcony, or sweeping out the common area in the hallway.

At a cabin or stand-alone home, this may include blowing off leaves from the picnic area or driveway. Tasks may also include cleaning up a fire pit.

At our cabin in Pigeon Forge, the cleaners need to be able to drain, sanitize, and refill the hot tub. Confirm that they know how to do it.

The cleaners may need to clean an exterior propane grill. Ask them if they are comfortable with doing that.

Again, you are not looking for something for free, simply ask them whether they would be willing to do that or not, and to include it in their fee for each cleaning. Some of the larger cleaning companies have a schedule, or list, and with each item added on, the cleaning fee slowly starts adding up, which is fine. Again, you do not want something for nothing.

The main thing is that you do not 'spring' something major or unexpected on them <u>after</u> they give you the quote for cleaning. Get it all out there right then.

Try and get everything that needs to be done out there, so that those tasks are covered in the initial quote for cleaning, a time when they are most likely trying to submit a competitive bid and get your business.

After walking through the vacation rental with several cleaning services, you will have a list ranking which cleaners you like best.

You will also find that pricing for the cleaning service varies greatly.

Price is not the sole and/or definitive factor in choosing a cleaner. Look at the entire package that each service offers. Do not let a small difference in price affect your decision making in this area, as their services for you *are extremely important*.

At that point, take the extra time and check references of other owners the cleaning team has serviced. Ask the references about the good, bad, and ugly. Assure the other owner that their comments will be in the strictest of confidence. You want a frank assessment of the cleaning service from the other owner's perspective. I know that if another owner called me about my cleaning service, I would be brutally honest with them about both the good and bad of the service and would be happy to help.

RULE: Always interview in person your prospective cleaning team at the vacation rental and ask as many questions as you can possibly think of. In addition, make sure that you fully list everything you want done before the cleaning service gives a quote, rather than 'springing' something unexpected on the cleaning team later.

Chapter 58

What is Resort Cleaning and why should I use it?

Your goal is for you to automate as many things as humanly possible as the manager of your own vacation rental.

A wonderful technique with that in mind is to automate the scheduling of cleanings for your vacation rental. It is one less step for you to worry about, and by having it automated, it saves you precious time.

Enter Resort Cleaning (aka Resort Clean).

Resort Cleaning is an online service (resortcleaning.com) that monitors your vacation rental calendar and bookings, and then enters any needed cleaning on your cleaner's calendar, automatically, through shared calendar integration.

Your cleaner can then see all their clients' bookings and needed cleanings, including the scheduled cleanings for your vacation rental, all in one calendar.

Further, Resort Cleaning will tell the cleaning company whether the cleaning is a standard clean (the vacation rental does not have to be ready by 4 pm), or whether it is a 'same day turn' meaning that the cleaning crew needs to prioritize the cleaning, as the vacation rental must be ready by 4 pm.

In addition, the cleaning crew then uses the Resort Cleaning app to show when they have finished the cleaning, and then you as the owner get a message that the cleaning was indeed done.

In this entire process, you have done nothing. The guest books. Your cleaner is informed on when to clean. You then get an email showing that it was done. This is perfection.

Most larger cleaning services use Resort Cleaning for all their clients, so that all cleanings are centralized onto one calendar, as described. It is an incredibly efficient and brilliant system to use.

On the flip side, if your cleaning company does not use Resort Cleaning, then you must manually tell them when to clean. This may mean emailing the cleaner every time there is reservation, and the cleaner then enters the clean on their calendar. It may mean you simply take a screen shot of your VRBO calendar and periodically text that photo of the calendar to your cleaner.

The downside of this manual system is that it is not automated, and you must remember to tell the cleaners when to clean in some sort of fashion or another – a real pain, and a procedure prone to error, especially if one is forgetful, like me.

How does one get set up on Resort Cleaning?

If your cleaning team, XYZ Cleaning, is on Resort Cleaning, you simply contact Resort Cleaning and tell them that you want XYZ Cleaning to be your cleaning company, and they will then link your VRBO or Airbnb calendar system to your cleaner's calendar. The cost is only $5 per month per property – a steal.

Once your calendar is linked to the cleaner's calendar, the cleaner will then have all your bookings populate on their calendar, and they will know exactly when to clean. A series of confirmation emails will then spool out to the owner 'confirming' all the scheduled cleanings.

If you get a last-minute reservation, no problem. As soon as you know, your cleaners will know. You will get an email confirmation from Resort Cleaning confirming that the cleaning team knows about the last-minute cleaning, and has it covered.

If a guest cancels, the reservation is no longer on your calendar. At that same instant, the same reservation is then no longer on your cleaner's calendar either. Resort Cleaning will then email you notice that they know about the cancellation and the cleaners won't clean that day.

The beauty of the system is that it is automated, with confirmation emails (all of which I ignore as there is never an issue). It is also instant. As soon as your calendar adjusts, so does your cleaner's, without you having to do anything.

If your cleaner is not on Resort Cleaning, and you have already screen shotted the cleaning schedule for a particular month, you will then need to send a fresh screen shot each time that calendar changes due to a new reservation, a cancelled reservation, or a last-minute change adding on a night to an existing reservation.

Manually telling a cleaner when to clean takes time. Texting a calendar for any given month to your cleaner every time there is a change will technically work, but it eats into our goal of spending as little time as possible on managing our vacation rental. Resort Cleaning saves you time.

With that being said, I continue to use my 'Mom and Pop' cleaning crew in Panama City Beach, and it is not a huge deal to just text them the calendar periodically for the next thirty days' worth of reservations. I would prefer that she get on Resort Cleaning, so she would instantly know when to clean, not only for the next four to six weeks, but for every cleaning that needs to be done for the next year.

However, we tried to load the Resort Cleaning app on her phone and get her set up, but it just did not work. Between the language barriers and not being that tech savvy, we just gave up and I simply continue to just text her a screenshot of our calendar. She has never missed a clean. I simply text her the calendar for the next six weeks every so often or when there is an update. That system works fine, and I am not complaining. I just wish our scheduling for those two properties were more efficient.

During the meantime, all our other units get cleaned without me doing anything, as all my cleaning services at the other vacation rentals use Resort Cleaning.

Have I ever reviewed the Resort Cleaning emails showing the scheduling, confirmation, and completion of any given stay? Other than when the system was initially set up, no.

Assuming three emails per reservation, and ten reservations a month, that is 30 emails per property per month. We have four properties. So, I do not keep up with those 120 emails per month. There is no need to, as the system works.

The cleaners set up on Resort Cleaning never miss a clean – without fail, so there is no need for me to review any of the Resort Cleaning scheduling and/or completion emails.

One caveat on Resort Cleaning.

If you block the VRBO calendar, perhaps for some type of maintenance that you plan to have done in the unit or because the resort needs the unit vacant to paint the exterior breezeway floors, Resort Cleaning cannot differentiate this type of block from a standard guest stay. It therefore populates the cleaning crew calendar for a cleaning on the checkout day, when in fact, you don't need a cleaning for that day, as you merely blocked off the weekend for needed maintenance.

To fix this, simply email your cleaning crew and tell them the specific date is the end of a block, and not a reservation, and not to clean. Your cleaners will then know not to clean, even though it is scheduled on their calendar.

RULE: If your cleaning company uses Resort Cleaning, simply contact Resort Cleaning and link your newly set up vacation rental listing to your chosen cleaning company, so that your cleaning company will then see all of your reservations on their calendar, and know when to clean, at the same moment you know, automatically, without you having to do anything.

Chapter 59

Who should provide linens and starter supplies?

One of the biggest decisions on which cleaning crew to hire may depend on whether the cleaning service provides linens and starter supplies or not.

For example, the first cleaning service provides all towels, sheets, and kitchen linens. They also provide all the disposable starter supplies including bath soaps, shampoos, detergent, dish soap, paper towels, toilet paper and so forth. Some services charge an annual linen fee, and some don't.

The second cleaning service provides nothing. You provide them and must somehow deliver to them three sets of towels, sheets, and kitchen linens, all of which will be stored by them at their home, laundry facility or business. You then must secure and provide all starter supplies – shampoo, bar soap, dish soap, dishwasher soap, and laundry detergent. You then must put those supplies into your owner's closet for the cleaners to access them.

Surprisingly, the per time cleaning fee between the two types of services (which provide dramatically different things) where one provides linens and starter supplies and the other one doesn't, is remarkably similar. We currently have two rentals where the cleaning service provides the linens and all starter supplies, and two rentals where we provide the linens and some but not all starter supplies.

I would recommend if possible that you hire the cleaning team where they provide all the linens and starter supplies. This is simple and removes you from the process of buying linens and starter supplies and providing those products. Instead, they keep up with all linens, and they secure all needed starter supplies, instead of you.

They also then must keep up with the multitude of ruined linens from stains, blood, and mascara. It is an expense they absorb, and it keeps you out of the process of having to secure replacement linens each time one is ruined.

On our two vacation rentals where our cleaning team has us supply the linens, inevitably, we receive photos of ruined linens. They then go to Walmart to replace them, and I end up constantly having to reimburse for ruined linens and the accompanying trip fee to Walmart. The good news is that the cleaner is motivated to replace ruined linens, but the bad news is that it is a constant thing to review pictures of nastiness in your vacation rental.

If possible, hire the team that provides the linen service. If you can find one that does that as part of their fee, without an annual linen fee or set up linen fee, that is a deal.

If you must get one that charges an annual fee, it is an understandable fee and is worth it.

The last or worse alternative is for you to provide the three sets of linens and all starter supplies. Again, replacing the ruined linens is a pain. Also, when and if you change cleaning services, it is a process to move all those linens from one cleaning service to another. It takes time to shop for, pick out, and then get shipped all the starter supplies, and then get them into your owner's closet. All of that takes time – time that you do not have.

However, one may want to use specialty linens for their guests like bamboo sheets or something luxurious. The owner may also prefer picking out super high end starter supplies, that may be specialty or truly unique (and likely significantly more expensive than stock starter supplies).

Yes, if you do not mind paying and paying a lot for specialty sheets, linens, and towels, and emotionally can handle having those linens routinely ruined, and don't mind going through the process of getting those specialty linens replaced, then go for it.

For the two units where we provide the three sets of linens, we started from the get-go simply using Walmart brand basic white and have stuck with it. White is our choice because we can wash them in boiling hot water with bleach, with no fading or worry of cross color contamination in the hot water and bleach. It is simple, inexpensive, and easy to replace. The linens will get stained and ruined so fast it is a revolving door, so if you must toss a linen, it wasn't expensive in the first place, and second, it is quick and easy for your team to run by Walmart and replace it on the fly as needed.

Where we provide the linens, we also provide guests black washcloths that say 'Makeup' on them, for ladies to use for their mascara or makeup. Having that type of towel available that does not show stains has helped reduce our white washcloth losses.

RULE: The best option for a cleaning crew is one who provides all the towels, sheets, and linens for you, without an annual linen fee or set up cost. Hopefully, the same cleaning crew will also provide the starter supplies as part of their cleaning fee. By hiring a cleaning service that provides both linens and starter supplies, it will over time, save you an enormous amount of time, which is our goal. This is because you will have outsourced the securing and handling of linens and starter supplies.

Yes, you can do specialty linens, or specialty starter supplies, but emotionally for you, and due to costs and hassle, it may not be worth it.

Chapter 60

Decision on quilts and blankets

This is a tough call.

On one hand, you want to have a pretty quilt or comforter on the bed with lots of throw pillows that really makes your vacation rental stand out from the rest, and the listing photos pop. However, the downside of the elaborate display is that they are large and cumbersome, they take forever to wash, and the pillows get nasty as they are difficult to clean (as the pillow cover must be removed each time).

Remember, your cleaning person will most likely arrive with everything they need to service your condo in a small wagon. They can only carry so much. It is physically not possible for them to carry with them large bulky comforters, quilts and shams and exchange all of that out, every time.

Similarly, for your cleaner arriving at a standalone home, such as a cabin, you are one of many stops on their route. It is simply not possible for them to be able to routinely swap out the comforter, pillow, and sham sets for cleaning.

We started with these beautiful quilts with matching shams and pillows. Yes, the photos really popped, and looked like it was right out of a magazine. This is great and gets the guests' attention. Then the guest goes straight to the reviews, and then boom, all that work is then negated when a guest complains that the quilts were nasty or had a stain on them.

I cannot tell you how many times with that fancy set of quilts and pillows and shams that a guest would call after check-in and inform us of a stain that they absolutely could not handle. When this happens, your cleaner must make a separate trip with a replacement quilt, or set, and then pull the stained quilt, and set it all back up again – a logistics nightmare and time sapping task for all involved.

Then, the quilt gets laundered, and guess what, the stain doesn't come out. That fancy quilt is then ruined. It's a no-win situation.

Our solution was simple. We have all white linens, and the bed is made just with the linens. We then purchased from Walmart simple microfiber dark grey blankets, that do not show stains, and can dry in minutes. They are then rolled up and tied, indicating that they have been freshly laundered. They also compact well in a bag, and do not take up much space. We then have those blankets laundered just like the sheets get laundered, every time. In other words, try and find a set up where your top blanket or quilt can be laundered every time, just like a sheet does, but doesn't take up much space, doesn't show stains, and is small enough to easily transport.

Yes, the photos are not as pretty. However, what is does show is a pristine white bed with bleached and clean sheets, with no stains, and a freshly laundered blanket to open and spread out.

Skip the throw pillows. Guests literally toss them on the floor. They get dirty quickly. Throw pillows are a nightmare to clean.

A close second alternative is to purchase quilts that simply do not show stains but are still good about drying quickly.

For instance, our mountain cabin has quilts that are left on the beds and are darker in color with the mountain theme of the cabin, but are quick and easy to wash, with no matching shams or pillows. If our cleaning crew spots a soiled quilt, they are supposed to have a spare in the vehicle or owner's closet ready to go.

In theory, that process works, if the quilts do not show stains easily.

To really make that process work well, offer your cleaning crew an extra $20 per quilt each time they notice a soiled quilt, and they launder it. In that way, they are inspecting the quilts for stains every time and are motivated to change them out to make the extra money.

RULE: Do not purchase specialty, expensive bedding sets with pillows, shams and down comforters. Your bedding needs to be simple, not show stains, and be easily and quickly laundered, without taking up a lot of space. The simpler and cleaner you keep this aspect of your vacation rental, the better. Resist the temptation. Keep it simple and easy to clean.

Chapter 61

Hiring a maintenance team

Second only to a quality and reliable cleaning crew is your maintenance team. You need to locate and interview multiple options for your maintenance person or team. You want a well maintained and routinely serviced vacation rental where everything works, and everything is fixed. You want operable light bulbs and fully charged remote batteries. Air filters should be fresh. The AC drain line should periodically be bleached. The maintenance team will cover items and or issues that a cleaning crew typically will not handle.

The maintenance person needs to be (1) proximate to the unit, (2) affordable, (3) experienced and (4) trustworthy.

On our vacation rental at the cabin in the mountains, the previous owner relied on a gentleman who knew more about every inch of that cabin, more than the previous owner did, and more than I knew just buying the property. I simply picked up where the previous owner left off – a seamless transition. His trip rates were and continue to be super reasonable. He always responds immediately and takes care of whatever happens to pop up. He is literally the clone of an owner jumping on something and fixing it. He is only minutes away, and literally, can handle just about any cabin maintenance issue that pops up. This type of maintenance availability is priceless.

If not fortunate enough to get that type of service right out of the gate, check on Facebook groups for area maintenance persons, and then interview as many of them as you can. Meet each maintenance person, and then create a list of preferred maintenance personnel from highest to lowest, with multiple backups. Eventually, you will settle down with that 'go to' person, who will always be there in a pinch, and come to the rescue. Like hiring the cleaning team, you may find the perfect match after a couple of tries, and that is ok. Having maintenance backups on standby is also key in case your primary person happens to be unavailable.

In other situations, your resort may have a maintenance team that you can hire for an annual fee. This too is an excellent option.

At Splash Resort, we pay $450 a year for 24/7 on call maintenance service to replace any dead remote or fire alarm batteries, change the air filters monthly, replace leaky toilet flappers, replace burned out light bulbs, unclog toilets, or bring in the balcony furniture if there is a storm.

One of the best perks of the onsite maintenance plan is that if a guest cannot figure out to operate the TV, they visit the unit and show the guest how to properly operate the TV, saving you, the owner, from having to try and fix the issue over the phone at 10:00 at night.

Another perk is that the maintenance crew is super cool about fixing something for me that may not be technically on their list of covered services. They then bill an extremely low rate for the repairs, significantly less than what a standard service call would have cost from any given offsite repair service.

RULE: Second only to a reliable and diligent cleaning service, your maintenance person is a crucial aspect of your successful vacation rental team.

Chapter 62

Should I use a physical key, Schlage lock, Resort lock, or KABA lock for my vacation rental?

In the old days, one would check into a hotel, and the front desk at check in would issue an actual physical steel key, typically attached to a plastic tag, with the room number on it. The physical key was necessary to access the room, and a deposit was required, which was returned upon returning the physical key at checkout.

Following in those footsteps, and many years ago, many vacation rental owners would make multiple copies of the physical keys to their vacation rental door locks, and mail with each reservation an actual physical key to the vacation rental. This was an immensely cumbersome, slow, and time-consuming task. This process also had a tremendous amount of risk to both guest safety and the owner's property if the key was copied.

Schlage locks then began to sell key code entry locks, that with the simple entry of a code, the door would unlock. This was a boon for vacation rental owners, as they could simply email the guest the 'secret' code to the door to allow access to their stay. The downside was that the Schlage door lock code was not unique, and the code worked even before the guest's designated check in / check out times. This led to abuse of the system. Like the hard key, the risk of that code being used for nefarious purposes by that one bad apple was also there.

For our vacation rental, I initially went with Resort Lock, which was a key code entry door, but I could program unique door codes for specific entry times and dates with every guest stay. Their online software at the time was free to use, and super user friendly. We would then simply take a minute or two with each guest stay to generate the unique code. Simply by entering the dates of stay, with the check in / check out dates already set, generating the code, and emailing the guest, the door code would then work from 4 pm on the day of check in until 10 am on the day of checkout. The code generating process took less than two minutes.

I loved the inexpensive cost of the Resort Lock, and visually, it looked great. The backlit numbers on the lock's keypad were cool and were especially helpful when entering numbers into the keypad at night. Punching numbers into a lit keypad is a lot easier than punching numbers into a dark keypad, especially in a dark hallway.

The bad news is that the batteries on the lock would wear out in just a couple of months. When that happened, the keypad became inoperable, thwarting the nifty system that you had set up. The guest then had to resort to a hard key backup, which was technical. As a backup, we would hide a physical key somewhere nearby in a combo magnet box, and simply walk the guest through on how to find it, enter the magnet box code, and access the hard key to the unit, if that emergency came up.

To combat the dead battery issue, we would schedule maintenance on a calendar to replace the batteries every three or four months, a real pain.

But then it got worse.

It may have been an aberration, but for me, these locks unfortunately physically broke down on us multiple times, and at multiple properties. The lock would either rust out in the saltwater environment at the beaches or simply the hardware would flat out fail, and the door would not lock or unlock at all.

One time, we had a guest get stuck inside the condo, and could not get out, as the door handle completely stripped from the interior mechanism. We had to get a locksmith out there on an emergency basis just to get the door open and allow them to exit. That was nuts.

We then moved to the KABA lock. OMG. It was like entering heaven. The lock hardware is solid. It never breaks. The battery lasts f o r e v e r – kid you not. Although the software to program the codes is functional, and a bit boring, and not super user friendly, the codes work - always.

The downside of the KABA lock though is cost.

You need to hire a locksmith to purchase and install the KABA lock, and then set up your software on a yearly contract. There is an annual fee to generate the needed codes for each guest stay. The lock costs nearly triple that of a Resort Lock or a Schlage Lock. I believe we spent about $600 - $800 per KABA lock with the installation included. The annual fee is expensive, approximately $200 per year.

However, I would never trade any of our KABA locks for anything. These locks never break down, never have a battery issue, and always work. It is money well spent for peace of mind and worth every penny. Do not go with anything else. Buy a KABA lock, have a locksmith install it, and buck up for peace of mind. You've got to do it. It's simply one of those things you cannot cut corners on in a vacation rental.

We now have KABA locks on all four of our vacation rentals. It is easy and simple to generate guest codes once it is set up, even from your smartphone, or on the fly if needed.

Out of habit, we still hide a physical key somewhere nearby in a combo lock box or magnet box. This is out of an abundance of caution as old emergencies of having to rely on a hard key are still recent in memory.

In other words, even the keycode KABA lock has a physical key that will unlock the door, so if the keypad quits working, or the lock battery dies, the door can still be locked and unlocked.

We also pay the locksmith to go out each year and adjust the time, lubricate it, replace its batteries and so forth, to be preventative and avoid a breakdown (about $100 a year). Again, set it up and let the system work. It's peace of mind.

Yes, I could perhaps figure out how to change the battery each year. However, due to infrequent visits, forgetfulness, uncertainty on how to do it, and the special needed proprietary tool needed to adjust the lock's time, just pay the service to handle it for you so it gets done and the battery never dies, and the lock's time is accurate.

A guest not being able to get into your vacation rental is a major deal – don't let it happen. Get the KABA lock.

RULE: Have a locksmith install a KABA lock and pay the annual fee for you to be able to generate guest codes. It is well worth the security, reliability, and peace of mind.

Chapter 63

Transferring a positive review record

Second only to photos are your unit reviews. Reviews are the most prized possessions of your vacation rental and must be handled with extreme care, prudence, and diligence, as the guests may hook into the most benign of comments or feedback and then decide not to rent your unit.

In other words, the guest, after seeing the photos and title, are literally 90% sure they want to book your unit, and the cursory review of the feedback is just to make sure that there is not some crazy reason out there to not rent the vacation rental.

The guest also wants assurance of prior guest history, an affirmation of their belief after reviewing the photos that they are indeed on the right track. Vacation rental listings with few or no reviews also raise a concern for the booking guest, due to the absence of that assurance. You want at least a couple of reviews right out of the gate with a five-star rating, to really get the calendar to book up quickly after purchase.

The lengthy review history will also help soften the sting of an unexpected or undeserved three- or four-star review, if that were to happen, due to the dozens of other five-star reviews - a real perk.

Manufacturing a positive review history is difficult, if not impossible to do - at least with VRBO. VRBO is pretty good at weeding out fake or manufactured reviews, as a friend or a family member staying for free, typically does not get the opportunity to review the property. The guest must be a legitimate paying guest.

If you happen to be buying an established vacation rental, look at their entire feedback history, and see if it is a history that you would want to adopt for your listing (and provide insight as to whether this is a good vacation rental to buy or not as well).

In other words, you have the option for VRBO to transfer the listing review history from the previous owner to the buyer, which is cool, especially if there are a lot of reviews with a strong rating.

Otherwise, you are starting your reviews from scratch - a precarious position to be in during your first year. Because of this, do not open for rentals or open for business until the vacation rental is completely ready and perfect for those first few incoming guests, as those initial reviews could significantly impact your first year in business.

Can the seller transfer to the buyer existing reservations? No. The seller cannot transfer existing or pending reservations. The seller will simply honor their reservations through the closing date but will need to cancel and refund any reservations for stays that are past their closing date, and then the guests would (hopefully) simply rebook with the new owner under the buyer's new VRBO listing. Airbnb is similar.

This is yet another reason for the buyer to get their listing up and running quickly as soon as the property closes, so that those cancelled guests could then immediately rebook with the buyer for their same dates of stay. Work with the seller to inform any of their cancelled and refunded guests of the buyer's new listing so that they will hopefully rebook with the buyer.

RULE: If purchasing an already established vacation rental, check with the listing service to see if the reviews can transfer over to your new listing, especially if that review history is strong.

Chapter 64

Should I add a video to my VRBO listing?

If so, how do I do it?

Yes. You or your professional photographer should put together a 2 to 3-minute highlight video of your vacation rental, the resort, and attractions in the area.

If you have an iPhone, you could shoot multiple three second clips of your vacation rental, the resort, and area attractions. You can then use iMovie app on your iPhone to stitch the clips you took all together, add background music, and captions. You can then 'publish' the stitched together video (again all of this can be done from your iPhone).

Once published, that video can then be uploaded from your iPhone to your YouTube channel (which is free and easy to set up if you don't already have one).

Unless you know how to shoot and produce a video, edit it, and upload it to YouTube, you may need to hire a professional video person or photographer to make a marketing video for your vacation rental. Most professional real estate photographers also know how to shoot and produce a short promotional video, in addition to standard photography.

The photographer / videographer will arrive and video your vacation rental, its interior, exterior, resort amenities, and may have some stock footage of area attractions.

Again, professional photos and videos should be taken after closing, and after all the improvements, painting, and theme selection has been done. Hopefully this is done within a month or less of closing, but preferably prior to the first guest staying.

The shots are then heavily edited and cropped down to make a couple minute video. It does not have to be any longer than that as the guest will appreciate brevity.

Appropriate background music is added. If drone footage can be included, it would be even better. Some may do captions as the scenes unfold, while others may allow for a narrative as the scenes scroll through. Note that captions with background music are better typically than straight narration, if possible. We have tried both ways. Background music with captions is the way to go. The video is probably more expensive as more that is added to the production.

The photographer / videographer can then assist you with uploading it to your YouTube account.

If I recall correctly, the video needs to be uploaded to your own YouTube channel, not someone else's. Otherwise, VRBO may not allow the shared link, out of concern that you may not 'own' the video you are incorporating into your listing if your video is listed on someone else's YouTube channel.

Again, if you are versed in how to make a video with iMovie, or perhaps even in Adobe Premier, you will then know how to upload that video into your free YouTube account.

Once the video is uploaded into your YouTube account, you then copy the shareable link to the video, so that you can paste that shareable link into the video option of your VRBO listing.

In the VRBO and/or Airbnb app, there is a section under 'Edit Property' titled 'Video' where you simply paste that shareable video link into the box for your video, and the video will then appear in the camera reel, as an option for a prospective guest to watch. The link to the video appears on our listings within the first few photos in the carousel, depending upon whether you also have a virtual tour in your carousel or not.

If the video is good, every guest that watches it will likcly book your unit. By having a video in your photo carousel, you will be setting yourself apart from most other similar listings, as most other listings will not have a video link like what I am describing. Further, the guest starts that mental process of picturing themselves and their families in the video.

Like photos, the vacation rental video needs to be perfect. All the tips for taking great photos must also be used before shooting the video – plenty of light, bright and airy, clean, tidy, spacious, and again, not shot on a rainy day! The video also needs to be happy, fun, light and informative. Think of the 30 second commercials advertising resorts in the Caribbean. Your goal is to create something along those lines in a few minute or less video.

One last thing – make sure that the actual vacation rental listing URL is listed on the bottom of the video screen or displayed prominently at the end of the video of your vacation rental.

For example, list 'For rates and availability, please visit www.vrbo.com/513462.' This will cover the situation in case someone watches the video from a Google or YouTube search, and they are not watching it through the carousel photo link in your listing.

For instance, if one were to google 'video of Phoenix on the Bay Orange Beach Alabama vacation rental,' and or google 'Splash Resort vacation rental condo Panama City Beach,' our promotional video of our unit at those two resorts should show up in the first page of search results, which takes the prospective guest to YouTube, where they watch our promotional video of our vacation rental.

If the prospective guest then likes the video, and wants to book, the guest simply follows the listed URL (i.e., For rates and availability, please visit www.vrbo.com/513462) to the VRBO vacation rental listing and then books the unit.

So, if you can prepare a promotional video, or your photographer / videographer can prepare one, the video will serve two purposes.

The first purpose is to provide a video to the prospective VRBO guest scrolling through your camera carousel of photos to find a video link on the vacation rental, the resort and area attractions. The goal is for the prospective guest to then watch the promotional video as they scroll through the photos of your listing, and then book the unit, as they are already on your VRBO page looking at the listing photos.

The second purpose of the promotional video is to show up in Google and YouTube search results for your resort or area and serves as a driver of prospective guests to your VRBO listing.

The guest googles your resort name and the word video or YouTube, and then finds your promotional video. The prospective guest then watches it. If the guest likes it, and wants to either book, check availability, or check rates, they then visit your VRBO listing page, and will then hopefully book. This is why it is critical to add to the promotional video the link to your actual VRBO listing. Again, we typically add to the promotional video, 'For rates and availability and to book this unit, please visit www.vrbo.com/########'

DO NOT DESPAIR: If this is all too much, and just getting 50 photos uploaded to your VRBO listing was a Herculean task, do not fret over not having a promotional video. It is helpful but not critical in the grand scheme of things, so don't worry if you end up not having a promotional video as part of your photo carousel.

RULE: Unless you already know how to create a video, hire your professional photographer to make a short marketing video, upload it to your free YouTube account, and then paste the shareable YouTube video link into your VRBO listing, so that the video will play inside your carousel of photos. Make sure the video is stored either on YouTube or another platform where it can be found by Google for people searching for your unit or units in your resort or area, as that is a great marketing tool. The YouTube video will then drive prospective guests to your VRBO listing.

Chapter 65

Should I get a virtual tour?

Yes, you should get a virtual tour done of your vacation rental property.

However, this is not something that you can do on your own or with a smartphone, as the process requires specialized equipment and training to do.

VRBO (and presumably Airbnb as well) will have a list of approved virtual tour photographers who can create a virtual tour for you of your vacation rental property. Simply contact them for the list of approved vendors in your area. By going through VRBO, you get a trusted, experienced vendor, who knows what they are doing at a competitive price.

The virtual tour typically runs a couple hundred dollars, and we have done it on some but not all of our properties. We have not noticed a huge difference in business whether we have the virtual tour or not. I will say though it cannot hurt. I am leaning towards having a virtual tour being done on all our vacation rentals, not just some of them, as I do believe that it is worth the expense.

The convenience and efficiency of using the VRBO approved vendor is critical. You literally do nothing (other than schedule the time for the photographer to do the shoot and give them a KABA code to get in), and they do everything else, including getting the virtual tour set up in your listing.

Like photos, and especially if there is no rush, try and schedule the virtual tour on a day when the weather will be good.

RULE: Try and get finalized super high-quality photographs, a promotional video, and virtual tour all done within thirty days of closing, but no later than within a few months of closing. For that guest that is about to book, the combination of those three items in your photo carousel will go a long way in convincing the prospective guest that your vacation rental is the one they want.

Chapter 66

After finishing all improvements, should I hire a professional photographer for my final photos, take the photos myself, or a combo of both?

After you have spent the first few weeks getting your vacation rental ready for guests, all of the furnishings ready, décor, artwork, bedding set up, and the dust has settled from all of the changes that you made since buying or acquiring the vacation rental, it is then time to have the vacation rental photographed (for the final time) for your VRBO or Airbnb listing.

When I say, 'for the final time,' these are the photos that you intend to keep for the foreseeable future and are not just 'temporary' photos.

As discussed in an earlier chapter on this same topic, the single most important thing in your listing, other than reviews, are super high-quality photos of your property. This is the number one thing that a guest will go to when looking at your unit. The quality of the photos will either make or break your success in attracting guests to stay with you.

If the photos are dark, the guest will assume the vacation rental is dark. They then move to the next listing.

If the photos are blurry, the guest takes mental note. This owner doesn't know what they are doing, or is using old technology, and the unit is probably dirty, and they are hiding something. They then move to the next listing.

If the photos show clouds and rain, and it's a beach front condo, the guest moves to the next listing. They want a sunny beach day, and do not want to stay somewhere that attracts rain and bad weather. Seriously, do not put photos on your vacation listing of a beach front condo of empty wintertime beaches, cloudy skies, or rain. You want to portray paradise, not grey and cold misery.

Please review our list of suggestions from our earlier class on how to stage great photos, and how many photos should be taken of the vacation rental itself, the resort, and area attractions. Please then also review how to sequence those photos in your photo carousel for maximum success.

In addition to those earlier suggestions, consider also doing more.

If possible, set up place settings with dishware and glassware. Yes, if possible, perhaps set up wine glasses with a cheese plate or board. These are all great 'staging' ideas for your finalized photos.

You may need to assist your professional photographer in setting all of that up. If not, your photographer may be able to do all of that for you.

Note that just because your photographer is a professional, does not mean that they will get every detail right. I remember one time a professional photographed one of our units, and I couldn't use any of the bathroom shots – because the toilet seat wasn't down in every one of them. It may be just me, but there is something that wasn't right about the photo with the open toilet seat. If it's icky to you, it may be icky to the prospective guest.

Indeed, when scouting out a photographer to use, check their photos. Use my pre-photograph checklist from our earlier chapter to confirm that the photographer is getting every single detail right. All these details are essential. Prospective guests will pour over every inch of your photos at the final decision stage, looking for that affirmation that yes this is the place we want to stay. You do not want to create a red flag steering them to another listing. The finalized photos are that important.

Yes, you can try to take the final photos yourself.

With the advances of the iPhone and Samsung phones, it is amazing how automated they have made photography and have allowed those with limited camera experience to take great photos. I would only do this if you upgraded to the latest phone with enhanced camera capabilities.

I am one of those in that category. Equipped with the latest Apple iPhone, one can take great photos, and then, using the Apple software, brighten and crop each photo. The line is now blurring between super high-quality photos on the newest smart phones, and the professionals.

The benefit of using one's own phone is that this may give you more days to choose from for that perfect Instagram worthy balcony picture of the vacation rental's view. In other words, over a several day period, you should have at least one day where the weather is perfect, the beach is beautiful, the sun is out, and the water is green and clear and free of seaweed. This is the huge advantage of taking the photos yourself versus hiring a professional photographer who is scheduled for a one-hour shoot way in advance without consideration for what the weather will end up being.

For example, I hired a professional photographer, and we made the appointment. During the appointment (as the photographer was booked solid for weeks), he arrived for the appointment in the middle of a rainstorm. The interior photos were amazing, and were significantly better than mine, but the exterior photos, and photos of the resort amenities were worthless, as it was RAINING. Do not use pictures with rain and inclement weather – just don't – unless you are marketing an Airbnb in a rain forest.

In summary, I recommend taking high quality photos of the interior, exterior, views, property amenities, and area attractions. Crop each of them and brighten them with your phone's editing tools. Hire a photographer and then let the professional do their magic with interior, exterior, view, and amenity photos.

You then pick out from the combined group the 50 or so best photos.

RULE: High quality photos are the single most important thing on your vacation rental listing. These photos should, at minimum, include the interior, exterior, views, resort amenities, and area attractions. Whether you are phone and camera savvy or not, it is good for you to have a series of photos of your own, to combine with or compliment what your professional photographer provides you.

SECTION IV – HOW TO SET UP ESSENTIAL EMAIL TEMPLATES, AND WHAT TO INCLUDE IN THEM

Chapter 67

How to set up an email response template to a guest inquiry and what should it include?

In an ideal world, the guest chooses the instant booking option, which is the process to make an instant reservation without the need for preapproval, and you are off to the races. You then simply move to the check in email / access instructions email, and keycode email (the next email template that we will discuss) that provides the guest rental instructions.

However, there are many guests who will instead click on 'Contact Host' and ask a variety of questions, before making the decision to book.

VRBO consistently says that the host who responds quickly to a guest inquiry has dramatically better booking percentages than a host who does not respond quickly.

If you have the VRBO owner app installed on your phone, you get a notification that someone just inquired, giving you the opportunity to then immediately respond. If you do not have the VRBO owner app on your phone, that inquiry will then sit unanswered on your desktop computer until you check your email again (whenever that happens to be), which results in a painfully slow response time. You really need to have a smart phone so that you can quickly use a template to answer an inquiry wherever you happen to be at the moment the inquiry comes in.

As luck would have it, that inquiry will come when you are driving, at dinner, or in the middle of a weekend or workout. How do you honor that need to respond quickly, but at the same time thoroughly answer the guest's question?

The answer is the email template system through VRBO and/or Airbnb. With the email template, and the VRBO and or Airbnb owner app on your smart phone, you can quickly answer a guest question or inquiry, show availability, provide a quote, all *in under thirty seconds*.

So how is this done?

The key to an inquiry response is to provide in the template the same highlights in your listing description, but a bit more abbreviated, as that will then answer 90% of guest questions.

For the remaining 10% of questions that are not answered, simply add, or edit your template each time during the first year, to cover those frequently asked, unexpected questions. Your goal is to NEVER have to type out the same answer more than once for prospective guest inquiries. By the end of your first year, your edited and finalized primary inquiry response will capture every possible scenario under the sun.

In addition, your inquiry response should also serve the dual purpose of showing off or 'selling' your unit. It is an opportunity for you to literally close the deal. It is your chance to make your vacation rental shine. The template needs to be polished, and reach an appropriate level of sales pitch, but at the same time, answer the guest's question.

Be careful with the language you use in your template response.

'If you want to book, just let me know.' This type of language does not close the deal. If anything, it leads the guest to further delay, not booking. The statement lacks confidence and does not instill a positive affirmation for the inquiring guest.

'When ready to book, click on the 'Book Now' button highlighted on this email, and simply follow the VRBO directions to confirm your reservation. The process is easy, quick, and your payment information is kept completely confidential.' This sentence is the type of language that needs to be used to close the deal. Instead of asking an open-ended question, or a question that solicits a yes or no response, simply assume that they are going to book your unit. It's not a question of if, it's when. So, use language like 'When ready to book, please simply use the 'Book

Now' button. You are moving the prospective guest towards action, not further contemplation, to book the unit. Direct the guest towards booking your rental unit, not somewhere else. You are providing the path or guide that you want them to follow.

One time I was waiting tables at a restaurant, and they had a contest for a new bike for the server that sold the most deserts in each month. At the end of each meal, I presented the table with a tray of desserts, and said, 'which of these do you all want?' Yes, that sounds brash, but it worked. I won the bike. The approach to not use would have been 'do you all want dessert?'

You too need to design that template response to sell your vacation rental, close the deal, and steer that guest towards hitting the 'Book Now' button.

VRBO and/or Airbnb have some starter templates that are already set up in the email system. You can use those and figure out what works for your vacation rental.

There are also lots of sample templates online that you could also use, and then try and build off those.

I am providing you with three very different examples of our inquiry responses. The first is for a bayfront condo where people bring a boat. The second is for a gulf front condo, and the third example is for a stand-alone cabin, or home for rent. Perhaps one of these options can be a good starting example for your vacation rental.

INQUIRY RESPONSE – BAYVIEW CONDO WITH SLIP FOR RENT

Phoenix on the Bay is our vacation rental on the bay in Orange Beach Alabama. It is not Gulf front, but rather bay front, with an amazing lazy river and slide. It also has an onsite boat ramp, boat slips for rent, and a harbor.

As such, we get a ton of questions including:

'Is this beachfront?'

'How far to the beaches?'

'Can I bring a boat?'

'I have a small dog. Can I bring him?'

'Is the unit available?'

'How much is parking?'

'I am 19, can I rent?'

Rather than answering each of these questions, capture all those answers at once in your inquiry response template email. Here is our inquiry response email for Phoenix on the Bay:

Thank you for your inquiry on vacation rental PROPERTY_ID, Phoenix on the Bay, Unit 1508, in Orange Beach, Alabama. The condo is available from AVAILABLE_DATE_PERIOD. We would be honored to have you as a guest!

BEST VIEW AT PHOENIX ON THE BAY: This is a luxurious, high end unit, with a breathtakingly beautiful view, with a large private open air balcony. Located in the popular Phoenix on the Bay resort in Orange Beach Alabama, this fifth floor two-bedroom condo has one of the best 2/2 views in the resort.

OUTSTANDING OPEN-AIR AMENITIES: Phoenix on the Bay boasts one of the longest outdoor lazy rivers in Alabama, outdoor water slide, multiple large outdoor pools, an indoor heated pool, and two hot tubs. In addition, this unit is accessed via an open-air breezeway directly from the same floor parking garage.

JUST IN TIME FOR YOUR STAY! New furnishings, new paint, new super clean barnwood style flooring, and more!

GULF FRONT BEACHES: Although most guests stay on property and enjoy Orange Beach's longest and fastest lazy river, water slide and pools, and other amenities, some guests still want to visit the Gulf front beaches at some point during their stay. We recommend the Gulf State Park beneath the Alabama Point bridge, which is visible across Terry Cove from Phoenix on the Bay and is only a short ten-minute drive away. The beach access includes elevated walkways down to the beach, restrooms, showers, lifeguards, and inexpensive parking.

MARINA / LAUNCH / BAY BEACH / SLIPS / TRAILER PARKING: The docks have been rebuilt, the beach restored, and the marina, boat slips, boat launch and trailer parking are all back in full operation for slip rentals, fishing, or kayaking. For those wishing to bring a boat that is 27' or less, our private, reservation only owner owned boat slip is available at the rate of $50 per night for boats under 27'. Availability of the unit's boat slip is guaranteed if you book with us. After you book the unit through VRBO, simply contact the owner to make the additional, separate payment for use of the boat slip, and to secure instructions on bringing a boat to Phoenix on the Bay.

Slips for boats 27' or longer, and wave runners, contact the front desk at Phoenix on the Bay at 251-980-5700 for reservations. Trailer parking is $10 per night, reserved in person through the front desk upon arrival at Phoenix on the Bay (trailer spaces unfortunately cannot be reserved in advance, and are subject to availability). NOTE: the front desk / security will require that you show proof of liability insurance on the boat upon check-in to receive a decal for use of the marina.

BOOKING IS FAST AND EASY: When ready to make your reservation, the fastest booking method is for you to simply hit the 'Book Now' button, and follow the online steps to confirm this reservation, through a secure, confidential, and easy online VRBO payment portal. Payment in full for the unit is required to book this unit.

Please note that this condo strictly prohibits smoking. Pets and parties are prohibited. Renters must be 25 years of age or older.

Please reconfirm before booking that there is sufficient space, beds, and or baths for your needs. This is a 2/2 (king bedroom with en suite full bath, 2nd king bedroom with en suite bath, queen sleeper sofa, Serta twin rollaway bed). For those traveling with babies or toddlers, there is additional space for you to bring a pack-n-play or crib if needed.

Please note that the attached quote is all inclusive of stay except for a single $48.67 plus tax ($55 total) payment due upon check-in, which covers unlimited amenity wrist bands, and one vehicle parking pass for the duration of your stay. A second vehicle pass is available for the same amount. Upon check in, please simply stop by the front desk and secure your wristbands, and parking pass or passes.

OWNER_NAME

OWNER_EMAIL

OWNER_PHONE

SAMPLE INQUIRY RESPONSE – BEACHFRONT CONDO

We have a 2/2 at Splash Resort in Panama City Beach, Florida. The condo stay includes use of the beach service, a wonderful perk, that unfortunately generates a lot of guest questions. We similarly get questions about the cost of parking passes, availability, and proximity to area attractions.

We also have questions about payment plans. <u>Don't do</u> payment plans. Make that clear in your inquiry response.

Sometimes a guest amenity may be down for maintenance. This unavailability should be listed in both the description (towards the bottom) and highlighted again in the inquiry response. This too will knock out a lot of questions.

Again, simply include all the answers to the most asked questions in your Inquiry Response template email, so that you don't have to type out the same answer every time there is the same question presented.

Thank you for your inquiry on our vacation rental PROPERTY_ID This condo is available from AVAILABLE_DATE_PERIOD. We would be honored to have you as a guest!

Please know that the west tower pool and hot tub and splash pad will be closed for maintenance from January 3rd and is expected to open by March 1. However, the east tower pool and Lazy River will be open during this time.

FREE BEACH SERVICE! For guests staying in our unit, receive complimentary beach service (3/1 thru 10/31), including two Gulf front beach loungers with cushions, drink table, and large canvas umbrella - a $35 per day value!

NEW FURNISHINGS! Freshly painted unit, brand new premium king bed, new barnwood style flooring, brand new premium sleeper sofa, and two new swivel rocker chairs - everyone's favorite chair to relax in!

OUTSTANDING OPEN-AIR AMENITIES: Onsite kids waterpark, hot tub, pools (shaded or full sun), lazy river, toddler splash pad, state of the art gulf front gym, plentiful covered parking, convenient proximity to Pier Park, and more. All Splash amenities are open year-round, and the pools are heated during the winter months.

COVID-19 CLEANING ADJUSTMENTS: As guest safety and security are our number one priority, enhanced COVID-19 specific cleaning procedures are now in place at no additional charge to the guest. We now have 100% easy to clean solid surface flooring throughout the unit - no difficult to clean area rugs or carpets, as well as easier to clean glass shower doors, and other improvements.

NEW COVID-19 LAUNDRY / UNIT PROTOCOLS: we have removed all throw pillows, quilts, shams and now launder everything between guest stays, so that even the blankets are all washed following every guest departure, in addition to the clean sheets towels and other linens typically provided. Our cleaning crew now exchanges the unit's air between guest stays. Even the linen sofa and cloth swivel chairs are sprayed with CDC recommended disinfectant between stays!

BOOKING IS FAST AND EASY: When ready to make your reservation, the fastest booking method is for you to simply hit the 'Book Now' button, and follow the online steps to confirm this reservation, through a secure, confidential, and easy online VRBO payment portal. Payment in full for the unit is required to book this unit.

$30 RESORT FEE: Please note that the attached quote is all inclusive for your cost of stay with the exception of a $30 resort fee which much be paid upon arrival at Splash Resort. The $30 resort fee is a onetime flat fee for the stay at the unit good for all your guests, and all your vehicles. The single $30 fee due is not a per guest or per day fee - it's $30 total for your stay. Once paid, you then receive unlimited guest wristbands for use of all Splash amenities, and also unlimited parking passes for all your vehicles, good for the duration of your stay.

Please note that this condo strictly prohibits smoking. Pets and parties are prohibited. Primary renter must be 25 years of age or older. ID reconfirming minimum age is required upon check in. Double check that this unit has sufficient bed capacity for your stay.

OWNER_NAME

OWNER_EMAIL

OWNER_PHONE

SAMPLE INQUIRY RESPONSE – STAND ALONE CABIN

We own Appalachian High cabin, a stand-alone vacation rental on top of a mountain near Pigeon Forge, Tennessee.

Questions include how far the cabin is from area attractions. Again, as these questions come in, simply add them to your email template so that you won't have to type out the answer to that question the next time it is asked again.

Thank you for your inquiry on vacation rental PROPERTY_ID, 'Appalachian High' located near Pigeon Forge, TN. The cabin is available from AVAILABLE_DATE_PERIOD

BEST VIEW AT THE PRESERVE: This is a luxurious, high-end cabin, with arguably the most beautiful view imaginable of the Smoky Mountains, with two floors of private open-air balconies. Located in the upscale The Preserve Resort, this three story, one bedroom cabin is the highest vacation rental unit located at The Preserve - located at the very end of the road and on top of the mountain!

BRAND NEW (2022) HOT TUB / ROCKING CHAIR VIEW IN TN: The new four-person hot tub is perched atop the top floor balcony with panoramic views of the Great Smoky Mountains. Super comfy rockers are available on both balconies for relaxation and taking in the views.

CABIN AMENITIES: For football fans, or those wanting Wi-Fi, our Comcast HDTVs provide a full lineup of channels and complimentary high-speed Internet. For family dinners, enjoy the views from our formal dining table for six and well-equipped full-sized kitchen, or eat at our picnic area outside. Cozy up at night in one of the two reclining lazy boy chairs and enjoy the giant flat screen TV. Kids will love the authentic log ladder to the third story loft, with informal futons. There is also a unique 'bears den' play area built beneath the living room stairs - a great 'hide out' for the kids. For those who love to cook, we have both a charcoal and a propane grill available for use, and outdoor picnic area.

Enjoy a true log cabin feel with 100% wood interior, stone electric (simulated) fireplace, cathedral ceilings, and rustic all wood furnishings!

CABIN GAMEROOM: For kids of all ages, enjoy our full-size pool table, full size foosball table, full size Atari driving simulator, or try a hand at our table sized authentic Atari multi-cade game which sports Pac-Man, Galaga, Centipede, Frogger and other 1980's favorites!

OUTSTANDING OPEN AIR RESORT AMENITIES: The Preserve Resort boasts a large mountain top pool and hot tub (open roughly from Memorial Day to Labor Day, weather permitting), gym, sauna and steam room, fireplace and pavilion - all of which are free for guests of Appalachian High - and just a short walk from the cabin!

PROXIMITY TO ALL PIGEON FORGE ATTRACTIONS: We are conveniently located within ten miles of Pigeon Forge and only minutes from the Great Smoky Mountain National Park. The scenic drive from the cabin to downtown Gatlinburg has zero traffic lights! There is also an onsite mountain top chapel available for weddings - simply inquire for more info.

PARKING: Free and secure parking available adjacent to cabin. 3 vehicles maximum.

BOOKING IS FAST AND EASY: When ready to make your reservation, the fastest booking method is for you to simply hit the 'Book Now' button, and follow the online steps to confirm this reservation, through a secure, confidential, and easy online VRBO payment portal. Payment in full for the unit is required to book this unit.

NO SMOKING / PETS: No smoking. No Pets. Renters must be 25 years of age or older and anyone under 25 must be accompanied by their parent(s). Parties, celebrations, events, or large gatherings are prohibited. Three vehicle max. All rules enforced via 24 hr. recorded video and RING surveillance of exterior.

GUEST CAPACITY: Please reconfirm before booking that there is sufficient beds/baths for your needs as follows:

1ST FLOOR / MAIN LIVING AREA FLOOR: Master Bedroom with King Bed; Living Room Queen Sleeper Sofa; Full Bath;

2ND FLOOR: Queen over Queen Bunks; Full Bath (walk in shower and jacuzzi tub);

3RD FLOOR / LOFT: Two Twin beds;

MAXIMUM CAPACITY: 6 adult max / 10 total guest max. Capacity limits are STRICTLY ENFORCED.

OWNER_NAME

OWNER_EMAIL

OWNER_PHONE

HOW TO CREATE THE PRIMARY INQUIRY
RESPONSE EMAIL TEMPLATE

Log onto VRBO while on your laptop or desktop computer. Go to your inbox. You will then see a button called 'templates.' Click on the template and then edit an existing, skeleton sample template to fit your specific needs. Again, it is typically simply providing an abbreviated version of your listing description in a condensed format. Airbnb is presumably similar.

I would just copy and paste your listing description into the template for an inquiry response, and then work on abbreviating it as much as you can.

Use the insertion tools on the top of the template titled guest name, owner name, dates of stay etc. for the automatic insertion of your name, the prospective guest's name, and proposed dates of stay. When creating the template, you will see where you can insert that wording to make the email automatically fill that space with your name, or the guest's name, and/or the dates of stay. By using those template insertions, the template will in turn create a more customized and personable email. They will also have no idea that you simply used a template. Even better, the prospective guest may think that you typed out the entire response just for them.

Remember too that you can attach a photo to the inquiry response, which should be either your primary listing photo, or perhaps the 2nd and or 3rd photos in your photo carousel. Simply click on the paper clip button at the bottom of the template box, and upload those photos, so that they will appear in the email response as well.

One of the reasons guests send an inquiry is to simply check how available you happen to be and how responsive you happen to be. This is important. By responding rapidly and thoroughly, you are showing this guest that you are available, are on top of it, and will respond quickly and efficiently during their stay as well, if an issue were to happen to arise. You then will set your listing apart from those listings where the owner may not respond as quickly, or are professionally managed, and inquiry responses are not given until the following day or Monday during regular business hours.

The old saying 'the early bird gets the worm' is true when it comes to response times. The speed of your being able to respond quickly after hours and on weekends significantly sets you apart from a professional management company, who only answers inquiries during regular business hours during the weekdays.

RULE: Set up an inquiry response in your email inbox. Copy your listing description and abbreviate it. This template response is your finalized and polished effort to show off your place, and your effort to close the deal. Use the insertable template tool to autofill names and dates of stay. Download and install the VRBO owner app, so that you can respond using the template within seconds of any inquiry.

Chapter 68

The perfect template to handle the bargain hunter looking for a last-minute discount or impossibly low overall stay budget.

Many guests will inquire about a last-minute discount, your 'best rate,' or will propose a capped budget for their proposed stay and ask you to discount the stay to fit within their desired budget.

When you get an email like that, this same guest has probably sent the exact same inquiry to 50 other similar vacation listings (kid you not), so the odds of you getting their business are slim.

If you do heavily discount the proposed stay, the bargain hunter still may not pick you if another owner similarly discounts or meets their desired budget. The endless back and forth negotiations sap your time and energy, especially if the prospective guest is negotiating with several owners. It is antithesis to our motto of streamlined mailbox money. Try and avoid back and forth negotiations like this if you can. It is typically not worth the hassle. Let me explain why.

The few times we got the bargain hunter's business, they were horrible guests. They nick picked everything, expected something for nothing, and left poor reviews. They immediately asked for a discount if any of the amenities were closed. They wanted to check out early and get a refund if it was raining. Even though they got a discount, they all wanted to check in early and check out late, another time-consuming process of last-minute code generation for the proposed extended time of stay.

If the unit wasn't perfectly clean, they asked for their cleaning fee to be refunded. There was always some type of issue on wanting a discount or further money back when and if we got a bargain shopper in the unit. It is better to just not go there if possible.

In addition, I have found that very few of the inquiries where guests are looking for a last-minute bargain-basement price end up booking with us, so we don't worry too much about not getting their business. The unit ends up typically booking anyway (albeit possibly at a discounted price but not a bargain basement price).

If it doesn't book, it's still a win as you avoid the hassle, time consuming negotiations, a negative review, and wear and tear on the unit. Look on the bright side – no one has taken advantage of you.

Further, you can discount your room heavily, and fill it 100% of the year if you want, but there is a downside to such volume, including a lot of time spent on making a small amount of money and enduring a lot of hassle – but it is up to you.

If I must reduce the published nightly rate last minute to fill a vacancy (which is a good idea, but just not too heavily discounted), that reduced, last minute rate is still typically much higher than what the bargain basement hunter would have paid anyway, with a lot less problems and hassle.

Again, you want people to just 'book it' so put your best rate out there, especially right before any given vacancy. It is better to do it that way than to have a high rate, and then enter endless negotiations on a low-ball offer on proposed stays.

In view of that, I recommend that the following paragraph simply be added to your standard inquiry response and saved as a second alternative inquiry response template. In that way you send this special inquiry response when you get an inquiry asking for a last-minute special or a capped low ball total amount for stay.

DISCOUNT ALREADY PRICED IN: You have requested if we can provide a last-minute reduced rate on our vacation rental. We appreciate the question and get this request often. The published rate is our last-minute, discounted rate, especially if we are within a month of the proposed stay. This unit will likely book for the requested stay dates, even last minute, at the listed, recently reduced competitive price. Use the 'Book Now' booking option sooner than later to insure availability.

HOW TO CREATE THE 2ND ALTERNATIVE
INQUIRY RESPONSE TEMPLATE

After you have created your primary, generalized email template response for when a guest contacts you, the owner, with a question, and includes your sales pitch, technical rules of stay, and the closing paragraph steering guests to 'Book Now,' simply copy that entire template, and then paste it into a new template. Call this second template the 'Inquiry Response – Discount Requested' template. You then paste the foregoing paragraph into that email template.

In that way, when you get an inquiry from a prospective guest requesting a discount or last-minute rate, you have a template ready to go to answer their question. This saves you time, as this is the most asked question by guests.

RULE: You may discount your nightly rate if you have a vacancy, and discount deeper the closer you get to that vacancy. I do not recommend giving out custom low-ball last-minute rates or trying to meet someone's impossibly low budget. Those guests tend to be problematic and unappreciative. Besides, the unit will likely book anyway as you slowly reduce your published price as you get closer to any given vacancy.

Chapter 69

The perfect template email response to a guest requesting a military, first responder, or senior citizen discount without hurting their feelings

Before I begin, you can provide your vacation rental guests a military, active duty, first responder, senior citizen, teacher, police and fire discount, or any other special class of people if you please. You can even advertise that discount on your listing description.

I am all for it as these are all well-deserved classifications and you may feel a moral obligation or sense of gratitude that you wish to share with that prospective guest thanking them for their service. If that is the case, good for you.

This assumes though that you have unlimited time to answer inquiries and send custom quotes with the discount applied. That's the first problem.

But the altruistic gesture gets worse.

As soon as you say we provide discounts for active-duty military, someone will inquire if you do a discount for the police, or a security guard at the mall. If you don't give them the discount, they literally will get their feelings hurt.

As soon as you provide a discount to first responders, then a nurse will email, wanting a discount. Are not all medical personnel first responders too? The questions about whether you will extend any given discount to their unique situation will explode. There will be endless associations and efforts to qualify for any given discount that you offer, putting you in a moral dilemma with each request for a discount. What about teachers, a principal, or a high school coach? What about an engineer or an inventor or a farmer or a chemist – are they all not amazing groups of people worthy of a break?

Due to the time-consuming nature of giving any given discount, and how providing or advertising that discount results in a tidal wave of requests for discounts of every shape, size, and worthy cause or not, we do not do them. We do not advertise them, and we do not do discounts based on someone's occupation or status. Period. We treat every prospective guest the same.

So how do we say that without offending the person or class of people who typically do get some type of discount on lodging or other service? The worst thing that could happen is that you insult them denying their request, and they then put you on social media and you end up with a mountain of backlash, not necessarily for not giving the discount, but how you handled turning down that request. Be careful in how you handle it.

So, you need to tread carefully with your response. Somehow you need to make them feel appreciated, but at the same time, gently let them down, without upsetting them.

Here is our response when we get a guest inquiring if we do military or senior citizen or first responder discount(s):

DISCOUNT REQUEST: You have requested if we can provide a veteran, active military, first responder or other special classification discount. We appreciate the request and get this request often. We are grateful for you and your family's service to others. However, we do not do discounts on any given stay. Our published rate is our lowest, best rate, which is generally available to everyone. This unit will likely book for the requested stay dates, even last minute, at the listed competitive price, so book sooner than later to ensure availability.

Again, like the bargain hunter inquiry response in the foregoing chapter, you gently let them know that the published rate is our best rate, and instead of them getting a discount, they need to book the unit now, as otherwise, it may be booked by someone else. You again flip the script and gently let them know that the rate is a great rate, and they better act fast, or it may get booked by someone else. It's a call to action, not a call to negotiate a reduced rate or to engage in a debate as to whether their circumstance should also quality for any given discount.

HOW TO ADD THE THIRD INQUIRY RESPONSE
TEMPLATE OPTION

To add the third alternative inquiry response template, which is to handle this specific discount request, again, simply log onto VRBO while on a desktop or laptop, go to your inbox, click on templates, copy your generic inquiry response template, paste it into a new template, and then paste the foregoing paragraph into the template just above the booking instructions.

Make sure all three templates have a similar name so they are lined up next to each other, and all stored in the same location, like 'dates available' section, so that they will all appear right next to each other on the top of the list of templates, for easy access when the inquiries start coming in.

Once done, you will then have three inquiry response options to choose from. The first is your general inquiry response that covers almost all questions. The second general inquiry response handles that prospective guest looking for a last-minute discount. The third general inquiry response handles that prospective guest looking for a military or special circumstance discount. These three templates will be your 'bread and butter' to work with in handling inquiries quickly and efficiently.

RULE: You are more than welcome to advertise and provide discounts for first responders, military, and others, but this will result in you spending a lot of time answering questions and providing customized quotes, which is opposite of our efforts for you to spend as little time as possible managing your vacation rental. For maximum efficiency, we do not do discounts like that and treat all our guests the same in that regard.

Chapter 70

How to set up a template for access instructions

to the vacation rental and what should be included?

Should I allow early check ins?

In an ideal world, all guests get their questions answered through the photos, the promotional video, the virtual tour, and your comprehensive listing description, and upon confirmation of availability, simply hit the 'Book Now' button. You get your calendar booked up without having to do anything.

Indeed, you may even get bookings while you sleep, or while out of the country, on vacation, or during a romantic dinner with your spouse. The feeling of making mailbox money and getting a reservation when you feel like you have done nothing is amazing.

Similarly, your cleaner will at that instant simultaneously receive notice of the reservation through the Resort Cleaning app, so the cleaners will know when they need to clean the unit. If your cleaner is a smaller 'Mom and Pop' operation that does not use Resort Cleaning, you may have to still periodically screen shot your VRBO or Airbnb calendar for them to know when to clean, but that too is a quick exercise.

At this point, after each instant booking comes in, the only thing you need to do is to email the guest the information to access the vacation rental, along with the unique KABA keyless entry code, for entry to the vacation rental. The entire access email is a form that is sent to every booked guest, in advance of their stay. The only thing that changes in that template form email for access instructions is the short, unique KABA code you generate for the guest's dates of stay.

As most reservations are not last minute, you will have time to get on your laptop or desktop and go to the KABA website and generate the keyless entry code, copy it, and then paste that exact code with times and dates of permitted entry, into the access instruction template, at a time convenient to you, but no later than a few days in advance of their stay.

If it truly is a last-minute stay, and you are not able to generate a KABA code for entry for some reason, you may as a last resort give the guest the permanent code (i.e., the one the cleaner uses), but only do that as a last resort.

When I get a booking, I know that I must send access instructions. **It is the only thing I must do each time there is a reservation**. Do not delay sending it as you may forget. The process to sit down, log into KABA, generate a code, copy it, and log into VRBO, pull up their reservation, and then paste it into your access instructions email template to that guest, takes a total of about five minutes, or less.

Once sent, you relax as you have then done everything needed for the guest's stay. Everything else – the cleaning, maintenance, or other needed services, is all automated or outsourced.

I then tell the guest to print the access instructions and all attachments and set the folder aside for their upcoming trip.

I then warn the guest that if they fail to formally print up the access instructions, and they cannot find the vacation rental or get in, that they then may be locked out until they can get in touch with the owner which may result in a delay in getting into the vacation rental. If they fail to follow directions, and fail to print out, at minimum, the access code and are therefore then inconvenienced, it becomes their fault, not yours.

What should my access instructions email contain?

The access instructions need to take the guest through a chronological virtual tour through the entire guest experience, from directions to the unit (including the address for GPS assisted directions), where to park, where to get a parking pass, how to get to and find the vacation rental (i.e. cross the pedestrian skybridge and turn right (not left) to the <u>west</u> tower), to the keyless entry code, to the Wi-Fi, to TV instructions, to location and use of resort amenities, area attractions, all rules of stay, and then conclude with checkout instructions.

What are some of the common elements used in all access instruction template emails?

You need to always include specific instructions about how to use the keyless entry system. Many, many guests leave off a # or * sign and the code will not work. You need to <u>tell them</u> not to leave those symbols out of the code sequence.

You need to always include a paragraph that instructs the guest to report damage immediately upon entry. That is important.

You need to always include a statement that cleaning oversights must be reported immediately upon entry, not hours later (after they themselves likely soiled the unit). This will then give your cleaners a chance to rectify a genuine cleaning oversight, versus something that the guests themselves did.

Tell the guest that everyone should have the keyless entry code in multiple locations to avoid an accidental lockout. It should be texted, written down, a stored screen shot or a spare copy kept in their wallet, purse or car.

Always include a paragraph that states that the code will not work prior to the check in time.

Many, many times guests think they can get in early with the code, and presumptuously think you emailed them a general owner code that allows for early access. Tell them that the code is unique just for their stay, and will not work prior to the check-in time, so that they are not then disappointed arriving early and finding that the code does not work for early entry. Even when we tell them that, many guests still try and access the vacation rental early, and then you get the call. You must then tell them again that the door code will not work until the scheduled check in time. It sounds harsh, but you must be consistent with your rules and instructions.

Also tell the guest that **no early check-ins are ever permitted**. We will discuss that issue in a later chapter. For now, remember that early check-ins are another time intensive, typically emergency task done on the day of check-in cast upon you without compensation. You must check with your cleaner or maintenance person or pest control or anyone else scheduled for that day to see if they are done. You then must log into KABA and generate a code. You then must text the code to the guest. This is all done on the fly and on an emergency basis without compensation. Don't do it. Don't take the bait. It's not worth it. Be clear. Be direct. There is no early check-in. Period. Never set yourself up for an uncompensated crisis mode situation that most guests will not remember or appreciate.

The other final reason to allow entry is that if you do, the guest may then say that you allowed early check in on a review, and then subsequent guests who read that review, then expect you to do the same for them on their stay. Why allow something that takes your time without compensation and then, in turn, cannot be appreciated or mentioned in a review?

Every vacation rental will be different, so you will need to construct your own unique access instruction email template that includes all the foregoing topics, plus many more depending upon your vacation rental.

For convenience, we provide three different examples of access instructions, from each of our units, for you to find one that perhaps matches your vacation rental. You can then see how we put the access instructions together and improve on them for your own access instructions.

You will find that some of the most common topics are repeated in each access instruction – no early check in, don't forget to use the * or # sign, don't misplace the keycode, and so forth, so you too should likely have those same paragraphs in your access instructions as well.

Please note that the templates we provided do not include the series of attachments that go along with the access instructions. The attachments are also important, and unique to your unit. We will discuss the attachments (and provide copies of those too) in a later chapter as well.

BAYFRONT VACATION RENTAL WITH BOAT SLIP

SAMPLE ACCESS INSTRUCTION TEMPLATE EMAIL

THIS IS YOUR KEYLESS ENTRY KEYCODE EMAIL. Please PRINT this email and PDF attachments, as this is the ONLY email that you will receive that contains the keyless entry code, directions to the unit, and other information regarding your upcoming stay.

RESERVATION DATES: You are booked for BOOKED_DATE_PERIOD, for PROPERTY_ID.

MAPQUEST INFO TO THE UNIT:

Phoenix on the Bay I

27580 Canal Road, Unit #1508

Orange Beach, AL 36561

GUARD GATE: When you arrive at Phoenix on the Bay, please show this confirmation to the guard at the gate (if the guard is present).

PARKING: Proceed to the west parking area (to the right as you enter the resort) and proceed up the car ramp to the fifth floor.

3pm CHECK IN TIME: On your day of arrival, you may arrive early and begin enjoying resort amenities, and secure your parking pass and complimentary wristbands from the front desk. However, your keyless entry code to the unit will not begin working until after 3pm. No access to the unit before 3pm is ever permitted - NO EXCEPTIONS, as 3pm is already considered our early check-in time. If the unit has not been cleaned upon arrival, call Diamond M Cleaning at 251-219-9606, and if unable to get through, the owner 251-209-9299 for status.

KEYLESS DOOR ENTRY CODE (INCLUDE * OR # CHARACTER IF APPLICABLE)

XXX-XXX-XXXX

Simply key in the FULL code, INCLUDING THE * OR #, if applicable. If the code doesn't work, you are either outside our check in / checkout times, or forgot to enter the * or # character, if applicable.

If you lose the access code or fail to enter the * or # sign if applicable, you may not be able to get into the condo until our next business day (if you are unable to get in touch with the owner). Use onsite security as a last resort only in the event of a lockout. We recommend texting the access code to yourself and others in your unit and keeping on your person an extra copy of the code at all times.

REMOVE SHOES: Do not track in black soot on bare feet or shoes from the breezeway or parking garage. Otherwise, the tracked in soot will cause your barefoot feet to quickly turn black, regardless of how clean the floor happens to be upon arrival.

DAMAGES: If damage or missing items are present upon check in, please report the issue immediately to the owner. Through timely reporting, this gives us a chance to fix it, to address the issue with the prior guest, and to document your assistance.

PARKING PASS / COMPLIMENTARY WRIST BANDS: Once settled, please proceed to the front desk on the ground floor of the resort, adjacent to the indoor pools / hot tub area (open 24/7). Please pay for and secure your $48.67 plus tax ($55 total) parking pass for each vehicle (good for one car for your entire stay, two maximum), and keep the parking pass displayed. Secure complimentary wrist bands for use of Phoenix on the Bay amenities.

SUPPLIES: As daily room service is not included with your stay, it may best to bring your own supplies if any complimentary starter supplies run out during your stay, such as laundry detergent, dish detergent, paper towels, toilet paper, trash liners, etc.

RENTAL SLIPS: If you are bringing a boat, please immediately email the owner to reserve the unit's boat slip ($50 per day for boats 27' feet or less). For jet skis, or boats larger than 27', please call 251-980-5700 for reservations.

TRAILER PARKING: $10 per night, reserved through the front desk in person upon arrival at Phoenix on the Bay (trailer spaces unfortunately cannot be reserved in advance, and are subject to availability).

RULES OF STAY / 10AM CHECKOUT: To avoid loss of deposit, please read and follow the attached rental agreement, all rules of stay, and checkout procedures.

OWNER_NAME

(251) 209-9299 (call or text)

ENCLOSURES / ATTACHMENTS:

      OWNER RULES OF STAY / CHECKOUT PROCEDURES

      PHOENIX HOA GUEST RULES

      PARKING GARAGE TIRE SOOT WARNING

      TV INSTRUCTIONS

      WARNING TO NOT SOIL FABRIC FURNISHINGS

SAMPLE GULF FRONT VACATION RENTAL
ACCESS INSTRUCTIONS TEMPLATE EMAIL

THIS IS YOUR KEYLESS ENTRY KEYCODE EMAIL. Please PRINT this email and PDF attachments, as this is the ONLY email that you will receive that contains the keyless entry code, directions to the unit, and other information regarding your upcoming stay.

RESERVATION DATES: You are booked for BOOKED_DATE_PERIOD for PROPERTY_ID

MAPQUEST / GPS INFO TO THE UNIT:

Splash Resort, Unit 902 west

17739 Front Beach Road

Panama City Beach, FL 32413

ARRIVAL: Unit 902 west is at Splash Resort in PCB, Florida. The parking garage is across the street from the beach and connects to the two gulf front towers via skybridge across the road. Park on the 2nd floor, as this is where the luggage carts are located. Proceed across the sky bridge and go to the west tower (the tower on the right as you walk across the bridge) and take the elevator to the 9th floor.

3PM CHECK IN TIME: On the day of arrival, you may arrive early and begin enjoying resort amenities. However, your keyless entry code will not begin working until after 3pm on the date of arrival. If the unit has not been cleaned upon arrival, call the owner at 251-209-9299 or 251-623-2287 to check status. No entry into the unit is permitted before 3pm - NO EXCEPTIONS, as 3pm is considered our early check in time.

KEYLESS DOOR ENTRY CODE (INCLUDE * OR # CHARACTER IF APPLICABLE)

XXX-XXX-XXXX

Simply key in the FULL code, INCLUDING the * or # character, if applicable. If the code doesn't work, you are either outside our check in / checkout times, forgot to enter the * or # symbol, if applicable, or you may be in the wrong tower (the unit is located in the west tower, not the east tower).

We recommend texting the access code to yourself and others in your unit, or keeping an copy handy. If locked out, call Splash Security for assistance (850) 960-0157.

DAMAGES: If damage or missing items are present upon check in, please report the issue immediately to the owner. Through timely reporting, this gives us a chance to fix it, to address the issue with the prior guest, and to document your assistance.

$30 RESORT / PARKING FEE DUE UPON ARRIVAL: Please note that the attached quote is all inclusive for your cost of stay with the exception of a $30 resort fee which much be paid upon arrival at Splash Resort. The $30 resort fee is a one-time flat fee for the stay at the unit good for all your guests, and all your vehicles. The single $30 fee due is not a per guest or per day fee - it's $30 total for your stay. Once paid, you then receive unlimited guest wristbands for use of all Splash amenities (wristbands must be worn by all Splash guests), and also unlimited parking passes for all your vehicles, good for the duration of your stay. This one-time fee may adjust slightly higher each year as it is set by our HOA.

Upon arrival, you will see an onsite Splash HOA office open during regular business hours that will accept your $30 resort fee. If arriving after hours, or during reduced winter hours, you simply pay the resort fee and pick up your wristbands and parking passes the next day.

ITEMS TO PACK: Guests should bring their own pool / beach towels, coffee supplies, and laundry detergent from home. The list of basic starter supplies is attached, which you may need to supplement depending upon your length of stay.

10AM CHECK OUT TIME: Checkout is no later than 10:00am on the day of departure. You may stay on property and enjoy resort amenities, as long as you timely check out of the actual unit. Late check out is never permitted.

TO AVOID LOSS OF DAMAGE DEPOSIT - PLEASE READ AND FOLLOW ALL ATTACHED RULES OF STAY / CHECKOUT INSTRUCTIONS.

HAVE A WONDERFUL STAY!

OWNER_NAME

(251) 209-9299 (call or text)

ENCLOSURES / ATTACHMENTS

SPLASH 902 INVENTORY

COMPLIMENTARY BEACH CHAIR SERVICE INSTRUCTIONS

TV INSTRUCTIONS

BE MINDFUL OF FABRIC FURNISHINGS WARNING

SPLASH RULES OF STAY / CHECKOUT INSTRUCTIONS

SPLASH RESORT OWNER / HOA POLICIES

SAMPLE ACCESS INSTRUCTION TEMPLATE EMAIL

STAND ALONE VACATION RENTAL / CABIN

PLEASE PRINT THIS EMAIL AND ALL ATTACHMENTS AS IT INCLUDES EVERYTHING YOU NEED / CRITICAL INFO FOR YOUR UPCOMING STAY

ADDRESS FOR GPS:

Appalachian High Cabin

The Preserve Resort (follow blue signs / double yellow line)

3127 Lakeview Lodge Drive

Sevierville TN 37862

NOTE: When the GPS says arrived, continue 100 feet higher up the hill to the highest cabin in the Preserve at the dead end / very top of mountain. Look for the sign '3127' and 'Appalachian High' posted on the 1st floor balcony railing.

CHECK IN TIME IS AFTER 4PM: Access to the cabin before 4pm is not permitted (the code will not work prior to 4pm). If the cabin has not been cleaned upon arrival, or if there has been an oversight, please immediately contact the owner through the VRBO app. Due its remote location, please allow the cleaners up to 24 hours to correct the oversight. If cleaners are running late, please be patient and await completion before entering.

NOTE: No entry to the cabin is permitted before 4pm - NO EXCEPTIONS.

KEYLESS DOOR ENTRY CODE (INCLUDE * OR # CHARACTER IF APPLICABLE)

xxx-XXX-xxx

Simply key in the FULL code, INCLUDING THE * OR # character, if applicable. If the code does not work, you are either outside our check-in / checkout times, or failed to enter the * or # character, if applicable.

If you lose the access code or fail to enter the * or # character (if applicable), you will not be able to get into the cabin (if you are unable to get in touch with the owner). We recommend texting the full access code (which may include a * or # symbol) to yourself and others in your unit, taking a screen shot of the access code, or keeping extra copies in your car, purse or wallet.

DAMAGES: If damage or missing items are present upon check in, please immediately contact the owner. Thru timely reporting, this gives us a chance to fix it, address the issue with the prior guest, and to document your assistance.

SUPPLIES: As daily room service is not included with your stay, it may best to bring your own supplies in the event that any complimentary starter supplies run out during your stay, such as laundry detergent, dish detergent, paper towels, toilet paper, trash liners, etc. The nearest Dollar General is at the bottom of the mountain in Wears Valley, about 7 minutes from the cabin.

GROCERIES: To save yourself a trip right back out after arrival, arrive with groceries already in hand. We have a fully equipped kitchen, full size fridge and freezer, stove and oven, a charcoal grill (you supply charcoals, fluid etc), a propane grill (bring a lighter), along with everything you need to prepare and serve meals in the cabin. We recommend Kroger, 220 Wears Valley Road, in Pigeon Forge, the nearest major grocery store to the cabin.

HOT TUB / LOFT / TOP BUNK WARNING: Due to risk of fall, those in poor physical condition cannot use the hot tub, top bunk bed, or loft area. Due to risk of drowning, and other risks, babies, toddlers, and unsupervised children cannot use the hot tub.

THE PRESERVE POOL, HOT TUB, GYM ETC: As a guest of Appalachian High, you and your guests have complimentary access to The Preserve's mountain top outdoor luxury pool and heated jacuzzi tub (open Memorial Day to Labor Day). You may also use the adjacent gym, steam room, sauna, and outdoor fireplace - all of which are complimentary (bring your own towels). Secure the gate code / door codes from the front desk at the building adjacent to the pool for access.

SERIOUS INJURY / DEATH WARNING: PLEASE PRINT AND READ ALL ATTACHED WARNINGS AND TELL YOUR GUESTS.

TIRE CHAINS: We recommend packing tire chains (typically under $75 on Amazon) if you are traveling during winter months. Please do not let perilous winter road conditions interrupt your stay - so come prepared!

RULES OF STAY / 10AM CHECKOUT: To avoid loss of deposit, please read and follow the attached rental agreement, all rules of stay, and checkout procedures.

Thanks so much and have a great stay!

James Dorgan

Owner

(251) 209-9299 (call or text)

ENCLOSURES / ATTACHMENTS

      RISK OF SHATTERING WINDOWS BEHIND ROCKERS

      FIRE RISK – NEED FOR GUEST TO SELF MONITOR EVACUATION ORDERS

      WIFI INSTRUCTIONS

      PRINTED DIRECTIONS UP MOUNTAIN IF GPS FAILS

      RISK OF FALL FROM LOFT, LADDER, TOP BUNK BED

      RENTAL AGREEMENT / RULES OF STAY / CHECKOUT INSTRUCTIONS

      GAME ROOM RULES

      HOT TUB RULES

I wish that VRBO had an option to send the keycode email a second time immediately before the stay (with access to all templates), so that the email is fresh in their inbox, right before arrival at the vacation rental. Hopefully that additional feature or capability will be added to the VRBO email template system soon, so that the keycode email could be sent again, automatically, just prior to guest arrival.

RULE: Always include specific directions on entering the keyless entry code, and how not to lose the code. Include specific directions to report damage or cleaning oversights immediately upon entry. Always include a statement that early check-ins are never permitted, and that the keyless entry door code will not work prior to the scheduled check in time. Attach your comprehensive rules of stay, cancellation policies, warnings, and checkout instructions as attachments. We will discuss those in a later chapter.

Chapter 71

What should I include in my

Rules of Stay / Rental Agreement?

What additional attachments should I include

in my access instructions?

RULES OF STAY / RENTAL AGREEMENT

The Rules of Stay and the Rental Agreement are extremely important. These are both prepared in Word and then saved to PDF format. At minimum, you state the rules that you must follow as a condition of your guest staying at your vacation rental. If they break your stated rules, they are then either thrown out or their damage deposit is charged.

After finalizing the Rules of Stay / Rental Agreement in PDF, you then upload them when prompted by VRBO when you set up your listing, so that the guest must agree to the Rules of Stay before booking the vacation rental. You then include the Rules of Stay / Rental Agreement as an attachment to your access instructions email.

What common features are present in the Rules of Stay / Rental Agreement for all four of our vacation rentals?

1   No smoking

2   No pets

3   No parties / celebrations

4   Booking guest must be 25 years of age or older and must actually be staying in the vacation rental

5   Capacity restrictions

6   Vehicle limits

7   Disclosure of exterior video surveillance cameras (if applicable)

8   Items to pack (beach towels)

9   Directions

10   List of provided starter supplies, supplement supplies to pack

11   Warnings / Dangers (i.e., falling out of a top bunk bed, children drowning in the hot tub, falling off a steep ladder to a loft sleeping area, etc).

12   How to handle cleaning oversights

13   How to handle lockouts

14   Procedure for forfeiture of damage deposit if rules are not followed

15   Rules forbidding red wine near fabric furnishings or flooring

16   Lash liner / eye makeup warning; availability of dark makeup remover towels to use; hot curling iron / flat iron and countertop damage.

17   How to handle soiled quilts or blankets

18   How to work the exterior grill(s)

19   How to work the hot tub, pool, or special amenity (if applicable)

20   General warnings, forest fire risk, winter storm risk, hurricane awareness, etc.

21   Information on wildlife (if applicable)

22   Inventory of unit

23   Reporting damage or missing items

24   How garbage is handled / location of garbage chute

25   Television instructions

26   Checkout procedures

The foregoing list of topics should be covered in your Rules of Stay / Rental Agreement at minimum, that the guest must agree to these conditions in advance before they book your vacation rental. A sample Rules of Stay / Rental Agreement for our cabin in Pigeon Forge is attached below.

I also attached a sample inventory, owner policies on cancellation, forest fire warning, and tire soot warning, as examples of various attachments that you can potentially include with your access instructions email template, depending upon your situation.

RULE: Prepare a detailed Rules of Stay / Rental Agreement for the guest to review before they book your vacation rental. They must agree to your rules of stay before being allowed to book your vacation rental. By setting your rules and expectations up front, guests are more likely to be on their best behavior, when they know the rules, and know the financial consequences if those rules are not followed.

SAMPLE ACCESS EMAIL TEMPLATE ATTACHMENT
RULES OF STAY / RENTAL AGREEMENT
STAND ALONE VACATION RENTAL / CABIN

'Appalachian High'
Rental Agreement, Rules of Stay,
Critical Information, FAQs, and
Check-Out Instructions

We hope that you have a wonderful, safe, and enjoyable stay with us at Appalachian High. **Please read and print this rental agreement / rules of stay / informational brochure as it contains critical information needed for your stay.** *It is critical that it is reviewed thoroughly prior to stay.* Safe travels!

Appalachian High Cabin
3127 Lakeview Lodge Drive
Sevierville TN 37862
NOTE: When the GPS says 'arrived,' proceed further up the nearest hill to the highest cabin in The Preserve Resort. There is a sign that says 'Appalachian High' posted on the front balcony railing. Motion detector lights should light the parking area upon arrival.

Winter Weather / Tire Chains: If traveling during the winter months, we encourage guests to purchase from Amazon for their vehicle *tire chains*, in the rare event of ice or winter storm that may impede travel through the region. Although an exceptionally rare event, we encourage for our guests to be prepared just in case. In the past five winters, there were only two occasions where guests were not able to get back and forth to The Preserve due to a winter storm, but the access issue resolved itself in less than 24 hours.

If a winter storm warning is issued for Wears Valley, we encourage guests to cancel their stay, or balance of stay for the portion of time effected by the winter storm warning. Otherwise, if a guest chooses to stay despite a winter storm warning, there is no refund for any inconvenience caused by the ensuing inclement weather, including hazardous driving conditions, losing power, losing heat, losing water pressure or other inconveniences caused by implement weather. If you stay, you pay. It's that simple.

Capacity Limits / Parties Not Allowed: No more than 6 adults are permitted in the cabin at any given time. Total guest capacity when traveling with kids is 10, with no more than six adults. **No parties are allowed.** Guests exceeding stated capacity or hosting a party will be asked to leave, remaining stay forfeited, and damage deposit forfeited.

Vehicle Limits: No more than three vehicles should be on premises at any given time unless owner approved. This rule is strictly enforced and actively monitored via video surveillance, and onsite personnel. Tampering with video surveillance equipment results in immediate forfeiture of stay. **Parties, Celebrations, Theme Events, or College Events are strictly prohibited at this cabin and result in forfeiture of stay and damage deposit.**

No smoking / No Pets / No Parties: Cigarette smoking, cigar smoking, or vaping inside the condo is strictly prohibited. Tampering with the multiple onsite smoke detectors is prohibited. If any of these strictly enforced policies are violated, there will be an automatic loss of security deposit, forfeiture of stay, a $2500 fine, and reimbursement for all costs of deodorization. No pets or parties are allowed. Do not exceed the number of guests as stated in your reservation.

RING Doorbell / Cameras: This cabin is equipped with a Ring Doorbell mounted at the front door that records both audio and video. There are additional video cameras mounted around the cabin that monitor the parking area and the areas around the cabin. By renting this cabin, you consent to both audio and video surveillance (a sign to that effect is also posted outside the cabin). There are no cameras located inside the cabin.

Age Minimum / Responsible Adult: The guest paying for the cabin should also be staying the cabin, unless the owner has granted an exception to this rule. For example, an adult parent paying for college age child and friends to stay unsupervised is absolutely prohibited. At least one parent or adult age 25 years or older must be always staying in the cabin and must be the same person actually paying for the unit.

Items to Pack: We recommend arriving at the cabin with at least 24 hours' worth of groceries already in hand, so the guest does not have to turn right back around to go to the grocery store immediately upon arrival. We recommend Kroger on Hwy. 321 in Pigeon Forge.

Although we leave out a starter pack of laundry detergent, Guests should also bring their own **laundry detergent**, if they intend to wash more than one load of clothes and or towels in the unit's washer and dryer during their stay.

Starter disposable supplies for each **bathrooms**:

- 1 small shampoo
- 1 small bar soap
- 1 roll of toilet paper
- 2 waste bin liners

Starter disposable supplies for the **kitchen**:

- 1 roll of paper towels
- 2 waste bin liners
- 2 packets of dishwasher detergent
- 1 dish soap

Depending upon your length of stay and or needs, you may need to supplement these starter supplies as needed. There is a Dollar General at the bottom of the mountain in Wears Valley.

IMPORTANT WARNINGS TO FOR YOU AND ALL YOUR GUESTS TO BE AWARE OF: THERE IS A RISK OF DROWNING FOR ANY TODDLER OR CHILDREN IN THE HOT TUB OR JACUZZI TUB. THERE IS A RISK OF FALL FROM THE LOFT LADDER. OTHER IMPORTANT WARNINGS ARE ATTACHED TO THIS EMAIL. THESE WARNINGS ARE SERIOUS – THERE IS A RISK OF SERIOUS INJURY OR DEATH – PLEASE READ AND OBEY THE WARNINGS AND SHARE THESE WARNINGS WITH YOUR GUESTS.

Cleaning Oversights: Upon the extremely rare event of a cleaning oversight, the cleaners will return for a touch up. There are no partial or full refunds for cleaning oversights, or credits on stay. Due to the cabin's location on top of a mountain, we ask that guests be patient to allow for travel time to correct any cleaning oversights. Simply contact the owner through your VRBO app to arrange for a return visit by the cleaning crew,

Please give us an opportunity to remedy any issues during your stay, and if not possible, in time for the next guest. ***Please do not let something that is within our control negatively impact your review of Appalachian High unless you have <u>first</u> given us an opportunity to remedy it!***

Lockouts: Please secure the keyless entry code and do not lose it. You should text it to all guests in the cabin, enter the code into the notes section of all phones and tablets, take a photo of the code, and keep an extra written

/ paper copy in your wallet, purse, car or other locations. The code is literally your cabin key. If by chance you lose the code or it does not work, please call, text and email the owner directly at 251-209-9299 and email at JamesRDorgan@gmail.com. The owner's wife cell phone as an absolute last resort is 251-623-2287 (call text or message), or owner's office at 251-928-0192 (call or message only).

IMPORTANT: If the owner cannot be immediately reached, you may be locked out until you are able to get in touch with the owner, as there is no onsite security, or a front desk in the area that can assist with that issue.

Carpets / Pool Table: We want guests to feel at home and to enjoy themselves. However, spilling red wine, drinks, or food on the pool table / felt and or the upstairs carpeting is not acceptable, and their account will be charged for cleanup costs, and if necessary, replacement of the pool table felt, or carpeting. PLEASE DO NOT PLACE DRINKS, SUITCASES, CLOTHES OR SHOES ON TOP OF THE POOL TABLE. CHILDREN SHOULD NOT CLIMB OR PLAY ON TOP OF THE POOL TABLE AT ANY TIME.

No red wine, food or drink in or on beds, lazyboys, loft, sofa, or kid's cavern: Please do not allow anyone, especially young children or toddlers, to have snacks, their meal, their cheerios, drinks, cool aid, milk bottles, juice bottles, sippy cups, or juice boxes in or on the sofa, their beds, the lazy boy chairs, the kids cavern, or in the loft area as the inevitable stains will ruin the provided furnishings, quilts and or blankets.

Red wine is prohibited in the bedrooms, game room and loft, as the inevitable stains will ruin / permanently stain either the carpet, bedding, or pool table.

Special laundering of soiled linens / replacing linens / steam cleaning the sofa or rugs or other fabric furnishings / re-felting the pool table / replacing the carpet are charged to guest's damaged deposit, and if insufficient, litigation.

Lash Liner / Eye Liner / Make Up Permanent Stains: Removing lash / eye liner and or makeup may result in permanent stains to the hand towel, wash cloth, or bath towel. Be mindful not to get lash liner or eye liner on pillowcases. **Do not use our linens or towels for makeup removal as it will permanently ruin them.** Special laundering of soiled linens / replacing linens is charged to guest's damaged deposit.

Sheet Stains: Permanent sheet stains, even if accidental, result in loss. Replacing linens are charged to guest's damage deposit.

Flat Iron / Curling Iron Warning: Please do not place hot curling irons, rollers, or flat irons on the cultured marble countertops, as the heat will permanently burn / damage / scar the cultured marble countertops. If countertop damage occurs, the guest's damage deposit will at minimum be forfeited, and cost of replacement charged to the guest.

Permission to Launder Blankets: With each cleaning, fresh bath towels, hand towels, wash cloths, floor mats, kitchen cloths as well as complete fresh sheet sets are provided for each guest.

If there is a concern with something needing to be laundered, you may contact the owner directly for him to arrange for a swap out. The cleaning service will then come to the unit during regular business hours, secure the item(s) and them launder the item(s) offsite and return it during regular business hours at a later time.

In the preferred alternative, you may simply use the onsite washer and dryer and launder the blanket yourself for a speedier turnaround.

During your stay, if an accident happens and a blanket or bedding or sofa is stained (accidents happen and we understand), please simply launder the item at your convenience with the provided washer and dryer, but no later than your departure.

Loft: The loft is accessed via a steep wooden ladder with no railings. Please supervise children at all times. Any guest with limited mobility should not use the loft. Due to the risk of fall, use of the loft is strictly at your own risk. All guests assume the risk if they use the loft and accidentally fall.

No food or drink is ever permitted in the loft.

Propane Grill: If you plan to use the propane grill (subject to availability), please confirm the grease trap can at the bottom of the grill is empty prior to use AND RETURNED. Turn on the gas at the tank first, then turn on the burners. Make sure the grease trap (a small silver can hanging) beneath the grill is empty and in position. Use your own lighter to light the grill (bring an extra lighter just in case the one in the cabin is empty). Please make sure all grease is disposed from the grease trap following each use (it's a small can hanging beneath the grill) **and returned**, otherwise grease will just drip on the ground and attract bears. Make sure the propane gas it turned off at the tank when done. If food is stuck to the grate of the grill, you may run the grates through the dishwasher. To prevent risk of fire, please do not move the grill or place it too close to the cabin or any wooden structures. **Please note the location of the cabin's fire extinguisher and or water hose prior to grilling.** Remember, do not use water to put out a grease fire – use the fire extinguisher. If the propane tank is empty, please contact the owner at 251-209-9299 for options. Plan B is to reimburse guests if the blue Rhino tank needs to be swapped out at the Dollar General Store in Wears Valley (with receipt), or work on some other arrangement. **Use of grill is at your own risk / subject to availability.**

Outside Charcoal Grill: If you plan to use outdoor charcoal grill, please bring your own charcoal, fluid and lighter. Please make sure all used coals are first disposed in the provided metal ash can (to make sure they are cool and not flammable), and ultimately, bagged and taken out with the trash. Please do not dump coals on or around the premises. **Please note the location of the cabin's fire extinguisher and or water hose prior to grilling.** Use of grill is at your own risk. As this is a permanent fixture, the charcoal 'park style' grill should always be available.

Sewer System: We are on a private, small sewer system built just for The Preserve that is not designed to handle anything but regular human waste and a small amount of toilet paper. We do not have a sink garbage disposal as food waste is not permitted in this private wastewater system. Please do not flush anything down the sinks or toilets other than typical human waste and a small amount of toilet paper. No paper towels, wipes, food, or feminine products should ever be flushed.

Appliance Breakdown: As most of our appliances are new, there are no refunds in the event of an unforeseen appliance failure. Please simply let us know so that the appliance may be repaired either during your stay or in time for the next arriving guest.

Hot Tub Cover: Guests must keep the hot tub cover on and secured at all times unless the hot tub is in active use (especially if there are children staying in the cabin). When not in use, the hot tub cover should be secured closed with the clasps to prevent being blown off the balcony or being opened without authorization by children. Failure to properly secure the hot tub cover may result in loss of the cover (due to frequent high winds in the area) and a corresponding charge to the guest for replacement. If the hot tub water level is low and dips below a jet, please use the provided hose to replenish it but no more than to cover the highest jet.

HOT TUB WARNING: Toddlers, babies, and young children are prohibited from using the hot tub due to fall risk. Children of sufficient maturity should only use the hot tub if carefully supervised by an adult at all times. NO TOYS OR OBJECTS ARE EVER ALLOWED IN THE HOT TUB AS IT COULD GET SUCKED INTO THE MOTOR AND CAUSE DAMAGE. Horseplay or standing up in the tub is STRICTLY FORBIDDEN. Those with limited mobility, and or strength or balance concerns, should also not use the hot tub due to risk of fall entering and exiting the hot tub due to wet conditions / physical difficulty of entering and exiting the hot tub. The balcony will be slippery when wet. PLEASE SEE ATTACHED WARNINGS.

DO NOT CLIMB ON TOP OF COVER AS IT WILL COLLAPSE AND BREAK – it's made of Styrofoam.

Hot Tub Concerns: The hot tub will likely be cold upon arrival. This is because the hot tub is emptied following every guest departure, sanitized, and refilled with clean water. It takes up to 24 hours for the hot tub to return to the 100–102-degree range. Please be patient. Do check though the temperature by pressing the up / down arrows to confirm that the hot tub is set to the desired temperature.

Once the hot tub is at temperature, and the guest turns it on, water will circulate, but **not vigorously** or to the extent that it causes foam type bubbles typical to other hot tubs. It is more akin to light jets moving the water around, like the jacuzzi tub in the upstairs bathroom.

After a day or two, **you may notice a small layer of fine sediment on the bottom.** This is normal. We are on well water and a small amount of sentiment that is suspended in the water will ultimately settle in the bottom of the hot tub. Do not be alarmed as this is normal. We have placed a water filter on the hot tub hose, and we hope that this will cut down on the amount of sentiment in the tub.

If for any reason you become dissatisfied with the hot tub, don't use it. Simply use the private jacuzzi tub in the 2nd floor bath. It too has views through the windows around it – simply open the shades. In the alternative, simply use the Preserve Resort's hot tub at the pool area in the resort – open from Memorial Day to Labor Day. It too has amazing views.

Even though the hot tub is emptied, sanitized, refilled with fresh water, and treated with bromine between every guest stay, there still exists inherent risks of use of a hot tub in a rental cabin such as this. Guests assume all such risks inherent to use of the unit's hot tub.

As there is an oversized jacuzzi tub available in the 2nd floor bathroom, and a large resort hot tub available during summer months, both with views, no refund / credit is ever permitted due to any given balcony hot tub issue.

Hot Tub in Winter / Freeze Damage Warning: The hot tub temperature should always be left at 76 or higher upon checkout, and the cover latched in place. Otherwise, the hot tub piping may hard freeze causing damage to the hot tub. Failure to follow these simple instructions which result in hot tub damage will be charged / billed against the guest's damage deposit.

Balcony Rocker Warning: Please be careful not to rock the balcony chairs back and into the large glass balcony windows. **Serious injury or death could occur if you rock backwards into a large window that shatters upon you.**

Wi-Fi: For complimentary Wi-Fi look for 'Appalachian High.' The password is **appalachianhigh** Wi-Fi is subject to availability. As most guests have smart phones, and cellular service is readily available, there is no refund / credit for inability to use the cabin's Wi-Fi.

Early Check-In / Late Check-Out / Unavailable: Due to cleaning and maintenance schedules that are set well in advance of every guest stay, and the corresponding commute time of the team of the cleaning and maintenance team who take care of this cabin between guest stays, **early check in / late check out is never available**. Check in is at 4pm and check out is no later than 10am. Please note that this cabin typically books back-to-back during busy times so your departure must be timely to allow sufficient time for our cleaning and or maintenance crews to ready the cabin for the next guest.

The Preserve Resort Amenities: All resort amenities are free for our guests to use and enjoy, including the Preserve's pool, hot tub, pavilion with large wood burning fireplace, gym (with treadmills), sauna, and steam room, all of which are less than a 5-minute downhill walk from the cabin. The resort pool and hot tub are typically open Memorial Day to Labor Day (these dates are approximate), subject to weather conditions. Please bring your own pool towels from home. As resort amenities are offered, but not guaranteed, there are no refunds due to any resort amenities not being available for any given reason.

Code for Preserve Resort Amenities: The gym, sauna, pool and hot tub are all accessed via private code on their respective door locks. To secure that code, please simply proceed to the large building by the chapel / pool area during regular business hours, and inquire within / in person through Heartside Cabin Company, for the needed code, upon arrival. Simply tell them that you are a guest of Appalachian High, and they will provide you all needed codes for all Resort amenities good for your entire stay. Unfortunately, the owner does not have these codes as they are unique and constantly changing. As such, you must secure a current code upon arrival as instructed, and not in advance of stay. As hours of operation, and availability of the various amenities vary by season, simply inquire upon arrival for those hours as well.

Wildlife: Although we encourage guests to explore the woods surrounding the cabin, please be mindful of area wildlife, such as snakes, ticks, chiggers, bears, biting insects, mosquitoes, and other inherent dangers. Wear bug repellant.

Resort Chapel: The resort chapel, meeting room and fireplace pavilion may be rented / reserved for guests planning a wedding, family reunion or special event. Contact Jim Whaley for rental info at 865-766-9595.

Excessive Cleaning Fees: Our cleaning team budgets a standard amount of time to clean a cabin of this size under normal use, with guest adherence to our checkout instructions, capacity limits, and use of premises limitations. If the cleaning crew requires an inordinate amount of time to clean due to violation of any of our rules of stay, or for any other reason, an excessive cleaning fee and administrative fee may be charged for that service, for which guest shall be responsible.

INVENTORY LIST:

KITCHEN: appliances, coffee maker, toaster, blender, waffle iron, electric can opener, fire extinguisher, rug, knife set, glassware, bakeware, dishes, wine glasses, silverware, paper towel holder, lighter, wine opener, grilling ware, salt and pepper bear dispenser (subject to availability), etc;
DINING: Table and six chairs; decorative bears centerpiece, rug;
LIVING: Two reclining chairs, sleeper sofa, TV w Xfinity remote (labeled), two lamps/tables, bears, coffee table, bear artwork, rug, Christmas décor (seasonal), broom and dustpan (laundry);
KIDS CAVE: stuffed animals, oversize Lego set, clip on LED flexible lamp;
1st FLOOR BALCONY: four rockers /two end tables;
MASTER: king bed (w quilt, shams, blanket, bed protector), two lamps/end tables, dresser, TV w Xfinity remote (labeled), luggage stand, bear décor;
2ND FLOOR: Pool table, sticks, cue, balls and accessories, foosball table w balls, Atari multicade w two stools, Atari Driving Simulator, bar set w three stools, bar fridge, decorative moose, Queen bunks (w quilts, shams, blankets and bed protector), TV w remote (labeled), vacuum, bear themed artwork, 2 luggage stands;
2nd FLOOR BALCONY: Hot tub w cover, rope tether, hose with sediment filter, pole with hook, two rockers/end table, hot tub steps;
LOFT: two twin beds, two blankets, extension cord;
OUTSIDE: : Picnic table, two wooden bears; Fire extinguisher; Propane grill and tank, grill mat, grill scraper, charcoal grill, ash / coal can with metal shovel, grill scraper; six person picnic table;

Damage or Missing Items: Damage or missing items should be reported to the owner at the beginning of your stay to allow us to address the issue with the prior guest, and or for the owner to start working on addressing the damage or missing item for either your stay or in time for the next guest stay. Simply email the owner through the VRBO app. Due to the cabin's location atop a mountain, please allow us plenty of time to fix any given issue, and we ask that guests be patient in that regard.

Guests are financially responsible for any and all cabin damage, lost or damaged items that occur during their stay, regardless of whether the damage or loss was caused by accident or not. This cabin is inspected for damage, photographed, and inventoried following every guest departure. Please again note video surveillance of exterior areas.

Furniture Position: Please do not move furniture. Move balcony rockers away from balcony windows so that they do not break the windows accidentally.

Black Bears and Garbage: Hungry black bears of all sizes inhabit The Preserve area. Garbage should be secured and placed only inside the fortified garbage boxes and **secured with a latch.** Guests who fail to secure their trash, then the responsible guest must clean it up – this is not something that is to be left to the cabin cleaners to clean up (who may or may not clean immediately upon your departure). **This rule is strictly enforced via video surveillance – guests leaving trash strewn by bears on or about the cabin premises will be subjected to a fine if not timely cleaned up.**

If you completely fill the provided cans during your stay (they are typically emptied until after each guest departure), please dispose of any additional trash off premises (info below). Do not leave next to the fortified cans any bagged garbage, as the bears will make a huge mess.

Free Drive Thru Trash / Garbage Drop Off: Make our housekeeper's day at the conclusion of your stay, or if the outside fortified garbage cans end up full, please simply drive thru the free trash disposal convenience center, located right off 321 on the way from the cabin to Pigeon Forge.

Pigeon Forge Free / Drive Thru Garbage Drop
447 Tiger Drive
Pigeon Forge, TN 37863

Monday – Saturday 8:00 am – 6:00 pm
All centers closed on Sunday

Black Bears and Vehicles: Bears have learned how to open car doors. Please lock your car doors, and also, do not store any food in your vehicle overnight. Further, do not put any food in the fortified outside garbage cans, as a bear may pick up and toss around the can trying to break into it which may then inadvertently damage your car. Owner is not responsible for any damage to your vehicle or personal property caused by bears due to guest mismanagement of their food and or food waste. YOU WILL LIKELY HAVE BEARS VISIT THE CABIN DURING YOUR STAY.

Snow Conditions / Fire Alerts: Guests should remain weather and fire aware at all times to make sure that they are staying safe and planning accordingly before and during their stay. It is the guest's *sole responsibility* to keep themselves and their family safe while on vacation, remain informed, and heed all local rules and guidance on evacuations, keeping informed on forest fires, winter storm warnings, use of tire chains if needed, and so forth. As the owner lives out of state, the owner is not able to give advice or recommendations as to weather conditions, winter storm warnings, fire conditions or road conditions in the area.

Further, guests should at minimum during all winter stays have sufficient food, bottled water, and emergency supplies (i.e., candles, flashlights, etc.) to get through winter weather, in case the roads become impassable, or the cabin's power goes out temporarily, as the nearest Dollar General is at the bottom of the mountain. Winter storm weather typically resolves quickly but we nevertheless encourage guests to be prepared for that contingency.

Due to the cabin's remote location on top of a mountain, the owner strongly recommends that guests err on the side of caution when it comes to either winter weather or fire conditions, and depart the cabin if necessary to stay safe, even if it may happen to interrupt, delay their check-in, or possibly shorten their existing stay.

Televisions: As the unit is equipped with multiple TV's, Xfinity cable, Wi-Fi, some or all of which takes some tech know how to use and operate. These amenities are offered but not guaranteed, especially for those who may not be technology proficient.

Typically, most TV issues can be resolved by pressing 'input' or 'source' and scrolling through the various inputs until the cable picture source or input appears. Once the cable TV source appears, simply use the cable remote to adjust volume or scroll through the channels. **If the remote is not working, the remote is most likely in the wrong room, or needs a fresh set of batteries.**

Please be mindful of the location and placement of remotes and do not let children play with them. Remotes are a critical component for the use and operation of the electronics in the cabin and they should not be misplaced (or moved between rooms or upstairs and downstairs as each one is set to operate only one TV), tampered with or damaged. Please do not unplug electronics. Please do not unplug or change the input on any given electronic unless you know how and or remember to return the electronic to its original setup and is fully operational for the next guest.

Xfinity Technical Assistance (Free): If you cannot figure out how to use the complimentary Wi-Fi or complimentary cable service, please contact 1-800-**XFINITY** for free technical assistance.

In Cabin Technical Assistance: If you need maintenance to come to the cabin to show you how to properly use the equipment, a service / trip fee of $75 is charged against your security deposit.

MISSING OR BROKEN OR MISPLACED REMOTES OR MISSING REMOTE BATTERIES WILL BE BILLED TO THE DAMAGE DEPOSIT. As most guests have their own iPads, laptops and or smart phones, no refund or credit is ever permitted for guests not knowing how to properly use our Xfinity television amenities.

Atari Games / Pool Table: **The arcade quality games typically do not break down unless there has been some type of abuse or misuse.** Damages / Replacement costs caused by abuse or misuse are billed to the guest. Please simply leave the Atari Multicade and Atari Driving Simulator on at all times, even upon departure. Damage to the games and or the pool table will be charged to the guest's damage deposit. **There is a minimum $700 fee to recover the pool table, in the event of a spill on the felt or broken side rail.** Please keep up with the foosballs, pool balls, cue and pool sticks and make sure they are returned to their racks or games upon departure to avoid forfeiture of damage deposit. We endeavor to keep all games operable for all guest stays. However, there is no refund or stay credit due to any inoperable games in the cabin.

Checkout Procedures: **Check out of the cabin is no later than 10am. Late checkout is never available.** While the bulk of towels, sheets and linens and general cleaning are all taken care of on your departure, there are a few things we ask guests to do at checkout.

1   All dishware, silverware, and bakeware should either be clean or left running in the supplied dishwasher.

2   Clean up any spills in the fridge, in or on the stove or on the floors.

3   Remove / pick up all trash off the countertops, tabletops, the floors, balcony, and immediate vicinity of cabin.

4   If you used the charcoal grill, bag up and place in trash the ashes. If you used the propane grill, empty out the grease trap (a small can located beneath the grill) and return it. Turn off the valve on the propane tank.

5   Do not make beds – it should be clear what linens were or were not used during your stay.

6   **The hot tub cover must be on and latched closed.** Set and leave the hot tub temperature at 75. Do not turn it off or unplug it as it may freeze the pipes. Move balcony rockers away from the large glass windows.

7   Heat should be set on 60 in the winter and the AC set on 80 in the summer.

***DO NOT TURN OFF THE HEAT OR THE HOT TUB AS OUR PIPES WILL OTHERWISE FREEZE IN THE WINTER ***

8   Please leave all shades down but in the open position (so natural light comes in).

9   Locate and secure each Xfinity labeled remove and place them in the appropriate room in a visible location.

10   Please rack the pool balls for inventory and hang up the pool sticks. Make sure the foosballs are left visible in the game. Please make sure the Atari Multicade and Driving Simulator are both left plugged in.

11   This list is not exhaustive. Please clean up anything that would take our cleaning crew additional time to clean beyond a standard clean. Please make sure furniture is returned to the position that it was upon check-in.

12   Please remember to turn out all lights upon departure, and all windows and doors should be tightly closed and locked fully secured as well (note that windows open from the top down).

13   Guests should remove all food and personal items from the cabin upon departure (it's ok to leave coffee filters, sugar, salt and pepper and related nonperishables behind). Old food or disposed food items should be bagged and taken with the guest to the free drop off / drive thru garbage dumpster conveniently located off Hwy 321 on the way to Pigeon Forge, located at 447 Tiger Drive, open every day but Sunday, and not placed in the outdoor garbage cans (due to hungry bears in the area who will destroy the fortified garbage cans if there is leftover food in them). This same rule to drop off your trash at the drive thru location applies if the outside fortified cans are full.

Leaving the cabin in a mess, throwing a party, leaving trash everywhere, failing to follow these instructions, leaving dirty dishes piled up, wasting utility use, breaking something, damaging something, stealing or losing something (including but not limited to a TV remote), causing temporary or permanent stains to linens or towels which result in additional laundering or replacement, turning the heat off in the winter, and or failing to follow these check out instructions and or all rules of stay could result in an additional cleaning surcharge / utility surcharge / damage or replacement claim charged to your credit card on file, forfeiture of your security deposit, and or litigation.

***The good news is that we typically have thoughtful and considerate guests who diligently follow all of our rules and there is rarely if ever an issue with return of a
damage deposit – please let that be you!***

At checkout, don't forget to take with you your cell phone charger(s), clothes accidentally left in the dryer, toys left under beds, extra pillows or blankets, hangup clothes, pool toys, pool towels, and other misc. personal items!

SAMPLE ACCESS INSTRUCTION ATTACHMENT
OWNER POLICIES ON CANCELLATONS
BEACHFRONT VACATION RENTAL

Splash Resort 704W / 902W Owner Policies
17739 Front Beach Road
Panama City Beach, FL 32413

OWNER POLICY ON HURRICANE / TROPICAL STORM In the event of a hurricane or tropical storm, you may cancel a portion or all of your stay without penalty, even at the last minute, or during your stay, and receive a full credit for any unused portion(s) of your stay, to be used towards a future stay with us. Unless there is a hurricane or tropical storm warning for the condo location, cancellations during your stay are otherwise nonrefundable.

OWNER POLICY ON MECHANICAL BREAKDOWNS On rare occasions, as most if not all our major appliances are new, an appliance may breakdown during your stay, requiring either a fix or replacement. We provide in our welcome email the contact information for our maintenance crew if that happens, and we will do all we can to remedy the situation as quickly as possible. Upon such event, there is no compensation for any inconvenience cause by an unexpected mechanical breakdown in the unit.

OWNER POLICY ON CLEANING ISSUE OVERSIGHT(S) On extremely rare occasion (as our new cleaning crew gets consistently excellent reviews), our cleaning service may have an oversight in the servicing of the unit. Similar to many hotels, we do not compensate for cleaning related issues or oversights that can otherwise be easily remedied by a return visit by our cleaning crew.

OWNER POLICY ON AVAILABILITY OF RESORT AMENITIES Finally, the resort may have an amenity that may become unavailable at some point during your stay. As there are typically many different amenity alternatives available, we do not compensate guests if any given resort amenity happens to become unavailable.

SAMPLE ACCESS INSTRUCTION ATTACHMENT
FOREST FIRE WARNING

RISK OF FOREST FIRES / GUEST MONITORING OF EVACUATION ORDERS

As this mountaintop cabin is surrounded by woods and adjacent to the Great Smoky Mountains, forest fires are always a concern. Orders to evacuate should carefully be monitored by the guest throughout their stay.

To insure accurate and timely notifications, the guest should set up their phones, at minimum, to receive important notifications from area emergency management.

Especially during low humidity / high wind / drought events, there may be an elevated risk of fire. When this happens, fire notifications need to be monitored carefully by the guest, and quickly evacuate as necessary or if ordered.

The remnants of the 2022 Hatcher Mountain Road / Indigo Lane fire in the distance, with The Preserve's pool and pavilion in the foreground, with fire protection personnel onsite. The Preserve was evacuated and fortunately spared from this nearby devastating wildfire, but it could have been much worse.

In view of inherent fire risk, outdoor campfires at the cabin are never permitted. Fireworks are also prohibited.

We also recommend that guests keep critical medications, an extra set of contact lenses, and or any critical items with them whenever they leave the cabin, especially if leaving the cabin for the day or to go to an amusement park.

For instance, an evacuation order could be issued for The Preserve while you are at Dollywood, and you might not be able to get back to the cabin to get these items if an evacuation order gets unexpectedly issued and or if roads close. You need to be prepared just in case.

We recommend that guests 'Favorite' the following Facebook page both immediately before and during their stay and set their phone to be notified of all posts, and or prioritize seeing page posts at all times during their stay, as the page provides accurate and helpful information on area fire risk, road closures, and or evacuation orders, if needed.

Sevier County Emergency Management Agency
https://www.facebook.com/SevierCoEMA

For those without Facebook, the agency may be contacted at 865-453-4919 and by email at ema@seviercountytn.gov for additional information.

As we value you and your family's safety, please diligently follow these recommendations, at minimum.

Few thought The Preserve would ever be evacuated and be at risk of fire, until it happened. Considering the recent nearby Hatcher Mountain Road Fire, guests cannot be careful enough on this life-or-death issue. We thus encourage our guests to actively take steps to keep themselves informed of reports of fire and or evacuations, throughout their stay.

SAMPLE ACCESS INSTRUCTION ATTACHMENT
DEALING WITH TRACKED IN TIRE SOOT –
SAME FLOOR PARKING ISSUE

<u>Parking Garage Tire Soot Warning</u>

The covered same floor covered parking, although convenient to the unit, has a drawback. When cars park, their tires leave a black soot on the pavement. A checking in guest then tracks the soot down the breezeway on luggage wheels, shoes, bare feet, and luggage carts and ultimately onto the clean floors of the unit.

Here is an example of a clean floor being tracked on by shoes and a luggage cart brought inside the unit *on just one visit from the parking garage*:

To prevent this from happening, wear shoes in the parking garage and then take them off *outside* the unit. Do not roll luggage through the parking garage – place them on the luggage carts. Do not roll luggage carts full of groceries or luggage into the unit – unload the cart outside. Do not roll soiled luggage wheels through the unit – carry them. Wipe your feet before entering, and if necessary, clean them with a paper towel upon entry.

The hardest part are children's feet. They typically roam the property with bare feet and come back with black feet, which then are tracked inside, or worse, rubbed onto the sofa cushions or sofa arms. It may be prudent to make it a habit for kids to wash their feet off each time they come in from outside, or wear sandals and leave them outside, *every time.* If it's a losing battle with the kids, use one of the spare sheets to cover the sofa cushions or swivel rockers for protection.

To help fight the tire soot issue, the owner has added washable area rugs and runners to help pick up the black soot that is inevitably tracked in. If any of these items soil during your stay, wash them in the washing machine and air dry them in the sun on the balcony.

Black feet, especially children's, should never come into contact with the fabric sofa, fabric swivel rockers, fabric quilts, or blankets, as the black soot will darken / stain the fabric and it is difficult to get out.

If at any times black foot soot is tracked accidentally onto the rugs, pillows, shams, quilts, sofa, swivel rockers, please either wash the item in the washer and air dry or use a damp soapy cloth or paper towel to scrub the item so that the soot is timely removed from the fabric.

Yes, our cleaning crew will return on a complimentary basis in the event of a cleaning oversight. However, our cleaning crews are not responsible for a checking in guest tracking in black soot upon arrival.

Please simply follow our suggestions to combat this issue unique to Phoenix on the Bay.

Thank you for your patience and understanding.

Chapter 72

How to extract from your departing guest a five-star review –

the ultimate follow-up email template

VRBO and/or Airbnb solicit guests to review their stay following every guest stay. Guests booked through VRBO have up to a year to leave a review, while guests booked through Airbnb have two weeks. Guest reviews are a critical part of your vacation rental platform, and you must go to great lengths to avoid any negative reviews.

We will discuss in a later chapter how to respond to a negative review. For now, let's focus on how to get those reviews – a lot of them.

By having a lot of reviews, you decrease the odds that a 'one off' review would hurt your overall average.

As mentioned previously, the search rank algorithm does factor in the number of reviews in its search ranking, so the more reviews the better.

Likewise, owners also have an opportunity to review their guests as well from one star to five stars. Getting your guest to think that the owner review rating you gave them is a big deal could be used to your advantage.

Think back to the time when eBay was all the rage. All sellers had star ratings, and all buyers had star ratings. Buyers and sellers on both sides of the transaction went to great lengths to keep a strong rating – a unique number and badge of honor in doing business. It represented trust and consistency and provided a sense of security to any given transaction. As soon as the person on the other side of the transaction left you a five-star review, you would ALWAYS reciprocate with a return five-star review, even though the transaction may have been less than perfect. It was sort of an unspoken rule that you always reciprocated a five-star review – or at least it felt that way to me.

On VRBO, neither side knows what type of review the other side has left or will leave when they make their respective review. The guest is in essence proceeding blindly as they are not sure what the owner is going to say about them. VRBO's stated goal in doing it that way is to insure a truly honest and uncoerced review.

In our template email to the departing guest, we tell the guest that we have left them a five-star review and make them think that the review is a big deal for them. We then ask the guest to reciprocate the same five star rating back to us. 'I scratch your back – you scratch my back' sort of thing. It's the same concept that generated so many reciprocal positive reviews in the eBay marketplace years ago.

In other words, you are almost guilting them into doing anything other than giving you a five-star rating back in generosity for the five-star rating you gave them.

This may sound like a sneaky way to a great review – but for whatever reason – it works every time.

The key though is that review template email must get to the guest before they leave their review, otherwise the plan fails. I have found that if the following template review email gets to the guest before they leave a review, we end up getting a five-star review 99% of the time in return.

Make sure you do include the quick disclaimer that the rating is 'subject to any damage or missing items being reported from our cleaning crew,' in case your cleaner comes in and they have made a mess of your rental. This disclaimer will then allow you to still claim their damage deposit despite the initial glowing review.

This email template is worth its weight in gold. It is also worth your 30 seconds of time to shoot the email template off upon checkout of each guest, as again, the reviews are extremely important to your booking success on both platforms. If thirty (30) seconds of your time consistently yields a five-star review from a guest, do it.

For returning guests, we do waive the refundable damage deposit and provide guest nightly rate discounts on non-holiday or off-peak stays, as a matter of course, and regardless of any given review. The timing of mentioning (as opposed to conditioning the discount, which is impermissible) that potential discount immediately following you telling a guest that you just left them a five-star review, further compels them to reciprocate the rating. They feel grateful. They almost feel obligated to reciprocate the rating.

We also ask the guest to 'tag' their photos on Facebook to our Facebook vacation rental listing page, or to like our Facebook vacation rental page as well. This invitation to join (like) a more personalized page, such as Facebook, sends a message of inclusion, not exclusion, and results in stronger odds that the guest will leave a better review, as they feel like they are now part of our team or a member of our vacation rental community.

A guest who feels welcome, included, and has been invited back to stay is more likely to leave a great review than a guest who hasn't been treated that way by the host.

On a final note, if you have more than one vacation rental, this is also an excellent spot to showcase your other property or properties. When guests are happy with any given stay, they tend to return to the same location again, or may stay at one of your other properties. Take advantage of that opportunity at this pivotal moment.

RULE: Always email the following template to your departing guest as soon as they check out. It will yield you great five-star reviews.

SAMPLE REVIEW GUEST TEMPLATE EMAIL
TO GUEST UPON DEPARTURE

Dear GUEST_NAME,

Safe travels and or welcome home! We hope you enjoyed your stay and that your vacation rental was everything you hoped it would be.

We have great news - you appear to have followed all our emailed check in instructions, understood the keyless entry system, and had from what appears to be an otherwise uneventful stay (which is what we want!), subject to any damage or missing items being reported from our cleaning crew.

In appreciation, we have provided you a 5 Star rating on VRBO, so that other owners will know that you are an ideal guest to have at their vacation rental!

When you come stay with us again, remind us of your prior stay and we will then provide you both a return guest discount (on any given non-holiday, non-promotional stay), and waive the refundable damage deposit on a future stay.

If you in turn loved your stay with us, please do let other vacationers know that this is a great place to stay when prompted by VRBO for a guest rating / review - your 5 Star reciprocated review of us makes a huge difference and is greatly appreciated!

If there were any issues or areas needing improvement, please simply email the owner directly at JamesRDorgan@gmail.com, or text the owner at 251-209-9299 and we will work on it for the next guest (assuming it is something within our control to fix).

We also invite you to become part of our Facebook community by 'liking' our unit's Facebook page (simply search for the unit's name and unit number on Facebook). We occasionally run last minute specials, provide informative information on local attractions such as concerts and or local events, and or provide interesting news on the unit and or resort. Please also feel free to 'tag' our unit on any and all vacation photos as well!

Thank you for staying with us and thank you again for being such terrific guests. We look forward to having you back for your next vacation!

Sincerely,

OWNER_NAME

OWNER_EMAIL

OWNER_PHONE

Please consider us for your next vacation in either Alabama, Florida, or Tennessee:

2/2 at Phoenix on the Bay, Orange Beach, Alabama with lazy river, slide, boat slips and launch. Sleeps 7. www.vrbo.com/513462

2/2 at Splash Resort, Panama City Beach, Florida with 9th floor direct Gulf front views, on-site kids water park, lazy river and free beach service. Sleeps 8. www.vrbo.com/873755

1/2 Splash Resort, Panama City Beach, Florida with 7th floor direct Gulf front views, bunk beds, on-site kids' waterpark, hot tub, gym, and free beach service. Sleeps 7. www.vrbo.com/873755

2/2 Appalachian High, Pigeon Forge, TN with amazing views, game room, balcony hot tub, and a truc log cabin experience all just a short drive from Pigeon Forge. Sleeps up to 6 adults / 4 kids. www.vrbo.com/2129848

Chapter 73

How to add 10-20% in gross rental revenues

with this one simple trick

As we do a three-night minimum, there are times that there is a one or two day 'gap' or vacancy between guest stays. What is the best way to fill that gap?

The answer is to simply entice the current guests on either side of that vacancy gap to extend their stay at a discounted rate, to fill that one-night vacancy.

About four to six weeks out before the one- or two-night vacancy, email the guests staying on the earlier side of the vacancy an offer to extend their stay by one night at a discounted rate. Ask them to respond quickly, as the extra night is first come first served. Four to six weeks ahead is still enough time for the guest to adjust their vacation plans. Waiting until the last minute to make this offer would be too late.

If those guests do not respond (and you state that a nonresponse by them to this offer means their reservation does not change), you then email the guest on the later side of that one-night vacancy and offer them to check in a night earlier at a reduced rate.

Hopefully, the guests staying on either side of that gap will 'snap' up the extra night, extending their stay.

Once they say they want it, you immediately adjust their dates of stay so that another guest doesn't book what you just offered. You then email the guest a payment request for the extra night, and after it has been paid, you then email them a new KABA code good for the revised dates and adjust the dates of stay on their reservation.

Remember, do not email the new revised keyless entry code until after the payment request for the extra night has been paid. This is consistent with your owner's job or duties. As soon as you get paid for a booking, you email the guest a code. As soon as you get paid for the extra night, you then email the guest a revised code.

Otherwise, the guest may never send the money for the extra night if you have already sent them the keyless entry code good for the revised dates of stay, or already adjusted their reservation. The KABA entry code is literally the 'keys to the kingdom.' Never send it out until the guest has paid in full for any given stay.

If there happens to be a two-night gap, you do the same thing – email the earlier guest to check out a night later, and the later guest to check in a night early.

Simultaneously, you also go into your calendar, highlight the two nights, and change the minimum night stay to just two nights. I also typically increase slightly the nightly rate for someone wanting to just stay two nights. I do this as two-night stays result in heavier wear and tear and create more generalized risks than having longer stays. I try and avoid that short of stay if possible. In other words, the guests on either side of the stay can take the extra night at the reduced rate, but a new guest just booking two nights would pay a premium, due to the increased wear and tear concern and generalized risks of having more guests than fewer in and out of the unit.

By taking all three steps, you are attempting to get that two-night gap filled in three different ways. The first to book is offered it first, as you always say, 'at this moment there is an extra night available' and that it is first come first served. This encourages action, not delay, and helps avoid a crisis mode situation of trying to adjust last minute stay dates, inconveniencing you and your cleaning team.

A final trick is working with an upcoming guest that is staying three, four or five nights. If there are considerable vacancies still present about a month away from their stay, you then can email the guest and tell them that they can check in a night early, and/or also check out a night later, with both extensions on either side of their stay at a reduced nightly rate.

In that way, the reservation balloons outwards in both directions, increasing your revenues from this single stay, and filling some of that vacancy on either side of the stay.

Another cool side effect of these email templates is that you are also reminding the guest that there are no early check-ins, or late check outs, if they fail to take advantage of the additional night. In other words, they must buy the extra night or nights to get an earlier check in or late check out.

For instance, if the guest wants to check in at 10 am in the morning after driving all night, the only way they can do that is to book the night before. Instead of checking in at 4pm that first night, they check in at 10am the following morning. These templates help make that point clear.

TRICKY TRICKY. Note that some super savvy guests have figured out exactly what I am saying in this chapter. They purposely then book a stay leaving a one-night gap on either side of their stay. A few weeks before their stay, they then contact the unsuspecting host and ask to extend their stay for the gap night or nights at a reduced rate, since it would 'sit empty' anyway. I have seen it happen and am surprised it doesn't happen more frequently.

RULE: Approximately four to six weeks out, always review your calendar and email currently booked guests offers to extend their stays at a discounted rate to fill any gaps between stays, or vacancies in your calendar. If there happens to be a two-night vacancy between two reservations, simultaneously adjust the nightly minimum down to two nights to try and fill that vacancy with a fresh reservation.

EMAIL TEMPLATE

CHECK-IN NIGHT EARLIER

GUEST_FIRST_NAME GUEST_LAST_NAME

At this moment, there is an available night between your check-in and the prior guest checking out.

If you would like to stay an extra night and come earlier than originally planned, we can offer you to do that for the discounted rate of $xxx plus tax.

If you wish to do that, let us know within 24 hours and we will then email you through VRBO a payment request for the additional night. Once paid, we will then email you a new confirmation with the new dates of stay, and a new keyless entry code good for the revised dates of stay.

If you want to leave everything 'as is' and as originally booked, you do not have to do anything. In other words, we will leave everything as is unless we definitively hear from you otherwise within the next 24 hours to change it, as availability is limited.

Please note that due to cleaning, inspection and maintenance scheduling, no entry to the unit is permitted prior to the designated check in time on the day of your scheduled arrival. In other words, the only way to get into the unit earlier than your designated check in is to book the prior night well in advance of stay.

Please note that we welcome all our guests to come early on the day of their check in to begin enjoying resort amenities. However, the actual unit is not accessible prior to their designated check in time on the scheduled date of arrival - no exceptions.

Thank you and we look forward to having you as a guest!

OWNER_NAME

EMAIL TEPLATE

CHECK-OUT DAY LATER

GUEST_FIRST_NAME GUEST_LAST_NAME

At this moment, there is an available night between your check-out and the next guest checking in.

If you would like to stay an extra night, we can offer you to do that for the discounted rate of $XXX plus tax. If you wish to do that, let us know within 24 hours and we will email you through VRBO a payment request for the additional night. Once paid, we will then email you a new confirmation with the new dates of stay, and a new keyless entry code good for the revised / extended dates of stay.

If you want to leave everything 'as is' and as originally booked, you do not have to do anything. In other words, we will leave everything as is unless we definitively hear from you otherwise.

Please note that check out from the actual unit is no later than 10am on the day of your departure (although you are welcome to stay on premises and enjoy resort amenities as late as you wish on the day of your departure).

Thank you and we look forward to having you as a guest!

OWNER_NAME

EMAIL TEMPLATE

CHECK-IN A NIGHT EARLY AND/OR

CHECK-OUT A NIGHT LATER

GUEST_FIRST_NAME GUEST_LAST_NAME

At this moment, there is an available night between your check-in and the prior guest checking out. There is also an available night between your check-out and the next guest checking in.

If you would like to stay an extra night on either end or both ends of your stay, we can offer you to do that for the discounted rate of $xxx plus tax for each night added.

If you wish to do that, let us know which night or nights you wish to add within 24 hours, and we will then email you through VRBO a payment request for the additional night or nights. Once paid, we will then email you a new confirmation with the new dates of stay, and a new keyless entry code good for the revised dates of stay.

If you want to leave everything 'as is' and as originally booked, you do not have to do anything. In other words, we will leave everything as is unless we definitively hear from you otherwise within the next 24 hours to change it, as availability is limited.

Please note that due to cleaning, inspection and maintenance scheduling, no entry to the unit is permitted prior to your designated check in time on the day of your scheduled arrival. In other words, the only way to get into the unit earlier than your designated check in time on the day of your scheduled arrival is to book the prior night well in advance of stay. Checkout is at 10 am on the day of your scheduled departure. Late checkouts are not permitted.

Thank you and we look forward to having you as a guest!

OWNER_NAME

SECTION V – READY FOR YOUR FIRST GUEST

Chapter 74

Time to test the system

You vacationed in this location and knew that the area will attract visitors. You ran the rental revenue numbers and there is serious 'bang for your buck' in exchange for what you paid. The vacation rental is within driving distance of your home. You started on your VRBO listing as soon as the Offer of Acceptance was signed. You were able to price the next year's rental revenues based on rates and occupancy levels from the previous owner. Your vacation rental passed all inspections with flying colors.

Within 24 hours of closing, you received your first 'Instant Booking.'

During the two weeks that you blocked off from stays after closing, you spent a good bit of time and effort getting everything ready by outsourcing as many things as you could. From paint, to appliances, to fixtures, to solid surface flooring, you hired professionals. You have replaced worn furnishings. You may have replaced the HVAC. Your locksmith installed a KABA lock. You have all brand-new dishes, silverware, pots, pans, and cooking accessories. You have a stocked owner's closet. You have an amazing cleaning team that uses Resort Cleaning. You have easy to wash quilts that do not readily show stains. You have a trustworthy and reliable maintenance person. You have planned out a theme for your vacation rental that matches the locale or unique characteristics of that area of the country. You have signed up for resort amenities and provide those amenities to all your guests. You have all your email templates, rental agreement, and attachments all set up in your VRBO email program, so that you never have to retype the same answer or same process more than once. You had a professional photograph your unit, who also provided you with a promotional video that you uploaded to YouTube, with the link added so that guests can see the video in your carousel of photos. You have a virtual tour booked or already done.

You are ready.

So, the book should end here, right? In a perfect world, absolutely.

However, we do not live in a perfect world. There will be many unexpected challenges, hardships, or circumstances that will happen. There will be difficult guests. There will be icy roads, hurricanes, and forest fires. There will be an occasional totally unfair review. There will be an occasional cleaning oversight.

So, I want to help prepare you for these things, so that when they do happen, you will know how best to handle them. You will 'stand on my shoulders' and instead of dealing with any given issue for the first time, you will have guidance, or someone to help 'coach' you through it. By anticipating some of the most common issues, it is my hope that you will say to yourself – 'oh yes, Dorgan said this might happen' and you will know exactly what to do.

RULE: Even though you have followed every single step on getting your vacation rental ready, there still will be many, many challenges. The remainder of this book is to help you anticipate those coming challenges, and 'coach' you through them.

SECTION VI – THE GUESTS START ARRIVING

Chapter 75

Top ten complaints or issues

and how best to respond to them

At this point, and if you have followed everything that I have recommended in getting your vacation rental ready for the first guest, even if you absolutely nail it, there are still going to be problem guests. You need to prepare yourself mentally for that unexpected splash of cold water. It is not necessarily anything you did or did not do – but rather, some folks are inherently unhappy or have a negative outlook on life.

There are always going to be guest personalities that you need to contend with to keep your sanity. The main thing by me telling you about these types of guests, is that you will anticipate it, and expect it, as opposed to being shocked or surprised by it.

You then will have ready and at your fingertips the best technique(s) on how best to respond.

As the following example list may not be exhaustive, the general thread through all these responses is to never argue with a guest, and never respond when frustrated or when your feelings have been hurt.

Rather, simply rehash the positive things that the guest has encountered so far, acknowledge the unfortunate issue, say thank you for letting us know, and that we will get to work on it.

That's the best response outline to follow.

The Nitpicker

So, the e-mail from the guest came in over the Thanksgiving holiday weekend. The guest stated that one of the twelve serving dinner plates had a chip in it, and that someone could possibly cut themselves on the plate, but fortunately, since she saw it, 'no one has been injured - yet.'

I also vaguely recall that there was also an extreme, immediate concern that there were only 10 cereal spoons instead of 12, or something along those lines.

After a several hundred-thousand-dollar investment of your own money, and then weeks, if not months of initial work, sweat equity, money, time and effort to get your vacation rental absolutely perfect for your guests, THIS happens? What the heck? As an owner, one literally feels like EXPLODING. This complaint is incredibly picky, and even petty, especially since the maximum capacity for the unit is seven guests.

It is at this moment that you need to breathe deeply, and not respond while angry or frustrated, or spin off a nasty fast text response. Do not call back the guest and speak with them in person, as they will sense a mile away that you are frustrated and or irritated, with what from your perspective, is a petty and ridiculous issue, especially in the middle of a holiday weekend.

If they texted you this, or even called you and left a message, do not immediately respond. Breathe deep. Sleep on it. Always, always, sleep on a non-emergency issue.

Rather, wake up the next day, and in your moment of quiet, peace and tranquility, as you sip on your morning cup of coffee, you respond, by email (not text) chuckling to yourself occasionally, as follows:

"I am so happy that you made it safely to our vacation rental. I am so happy as well that you got to spend Thanksgiving Dinner at our vacation rental and enjoyed good times with your family and friends. I am also happy to hear that the accommodation is otherwise satisfactory to you with the exception of the two issues you have brought to our attention.

Yes, absolutely, we want our guests to be safe, and appreciate your genuine concern.

Please throw away the chipped plate. You will not be charged for the disposed plate in our inventory.

By alerting us as well to this safety issue, we can then replace the chipped plate (and also any missing silverware as needed) in time for the next guest, and we appreciate your bringing that to our attention.

Thank you for keeping you and your family safe from this potential hazard and alerting us to this situation, so that at minimum, we can have this situation taken care of in time for the next guest.

Thank you and have a great remainder of stay!"

So, the number one rule is to not respond by text, or direct telephone communication, while angry, as the guest will pick up on your anger or frustration and that makes the situation worse.

Also, an agitated confrontational or argumentative response unfortunately may lead to additional petty complaints, and the cycle goes round and round. As badly as you want to scream at the top of your lungs THIS IS THE MOST PETTY COMPLAINT IN THE ENTIRE WORLD – don't do it.

Rather, since it is not an emergency, wait 24 hours and respond through your VRBO email template in a calm, cool, and respectful manner, regardless of how petty the complaint may be. Attempt to move the conversation away from texts, and instead, to more contemplated and carefully drafted emails, all within the VRBO reservation and accompanying correspondence.

Always, always, find something positive to highlight at the beginning and again at the end of the correspondence. Sandwich in the middle the negative issue presented. This is called the poop sandwich response. Put the yucky part in the middle, with the beginning all positive and happy, then bury the negative in the middle, and always end on a positive note.

The guest will check out, and you will then at some point in the next few weeks, see about replacing the chipped plate, and replenishing your stock of silverware, on a non-emergency, when you can get to it, basis.

Just shake your head and keep on going.

The Naysayer

As soon as the guest checks in, the guest emails you or texts you a message that it is raining, or that there was a lot of traffic getting there, or that the elevators are backed up, or there is seaweed on the beach, or some other complaint that is completely outside of your control.

Like dealing with the nitpicker, just relax.

Do not respond instantly to a text as they stand outside the elevator in a long line of people. Responding to them at that instant by text will not speed things along with the elevator cue. If a speedy response cannot help them anyway, do not respond quickly.

Again, reply by email through the email app, not by text, the next day.

Highlight all the good things first – they have had a safe trip, they are in a great unit, the resort has awesome amenities, and so forth.

Then briefly address the issue raised by the complaint, which is simply a grievance about hassles of travel generally, or the weather.

You simply explain that this is something outside your control and hope that they otherwise have a wonderful remainder of stay. Keep the beginning and ending of the correspondence positive.

Do not become the on-the-spot text recipient or punching bag of every slight, inconvenience, hassle, or issue that may come up incidental to any given vacation day. Don't take the bait. You are not a punching bag for any given frustration that they encounter during their stay.

If the guest is going to be miserable and complain about everything, just let them. Steer them towards communicating with you by email. Simply respond the next day and let them be. By not responding instantly, they will likely move on and find someone else to be their punching bag.

The Freeloader

The freeloader is that guest who low balled in the offseason and proposed an impossibly low total stay budget to stay in your vacation rental. Regrettably, you agreed to their proposed impossibly low budget, and they have now checked in.

The next message will be that the room is not sufficiently clean. You offer to send out the cleaning crew to correct the cleaning oversight. They don't want that. But can you do a full or partial credit instead?

The next message is that the splashpad is closed due to a brown out. Can you do a full or partial credit instead? They have a toddler that really had their heart set on spending time in that specific splashpad, and that is why they chose this resort. You explain that you had put in your description the dates that the splash pad would be closed, but they nevertheless booked anyway. They missed that disclaimer. Can we still get a refund?

The next message is that since it rained one of their days, can you extend the stay for free?

The list goes on and on and every year gets even more creative. It's pretty amusing at times.

Guests like this have zero shame in asking for credit, or refund, or something for nothing. Be prepared for that. You cannot just start giving away nights or refunds.

This is the truth – the guest who pays the highest, peak season rate is typically the most uneventful stay, with no issues. The guest who comes in at a bargain-basement off-season rate, is typically a nightmare stay, with multiple complaints, and repeated requests for some type of credit or refund. It's literally an inverse relationship – the higher the price paid, the less problems. The least price paid, the more problems. Kid you not.

If you are prone to having difficulty saying no to someone or somebody, you need to practice saying no. They will ask – especially those in your unit on a discounted rate. You need to be prepared mentally to say no to the freeloader.

Like all responses, keep it professional and courteous. Also, since this is a non-emergency situation, take your time in responding.

The Trasher

Our cleaners walked into our cabin following a check out, and the departing guest had literally exploded a 'party ball' of paper graffiti in the top floor of the unit, most likely the loft, as the mess was spread on all three floors of the cabin. The thousands of tiny pieces of colored paper landed on the pool table, behind the sofa, on top of the ceiling fans, windowsills, and were sprinkled among the window shade slats of the unit. Incredulously, the guest made zero effort to hide it or clean it up. Absolutely zero shame.

Fortunately, the cleaners documented the mess with photos, and only charged us an additional $100 for the excessive cleaning. To this day, and it's been more than a year, we still find bits of graffiti in the most unusual of places.

When we presented the photos and the excessive cleaning charge to the guest, as a claim against their damage deposit, the guest was absolutely enraged, if not offended, that we dared to charge their damage deposit for the excessive cleaning.

Be prepared for that.

Guests in their own mind can NEVER do wrong, especially when there is a claim against their damage deposit – so plan accordingly. No matter how badly they have treated your vacation rental, the guest will never, almost invariably, own up and be responsible for the mess.

As such, you must document what they do, and be prepared with photos and/or testimony to back up the reason why you claimed some or all their damage deposit. Your cleaner should do this for you (and pay the cleaner extra to do this).

Once that line is crossed, and you decide to make a claim against the damage deposit, the guest will always be unhappy. Claiming some or all of a guest's damage deposit is akin to a declaration of war. Do not go there unless you absolutely must.

In view of the likelihood that seizing their damage deposit will result in WWIII, do not go there with a guest, or cross that line, unless the claim is above a minimum threshold amount – say $300.

Otherwise, the negative blowback from going to war with the guest makes it otherwise not worth it to make the claim. Just consider it a necessary expense of doing business and move on. I should have just let the exploding ball of graffiti go – but I didn't. I got reimbursed for the $100 and won the battle, but ended up with a negative review, so lost the war. I should have just blown it off.

Remember the old saying 'Don't sweat the small stuff. Everything is small stuff." Don't go to war with a guest unless it's unavoidable.

The Smoker

The smoker will know that you have a nonsmoking unit. They appreciate how clean the unit is, and that the smell will not saturate their clothing and luggage. After a few drinks, they then light up inside to watch the game even though it is a nonsmoking unit.

If it's too cold outside, or raining, they just smoke inside. They simply don't care and think they will not get caught.

The slick smokers bring some type of spray or aerosol to cloak the smell as well and go to great lengths to hide any evidence of smoking.

When your non-smoking cleaner comes in, and smells the smoke, you need to be prepared to tell the cleaner what to do to document the smell, in as many ways as you humanly can, as smell is a subjective thing, and the smoker is banking on that.

1.   You tell the cleaner that you will pay them for this extra work to document this issue.

2   The cleaner should go through all the trash and look for disposed cigarettes, cartons, or packaging, and ashes. They should also scout the grounds around the exterior of the vacation rental.

3   The cleaner needs to pull all air filters and photograph them. Sometimes the smoke will leave a residue or dark imprint.

4   The cleaner needs to call their supervisor, or inspector, and get them out to also do the 'sniff test.' The more folks that can say, 'Yes, I smelled smoke in the unit following departure' bolsters your claim. There is power in numbers.

5   Have your cleaner take a white cloth and wipe solid surfaces. The oily residue from someone smoking then needs to be photographed on the damp white cleaning cloth.

6   Check all smoke detectors in the unit and see if they have been tampered with or were left unplugged.

There may be other techniques to prove that someone smoked in your unit. Whatever those techniques are, use them, as the guest will ALWAYS deny that they smoked inside the rental.

With the foregoing information in hand, and if your team is absolutely convinced that the departing guest smoked, make a claim against the guest's damage deposit.

Get the carpets cleaned, order a deep cleaning for the walls and ceilings and all solid surfaces to be scrubbed. Replace all air filters, and hire a carpet cleaning company to dry clean all furnishings and carpets. Have your cleaners pull all linens, pillows, quilts and bedspreads for laundering. Keep track of every expense.

VRBO will back you on your damage claim as long as you have sufficient evidence to support your claim. Make 'em pay. Do not just let a smoker slide. The next guest will smell it and it's just a downhill slide from there on unhappy guests and negative reviews.

Also, if a smoker smells smoke upon entry (left uncorrected from a previous guest stay), they will report the smell of smoke on entry, and then smoke it up during their stay, as they now feel like they have a 'free pass' to smoke inside and blame it on the prior guest. It's a vicious cycle. You must catch it when it happens, treat it, and get that smell out if and when it happens to keep it from happening again, and to avoid a negative review.

Fortunately, in ten or more years, at all six vacation rental properties we have ever owned (we own four currently and have sold two), we have only had to make a claim for a smoking violation one time. I firmly believe that the risk of a high fine of $1500-$2500 is the only thing that keeps smokers from lighting up. The placards on the inside of the front door may help too – but in the end – your ability to charge for deodorizing costs up to $2500 is typically the only sufficient motive to keep the most hard-core of smokers from smoking inside.

The late night texter

Every now and then you will have an unusually chatty guest stay with you. They constantly text you with questions, when the answers are clearly stated in their access instruction email template, with accompanying attachments. These texts start coming in prior to stay, starting with a request for an early check-in, and they continue texting throughout the stay, almost daily, until you received the text request to check out late. It's endless. Responding to each text is opposite of your goal of the one-to-two-hour workweek on managing the vacation rental.

Basically, this guest is too busy or too proud to read your access instructions and the accompanying attachments, and would rather, just wing it, and simply text you at all hours of the day and night to get the most mundane question answered.

At some point, to put an end to that type of guest, simply do not respond if it is between the hours of 8 pm and 8 am.

In addition, allow 24-hour response times on a non-emergency issue. Again, steer them towards communicating with you through the VRBO email app.

A text or two is fine. By the third text at 10 at night with yet another question that has been addressed in your access instructions, it is time to lay down the law.

Here is a proposed email template response:

Thank you for reaching out to me for help.

Although I am happy to assist, this question and many more are addressed in the access instructions and attachments that we provided with your keyless entry to the unit. We encourage you to read that information so that you will have a more timely response and answer to your questions, instead of having to wait for me to respond by text. Unless an emergency, please direct further inquiries by email through the VRBO app.

Thank you again for being our guest and have a wonderful remainder of stay.

The Inept

This is a situation where you really need to be patient and understanding. The guest is simply not capable of understanding or handling simple instructions on stay.

For example, the guest simply cannot figure out the remote or get the TV to work. Simple questions like have you checked the battery falls with a dud or numbing response, 'where do I find the batteries on the remote?'

Another time, and despite detailed instructions on where to park, and how to find the condo, the guest is standing at what they think is our unit door and is trying to enter the keyless code entry into the lock, but it won't work. We then realize the guest is not even at our door, but rather, is standing in front of our storage closet, that if you could see what I am talking about, is CLEARLY a row of storage closets in a hallway, and not an entrance to any given condo unit.

At Splash, and this happens frequently, the guests traverse the long skybridge from the parking area across the road, and over to the two Gulf front beach towers. We are in the west tower, or to the right, as you cross the sky bridge.

I cannot tell you how many guests go left and try to enter the door code to unit 704 east, rather than unit 704 west. We tell them to go right, and not left, after crossing the sky bridge, but they go the wrong way anyway – a lot. When the code doesn't work, we tell the guest that it is probably because they are in the wrong tower. They still cannot figure it out. How do we get there?

Fortunately, this type of guest is rare. Simply breathe deep and be patient and kind. They really are lost. They really have no clue on how to follow simple instructions. It is not intentional. They are just inept. Don't take it too seriously and just be as patient as you possibly can. Bless their hearts.

College Student / Underage Shenanigans

The college kids or fraternity friends will typically not reach out and do an inquiry prior to instantly booking your unit. They tend to just book it and ask questions later, as they become increasingly nervous about the potential loss of their damage deposit.

Rather, questions like the following will trickle in prior to their stay.

Does anyone check ID when we check in?

What is the maximum number of guests that can stay in the vacation rental without their being a violation?

What are the maximum number of cars that we can bring?

Can we have a few friends over for the day at the resort?

What is the maximum number of guest wrist bands that we can get on each day of our trip?

Are coolers allowed at the beach / pools?

The foregoing questions asked may be a potential cue or signal that this may be a college or high school person staying in your vacation rental.

Other clues may be that they list all adults staying, and no children, another potential red flag.

Also, the time of year or weekend booked may also draw concern. If the booking is during Spring Break, or if the booking is for all adults for a special teen or young adult concert weekend known to attract teens and the early 20's crowd, you should be suspicious.

If you get in any way suspicious of any given stay, simply email the guest that you look forward to receiving a copy of their valid driver license that matches the name of the guest who booked the unit. Tell them that this is your standard process and not a big deal (even though you typically do not check ID's prior to arrival).

If they do not respond, or balk at honoring the request, contact VRBO and get them to either investigate further on your behalf, or to cancel the stay, as it is likely a group of kids staying who are trying to circumvent your rules of stay. VRBO, and presumably Airbnb too, will back you up on this.

The scary cockroach

The guest texts or emails you that they just saw a cockroach in the vacation rental and were alarmed and concerned and were freaking out and did know what to do and were contemplating checking out.

Relax.

If it is an after-hours thing, simply wait until the next day to respond. When you do respond, ask them whether it was fully alive and running around or half dead, or already dead. Yes, express concern and understanding of such a horrible thing happening.

You then politely explain in detail that you have regular and consistent pest control in the unit and if they are half dead or already dead, your preventative pest control is indeed working.

If it's a live and super-fast one, you then simply say we will get pest control out right away to take care of the issue on a complimentary basis. We go to great lengths to combat pests and will send out the professionals right away.

Many pest control companies will do a return visit if you are on a contract with them, for a situation exactly like this. It does not cost you anything for them to come back out and spray, typically within 24-36 hours of getting the complaint. Either way, tell the guest that they will be 'right out.'

Often, when the guest realizes that they are not getting a refund, future stay credit, or other compensation for 'finding' any given pest, the scary roach is then not so scary, and they even ask to delay the pest control from spraying until after they have checked out. Problem solved.

It's simply 'not clean'

Your cleaners cleaned the unit in time for the 4 pm check in. Tasteful and high-end starter supplies were provided. Fresh towels were placed out and some were even made into towel animals. Fresh sheets are on the beds. All appliances are clean. You have a schedule where quilts are rotated out and cleaned. The unit was even inspected as well by a supervisor.

Despite all of this, the guest then texts you at 10 at night a photo of the baseboard covered in dust.

The guest is disgusted, and rants about how they picked your vacation rental based on the reviews on how clean it was. They are very, very disappointed. They just don't know what to do and are contemplating checking out. In the meantime, they are washing linens. They paid $175 for cleaning and that was a lot of money for them. The unit 'simply isn't clean.'

Again, relax.

Their mentioning how much they paid for the cleaning deposit, along with the purported cleaning oversight, is nothing but an attempt for them to extract some type of refund out of you, stay credit, or complimentary extension of stay. They likely pull something like this every time they check into a vacation rental.

Here is a proposed template email response:

We are so pleased that you had a safe trip to the vacation rental. We are also so happy that the unit was timely serviced and ready for your 4pm or later check-in, despite the busy holiday peak season weekend during a time when our cleaners are pushed to the limits of endurance. Fresh sheets, fresh towels, and starter supplies were all supplied to your unit.

You also obviously were able to figure out our keyless entry system, are in and settled, and perhaps have already started to enjoy our resort amenities, and otherwise having a wonderful stay.

On the cleaning oversight you presented, we will immediately contact our cleaners, including the supervisor who inspected the unit immediately prior to your check in, to come back out, and take care of the oversight right away.

The return visit to take care of the cleaning oversight is completely complimentary. Please also allow a reasonable amount of time for our team to revisit the unit.

Please note that there are otherwise no refunds for cleaning oversight(s).

If for any reason that you would rather the cleaner / supervising inspector to not come back out to take care of the listed cleaning oversight, please simply let me know. We will then take steps to make sure the same oversight does not happen again for the next guest.

Thank you for bringing this to our attention.

I firmly believe that if a guest figures out that you are 'new' to the vacation rental business, they will pull something like this to try and get the cleaning fee refunded. Do not do it. Don't take the bait.

Others simply do it every time they stay somewhere regardless of how clean a place is or not. Through volume, they sometimes win a refund.

By the way, our cleaners did return to take care of the cleaning oversight, and after much questioning as to the location of the dirty baseboard, the guest pulled the fridge out and showed them a dirty baseboard. Kid you not.

RULE: On nonemergency texts, move the guest to email correspondence with a 24-hour turnaround time. Avoid phone calls and texts if possible. Never argue with a guest, and never correspond when frustrated, angry or with hurt feelings. The email response should start positive, address the complaint in the middle, and then end positive. Keep everything professional.

Chapter 76

Bed bugs – what to do if it happens

Bed bugs simply hitch a ride in a suitcase, and that is how they are spread. They may arrive in an expensive vacation rental, a high-end hotel, a low-end hotel, or even a relative's home.

If it happens, the fact that it did happen should not reflect poorly on the vacation rental, hotel, or family member, as it is something that cannot be prevented – but only treated.

Bed bugs do not cause disease or permanent injury. Despite that, being bitten by one is a whole different level of distress for folks than being bitten by a mosquito, chigger, scorpion, or other biting insect, due to its stigma.

There is also the concern that the bed bugs will hitch a ride back home with the guest and then be extremely difficult to remove from the guest's own home, a legitimate concern.

What you do not want to ever happen is for there to be a guest bitten by a bed bug or have a situation where they take home bed bugs with them.

If one of your guests get bitten by bed bugs, or they bring bed bugs from your vacation rental home with them, it could potentially trigger not only an inflammatory bed bug review, but also a personal injury lawsuit. It's a serious issue and you need to know how to handle it if it were to happen.

You never want a bed bug lawsuit, or a bed bug complaint in your reviews. Such a review could irreparably devastate your vacation rental.

As discussed in an earlier chapter, be preventative and set up routine bed bug inspections by a bed bug professional. You want to catch them before they bite a guest, and well before it turns into an infestation.

Your cleaners should also be versed in knowing what bed bugs look like, and how to check for them, every single time they clean.

I recommend that all vacation rental owners get versed in knowing what to look for with bed bugs. Bed bugs can typically be spotted at night between the mattresses or creases of a mattress. Bed bugs look like small sesame seeds, and sometimes are light in color, and sometimes dark red in color. The bed bugs leave excrement stains wherever they go, or tiny blood stains, that leave dark tiny streaks across the bedding. Bed bugs typically hide in direct proximity to a bed in the mattresses, box springs, and bed frame. They may also take up residence in a sleeper sofa, or potentially a recliner as well – anywhere a person can be found sleeping.

Again, you, your cleaner or your inspection team need to spot them before a guest does, and never, never the other way around.

If bed bugs happen, you need to first confirm that there is indeed an issue, by having your bed bug specialist confirm either way once the guest complains.

I have heard that there are guests out there who travel around with dead bed bugs in a zip lock bag, and then show the bed bugs to the owner at some point during their stay, in hopes of a full refund, or even compensation beyond a full refund.

Unfortunately, scams like that have happened before and so be careful with that.

Also, just because a guest has bites on their body, does not necessarily mean that they were caused by bed bugs. They may have been bitten by fleas, chiggers, mosquitoes or any other number of biting insects, bites of which are very difficult to distinguish at times from a bed bug bite.

This is why you need your own K-9 dog and specialist to confirm definitively either way if there is ever an accusation of a bed bug issue. Often, the guest was simply bitten by chiggers, fleas, or no see-ums, and the bite mark was caused by something other than a bed bug. Don't instantly jump to a bed bug conclusion if someone says they were bitten by something, especially when the guest complains about the bumps sometime after checkout.

In other words, it is hard to tell what insects may have caused a small red welt or welts on the body. Indeed, even doctors have a difficult time concluding whether a bite mark is from a bed bug or some other insect, as the welts are difficult to distinguish.

However, it is not debatable if the $12,000 K-9 dog finds bed bugs. A bed bug complaint or accusation is extremely serious, so spend the money and get a bed bug trained K-9 out to the vacation rental immediately so that you definitively know either way, right away.

If there is indeed a live bed bug issue in your vacation rental (and it's not a scam artist trying to get a refund or simply a guest bitten by something while hiking), you will need to cancel and refund the staying guest, and then instruct them to be careful not to take any bed bugs home with them. Look up and provide them with the steps that need to be taken to prevent any bed bugs from hitching a ride with them to their alternative lodging or their home.

This may include bagging up all their personal property in sealed garbage bags, separately laundering everything they own on high heat, and drying everything they own on high heat. Anything that was inside the vacation rental needs to be heat treated before it enters their alternative lodging or home.

For suitcases, they can be thermally treated inside their vehicle if the vehicle with the windows closed heats up to at least 135 degrees for an extended period. A hot attic may also be able to reach that needed temperature. The departing guest may simply need to just throw away anything that cannot be laundered on high heat. Treating personal property with high heat is easily accomplished in the summer by using a hot car or a hot attic.

The winter is a different story, and attempting to thermally treat personal items during that time of year is much trickier.

Your pest control service will then come in to perform a thermal treatment on all affected areas. This is where the pest control company brings in large industrial size heaters and heats up all affected areas to 135 degrees or more for several hours.

They then apply the Apprehend pesticide to the bed frames in the affected areas, for any stragglers that may have survived the impossible. Bed bugs cannot handle heat, and that is about the only thing that will quickly kill them. Thermal treatments are always necessary if there is an infestation.

You will then need the unit deep cleaned, as a dead beg bug laying around or found in the cabin is just as scary for most folks as finding a live one.

Thermal bed bug treatment with the corresponding application of Apprehend can run thousands of dollars and may even approach $10,000 for larger properties. Again, the nature of how bed bugs spread is something that you cannot control. All you can do is monitor it, and if it happens, do what it takes to protect your guest, get it treated, and move on.

If a guest is bitten by a bed bug, and you confirmed it with the K-9 inspection, and you refund the guest, and they then want additional compensation above and beyond a refund for their stay, immediately contact both your homeowner's insurance carrier and VRBO to handle the potential liability claim. You cannot negotiate anything other than a full refund.

Otherwise, to negotiate anything beyond that may result in your losing any available liability insurance coverage that you may have to cover the potential claim. That is your insurance company's job, not yours, for any type of liability compensation above and beyond a simple refund.

Hopefully, by explaining to the guest that you go to great lengths to proactively monitor for bed bugs, and take guest health and safety seriously, they will in turn hopefully be understanding. They will simply depart and accept their refund in full and chalk it up to an unfortunate incident.

You then tell the departing guest all of the things that you have done to make sure that the issue is resolved – the thermal treatment, the pesticide, and so forth, so that this does not happen again with the next guest. That communication will help go a long way in keeping the departing guest from suing you, if they know you took the complaint seriously, and immediately took remedial action to cure the issue for future guests.

This communication may also result in the guest not being hard on you in a review, or they may just skip the review completely, which would be a miracle, but it is possible if you handle it correctly.

For those guests though that immediately escalate to threatening an attorney, litigation, or all types of demands for additional compensation beyond a simple refund on stay, simply refund them, and then turn it over to your homeowner's insurance company and the VRBO insurance company to handle it. If they are vindictive and leave a nasty review despite all your gestures and overtures to make it right. I will explain how to handle that type of review in a later chapter.

RULE: A bed bug claim is an emergency and demands your full and complete attention. Assuming bed bugs are indeed found, guests should immediately depart, and then be instructed on how not to take the bugs with them. Guests should receive a full refund, at minimum. Hire a professional bed bug treatment team that utilizes thermal treatment and Apprehend pesticide. Cancel all guest stays until the bed bug issue has been resolved, and the specially trained K-9 has confirmed their complete eradication. If the guest seeks additional compensation beyond a stay refund, contact your insurance company and VRBO for insurance coverage to cover their potential claim.

Chapter 77

Should I refund a guest if a resort amenity is unavailable?

Inevitably, one or more of your vacation rental amenities will go down at some point during your guest's stay.

At the beach, it may rain, or seaweed may come in, or there are frightful jellyfish, and the beach is temporarily closed. The pool or lazy river goes down for emergency repairs. Up in the mountains, the hot tub on the balcony breaks, or the outdoor grill runs out of propane.

Whatever amenity happens to not be available, the guest promptly informs you that 'the only reason' the guest booked this stay was for use of this amenity, and that because of the unavailability, their stay has been 'ruined.'

Plan for this contingency. It will happen and you are not a guarantor that any given amenity will ever be available and functioning during any given stay, regardless of whether the amenity is or is not within your control. For instance, our hot tub at the cabin is within our control. However, the resort pool and gym are not within our control. Either way, you do not guarantee that any given amenity will be available.

In your description of resort and or area amenities, or in your inquiry response email template, conclude the description of all of the wonderful resort amenities with a disclaimer - 'All amenities are subject to availability.'

Expanding on that, as the guest goes through the Rules of Stay, again list that disclaimer.

Finally, when you email the guest the keyless entry code which they need to enter the vacation rental, attach to that email a special PDF attachment that highlights in crystal clear language, that if any given amenity goes down during the stay, that there will not be a refund.

Here is an example from our unit at Phoenix on the Bay, in Orange Beach, Alabama, a lagoon front vacation rental resort with lazy river, water slide, and multiple indoor and outdoor pools.

OWNER POLICY ON AVAILABILITY OF RESORT AMENITIES: The resort may have an amenity that may become unavailable at some point during your stay. As there are typically many different amenity alternatives available, as well as Orange Beach's many area attractions, we do not compensate guests if any given resort amenity happens to become unavailable.

Occasionally, resort amenities may be closed for an extended time. For example, our waterpark needed maintenance at Splash. The maintenance was scheduled for January and February, the two slowest months of the year, and during a time when it's freezing cold out and very few if any children use the waterpark.

Simply list the closure on your listing description, on your keycode email template, and your keycode email template. The main thing is that the guest is informed of the closure in advance of their stay, and the closure is not 'sprung' on them. If they proceed to book or stay despite the closure, then there is no refund. If you stay you pay.

RULE: Anticipate that resort amenities will at some point be down for any given guest stay. Clearly state in advance of the guest's arrival that there will be no refund if an unexpected amenity closure becomes unavailable. For extended amenity closures scheduled way in advance, list the closure so that the guest knows about the closure prior to booking, and in advance of their arrival. If they choose to book and/or stay anyway, then there are no refunds.

Chapter 78

Should I refund a guest if an appliance breaks?

Guests sometimes get giddy with excitement when an appliance, toilet, fixture, coffee maker or blender breaks down during their stay. They automatically begin to think that this may be a means to get a refund.

One time a guest literally broke our washing machine, most likely from overloading it with towels. In alerting us to the breakdown, the guest explained that the presence of the washing machine was the main reason they booked our unit. This guest was fishing for a refund or some type of compensation.

To combat this inclination, nip this issue in the bud from the get-go. Include in your keycode email the following disclaimer on appliance breakdowns:

OWNER POLICY ON MECHANICAL BREAKDOWNS On rare occasions, as most if not all of our major appliances are new, an appliance may breakdown during your stay, requiring either a fix or replacement. We provide in our welcome email the contact information for our maintenance crew if that happens, and we will do all we can to remedy the situation as quickly as possible. Upon such event, there is no compensation for any inconvenience caused by an unexpected mechanical breakdown in the unit.

By having this disclaimer, the guest then knows that if something breaks down, that the owner will work on getting it fixed or replaced, but that no compensation is due. By having this policy, the guest is less likely to make a big deal out of the breakdown, as such theatrics will not get anywhere.

The exception to this rule is if there is an interruption in an essential service, causing the guest to have to depart.

For example, the air conditioning goes out during a summer stay at the beach, causing the guest to have to check out. If the guest does not stay, they shouldn't pay in this type of situation.

RULE: Disclaim prior to arrival that if there is a mechanical breakdown in the unit, there will be no refunds or compensation for the inconvenience of the breakdown. Allow exceptions when necessary and reasonable.

Chapter 79

Handling hurricanes

If you have a beach vacation rental, there is always the seasonal threat of hurricanes and tropical storms. Folks tend to be wary of vacation rentals that do not offer any type of refund or credit due to a cancellation caused by a hurricane or tropical storm.

To stay competitive, we simply state the rules of compensation in advance, if that contingency were to happen. In that way, the guest knows what the rules are if a hurricane or tropical storm comes through. They know that they will not completely lose their stay costs due to the storm.

Although I offer credit towards future stay, sometimes it is simpler to just refund the guest, so you don't have to keep up with the credit.

For example, a guest was staying at our beach condo, and a named storm was heading that way. Instead of immediately departing, the guest waited and enjoyed the pretty weather until just before the storm came in, and departed as soon as the evacuation order was issued. We ended up refunding a single night plus tax – a win win for everyone.

Here is the language used on an attachment to our keycode email that deals with this specific issue:

OWNER POLICY ON HURRICANE / TROPICAL STORM In the event of a hurricane or tropical storm, you may cancel a portion or all of your stay without penalty, even at the last minute, or during your stay, and receive a full credit for any unused portion(s) of your stay, to be used towards a future stay with us. Unless there is a hurricane or tropical storm warning for the condo location, cancellations during your stay are otherwise nonrefundable.

Please note that the disclaimer is written so that the guest can bail and get a stay credit if the storm affects the vacation rental destination, not necessarily where that guest lives. In other words, if their home comes under a storm warning and they need to immediately leave, resulting in an interruption of their stay at your vacation rental, that is on them and there are no refunds.

RULE: Clearly explain your rule on annual potential trip interruption events that may impact any given guest stay. Be flexible in your policy as the guest wants reasonableness, and not to have to solely bear the entire loss if a typical severe weather event happens. The odds are in your favor that the severe weather event will not happen, so you want that unit booked, not empty, simply because of a guest's reasonable concern of what 'might' happen. Once that fear is addressed, the guest is then more likely to book.

Chapter 80

Handling winter storms and hazardous roads

I am relatively new to renting our cabin up at Pigeon Forge and knowing how to handle winter Storm Warnings, so this may or may not be the best advice.

If the power goes out, and the guest spends the night in a subfreezing temperature cabin, what is the policy?

If the roads are iced over, and the rental guests cannot get in or out as they failed to pack or do not have the ability to use tire chains? What is the policy?

What if the guest is delayed on arrival due to iced over roads and must stay in a hotel down the hill?

What if the guest wants to leave and stays past checkout as they simply cannot safely make it down the mountain – do they pay for the extra nights?

These are all tough questions, and I am not sure I have all the answers.

The few times I booked a vacation rental out West to do a ski trip, the rule was crystal clear, if you did not make it to the unit for any given reason, even if due to a winter storm, there was no refund, as the unit would just sit empty.

This seems a bit harsh but is an understandable rule and is probably the rule that I should adopt. I remember trying to get to Breckenridge from Denver during winter on I-70 and the Eisenhauer Tunnel closed, keeping me from getting to our $500 per night slope side condo, which sat empty.

No refund was provided to us in that situation.

However, I have a hard time charging a guest for a night's stay when they don't even stay in the vacation rental. I also want guests to be safe in getting there and not to try and 'force it,' putting themselves at risk during hazardous driving events to try and make it to the cabin, which was bought and paid for.

Further, if the guest spends the night without power or water for an extended period, I feel that there should be some compensation.

If the guest gets pushed past checkout due to inclement weather, and there is power, the guest needs to pay the nightly rate plus tax for their staying past the checkout date for any reason (fortunately this has never happened at any of our vacation properties – ever). The guest is just as motivated as anyone to get home to their planned schedule and back to work so they typically have little, if any, motivation to try and 'milk it' past their checkout date.

Our winter storm policy has (loosely) evolved into the following, and is still a work in progress.

If the guest cannot make it to the cabin due to iced over roads, and their failure to bring tire chains, then there is no refund.

If the guest stays past checkout due to icy roads and their failure to bring tire chains to make it safely down the mountain, they pay.

If the guest stays, and power or water goes out for an extended period, there is no refund. If you stay you pay.

If the guest must depart early due to lack of power or water, we provide a 100% refund for all unused nights.

As we are new to handling winter storms and travel, this is an evolving policy. I recommend checking with other vacation rental owners for their policy on situations like this, and also area hotel policies. There may also be a forum on Facebook for your resort or vacation rental community where you can pose this question and see if you can find a common middle ground for a reasonable and fair policy.

RULE: Make a plan on how to handle foreseeable contingencies that come with any given winter storm, hurricane, wildfire, or other perennial event. Be flexible, reasonable, and fair. Look to other lodgings, owners and the hotel industry on standards and norms when unsure.

Chapter 81

How to claim some or all of a guest's damage deposit

As indicated in an earlier chapter, always mandate that every guest must provide a refundable damage deposit incidental to any given stay. By having some 'skin in the game,' guests are more likely to follow rules of stay, not trash your vacation rental, or steal anything.

The next question is understanding how the process works for the owner to claim some or all the guest's damage deposit.

The process starts with your cleaning team documenting the damage, missing item, or failure to follow check out instructions, or Rules of Stay. Documenting damage consists primarily of photos.

As you want to go to great lengths to avoid a negative review, you need to have a threshold amount in your mind, say $300, that you refuse to claim against a damage deposit, and simply blow it off. Do not stand on 'it's a matter of principle.' Rather, think of it as simply avoiding a negative review. As stated earlier, if you seize even .10 cents of a guest's security damage deposit, you have then just triggered World War III, so don't cross that red line unless you absolutely must.

Assuming that your threshold amount has been met and the damages or missing items are significant, you proceed with claiming the damage from the security deposit, and boom, just like that, the funds are transferred from the damage deposit straight into your bank account.

You will need to provide incidental to this claim against the damage deposit a summarized description of the reason for the seizure. Keep it simple, non-emotional, and all business. Inflammatory language must be avoided. At this point, it is not a debate, or a situation that is up for discussion.

The email to the guest when the damage deposit is seized can go as follows:

Thank you so much for being our guests at our vacation rental. It appears that you located our vacation rental, utilized our keyless entry system, enjoyed resort amenities, and were able to enjoy all of the amazing attractions in the area, during your stay with us.

You must have found everything to be satisfactory, including the condition of the unit upon arrival, as we have not heard anything otherwise from you, either during your stay, or upon your departure. We require that all guests report any damage or missing items within one hour of arrival, which was not done in this case.

When our cleaning team arrived at our vacation rental, they noticed multiple violations of our Rules of Stay, damages, and missing items. These include (LIST)

We have applied the dollar-for-dollar cost for the Rules of Stay violations against your refundable damage deposit totaling $____. We are not making any money on what was most likely an accident, but simply trying to be made whole again.

The good news is that the security deposit was sufficient to cover everything. We know and appreciate your wanting to make sure that these accidental issues are taken care of. You do not have to do anything further and we appreciate you being responsible for the accidental oversights, missing items, and or damages.

Thank you again for being our guest and safe travels.

At this point, the guest can simply lay low, and not challenge the seizure of their damage deposit.

However, we have NEVER had a guest lay low when we seized some or all their damage deposit. Again, it is akin to a declaration of war, so put your seatbelts on as it's about to get crazy.

The guest will likely immediately contact VRBO and declare that the owner has unjustifiably 'stolen' their damage deposit. According to the aggrieved guest, the owner should be thrown off the platform for such a heinous and underhanded theft of their damage deposit.

VRBO will then write you the following high-handed email, which immediately catches you off guard, and immediately puts you on the defensive:

We received a serious complaint from your traveler who has not yet received a refund of their deposit. We take these reports seriously and appreciate your prompt response. If you need assistance refunding, you can refer to our Help Center article How do I refund a damage deposit?

We understand there are two sides to every story. We have documented details of the traveler's experience on your account, and now we need your side of the story. Provide us a full response on the action you plan to take to resolve the complaint.

Please reply to this email, using your email providers reply option, within **[2]** days from today with a response to this complaint. **Please answer all questions:**

1. Why has the traveler's deposit not been refunded?
2. If the traveler has not received their full deposit refund, when can they expect it?
3. If you are not providing a refund **we will require documentation** to consider the matter closed, which includes:

- Repair or replacement receipts, and/or related documentation.

If you have not already notified your traveler that you plan to keep any part of their deposit please contact them with this evidence.

If we do not hear back from you by 08/19/2021, we will be forced to suspend your listing until this matter has been resolved. Your listing may also be taken down if the evidence requested above is not sent by the deadline.

We appreciate your attention to this matter and look forward to your reply.

Visit help.vrbo.com for answers to frequently asked questions.

Best regards,
Quinn
Vrbo.com Customer Support

Wow. It seems right out of the gate that VRBO has taken the traveler's side of what happened and is *threatening to suspend your listing* unless you respond within forty-eight (48) hours.

Dorgan says, 'do not panic.' This is a standard form email that goes out every single time an owner claims some or all of a guest's security damage deposit, and the guest then objects.

An important lesson is that if you claim the damage deposit, you will need to be able to justify the claim with receipts, photos, inventory, Rules of Stay, receipts, cost estimates and any other documentation *within 48 hours.*

I do not work in crisis mode. Avoid putting yourself in a situation where you are working on an emergency basis. You have two full weeks or 14 days following a guest's departure to make a claim against the refundable damage deposit. I recommend that you use all of it. Use that 14 days to build your VRBO response, with the needed documentation, so that it is already ready to go, even before you make the actual claim with the guest. That way you can provide the demanded substantiation quickly when you get the VRBO notice that the guest objected to your claim.

Further, the more time that passes between the guest checking out and the time that you make the claim provides multiple benefits to you as the owner.

During the 14-day span, the guest never complained about anything about their stay. VRBO will note that.

Further, the guest is prompted by VRBO on checkout day to leave a review. Waiting 14 days puts some time and distance between when you make the damage claim, and their being notified that they should leave a review.

Ideally, from the owner's perspective, the guest leaves a review in an immediate response to the VRBO prompt following checkout, or within several days at the latest. This review will then be left without the taint or bitterness that you seized their damage deposit (as you haven't – yet) and is more likely to be a more honest review than it would be otherwise.

Please remember though, that if a guest does not leave a review, and you claim the damage deposit on the 14th day following departure, the guest still has up to a year after their stay to leave a review on VRBO. It's a two-week limit on Airbnb – a notable difference.

Strategically, a VRBO guest who damaged the property should wait until the 14-day window expires before leaving an owner review. The owner will know that the guest has not yet left their review, and that, in turn, may weigh against the owner from making a claim. Something to consider. Ideally, the guest leaves the review immediately following checkout, so that you then know that if you make a damage claim, you won't be subjected to a retaliatory review.

Again, assuming the guest did not submit a review before you made the damage claim, you must ask yourself if it is worth a negative review to seize this damage deposit? It is almost guaranteed that the guest will leave a retaliatory review if you seize any of their damage deposit.

Is the damage claim also worth the risk of having your listing shut down if you don't respond on an emergency basis within 48 hours?

The answer is sometimes yes, it is. If the damages are significant, you must do it. Be prepared and have on go all your receipts, photos, estimates, Rules of Stay, inventory and so forth, as you will need to be able to provide that needed response to VRBO quickly.

This brings up another issue. Do not claim a guest's damage deposit just before you go on a cruise or on vacation or will be away from your computer. You must have the ability to provide that needed response within 48 hours of the VRBO letter demanding justification for the seizure.

The good news is that VRBO will back your damage claim, if the issues are well documented, and the damages amount seems reasonable and fair. In the very few instances that we have ever had to seize a guest's damage deposit, we always won the issue, when and if the guest appealed the seizure with VRBO. You simply tell VRBO your story, what happened, and how much it cost to fix the issue. If it is documented, and reasonable, you will win the issue on appeal.

RULE: Do not go to war with a guest over taking some or all their damage deposit, unless it is over a certain threshold amount, and is worth your time and effort to back up the claim on appeal with VRBO and outweighs the substantial risk of picking up a negative review. The good news is that if you document everything, and your damage claim is reasonable and fair under the circumstances, VRBO will back you up on appeal.

Chapter 82

Ten essential steps to follow

to create the perfect response

to a negative review

Even if you follow all the steps as outlined in this book, and everything in your vacation rental and the process to rent the unit is 100% perfect, there will still be the one-off review that catches you by surprise, is completely unfair, or is inaccurate.

What is the best way to handle the review?

First, as the negative review will feel like a personal attack, you must not give in to the temptation to blast back at the guest in your response. Never, ever respond to a review on the first day. Sleep on it and cool down. You will feel compelled to respond quickly, to right the wrong. Again, calm down. The negative review will not be published immediately. You will be given an opportunity to respond before they make the negative review public or included on your listing, so take your time.

Second, once the review has been submitted, you must not give in to the temptation to contact the guest directly through the VRBO platform, via text, or call. Contacting a former guest when you are hurt, frustrated, or feeling wronged by the review will not yield any positive results. If anything, it could escalate matters and then further motivate that guest to leave additional negative reviews on additional platforms, like Google, Facebook, or other sites. Just let them go. One negative review is enough. Don't stir up a dozen more negative reviews by blasting the former guest.

Third, you must not frame your review response in terms of answering the complaining guest, or speaking to the complaining guest through your review, or by lodging personal attacks against the former guest. Indeed, the complaining guest may or may not ever even see your response to their negative review.

Rather, you must focus your response on the future, to prospective guests who have read the negative review, and want to hear your side or version of it. They want to hear your perspective, which may be radically different from the guest's perspective. Then, the prospective guest can make up their own mind on which to believe.

The good news is that prospective guests do tend to give the owner the benefit of the doubt, especially if the negative review is poorly worded, poorly written, or riddled with spelling and grammatical errors. Your job is to reinforce that inherent bias.

Fourth, comb through the negative review to find anything positive that they have to say and create a list of those comments. These positive comments will be restated at the beginning of your response.

Fifth, characterize what happened as unfortunate, but you have a system in place or a policy in place to handle the subject of the negative review. You explain that the guest failed to avail them of your procedures to correct the issue, or finally, declined your tendered assistance to take care of the issue.

In other words, you want to acknowledge what happened was unfortunate, but then focus on how you either fixed it, or explain that the guest failed to let you know about it to give you an opportunity to fix it. You flip the script – it is their own fault for not following your procedures to take care of the problem, or you took care of the problem and they still complained, or the issue was a temporary anomaly.

Yes, admit when needed that something wasn't perfect.

For instance, if the towels and sheets were old admit it and then state that they were subsequently replaced. The prospective guest will appreciate your candor. They then know the issue was fixed and they then disregard the complaint – which is what we want.

Sixth, it's all about perspective. The guest is mad about the wait for the elevator. Explain why there was a wait and how this was a one-time thing. The guest says the AC doesn't work. Respond that the AC worked perfectly for the guest both immediately prior and immediately after this guest stay, and is a new system, with a state-of-the-art dehumidification system. In other words, after the prospective guest reads your answer to the review, they say to themselves 'Aha' that makes sense. They then understand that the complaint is either unfounded, unreasonable, or retaliatory. There are always two sides to the story so make sure your story or perspective is told.

Seventh, it is ok to bite back, a little. It is alright to mention at the conclusion of your response the really bad things that the guest did. It helps frame or solidify why their negative review was unjustified, unfair, or retaliatory. Keep it brief though.

Eighth, you then finish on a positive note by describing how this issue was remedied in time for the next guest checking in, or highlight all of the efforts that you took to address the problem.

Ninth, have a friend or co-worker or another vacation rental property owner or a teacher friend review the negative review and your proposed response. Make sure your response is grammatically correct, with no misspellings. It needs to be a professionally sounding response.

Tenth, do not respond to every less than five-star review. The only time we ever respond is if there is a serious complaint that might potentially persuade a prospective guest who happens to see the negative review, to not book your vacation rental. Otherwise, leave the 'almost perfect' but not entirely perfect reviews alone. To get a response out of you, the negative review needs to be bad. Focus on the substance of what they complain about, not necessarily the number of stars.

Assuming you have followed all of the guidance in this book, negative reviews should be few and far between. However, when and if they do happen, you will be prepared.

I have pulled several real-life negative reviews from each of our properties, and then provided our response. In each, see how each of the foregoing techniques are used in the Host's response (i.e., my response).

These are actual, real reviews, with my responses, which (hopefully) incorporate the listed techniques.

FROM PHOENIX ON THE BAY

Great

4/5

Stayed Jan 2022

Carter M.

It was a easy process and host was very Accommodable to our needs. I have four stars as the floors were dirty and the pools weren't kid friendly. But overall I would say it was a great stay and we enjoyed our time. I felt like a second home.

Published Feb 9, 2022

Host's response:

We are pleased this guest thought of the condo as their 'second home' and found the booking process to be easy and accommodating. This family with children were coming in January, the peak of snowbird season, and during a time that the water slide, lazy River and other children's amenities were temporarily closed for repairs. Within an hour of their booking the unit, we offered free cancellation so that they could stay somewhere else. After contemplating their options, they chose to stay anyway. This review is unfortunate as they knew in advance that they would be staying in the middle of winter / snowbird season, at a resort where the most popular children's amenities would be closed, and then complained about it in a review. We also have a 24/7 hotline to call for a complimentary return visit for cleaning oversights, which this guest did not use, which is unfortunate. We respectfully request that if a guest is informed of an amenity closure in advance, and chooses to stay anyway, that they then not ding us in a review about the closure.

FROM APPALACHIAN HIGH CABIN:

Great place to stay

3/5

Stayed Mar 2021

alicia a.

How ever the hot tub wasnt clean and gave my children and I a rash but other then that its a beautiful place

Published Mar 19, 2021

Host's response:

We are pleased this guest thought the cabin was beautiful. In regard to the hot tub, it is completely emptied, sanitized, filter rinsed and bleached, between every guest stay, and the clean water then treated continuously with bromine in a floating dispenser. We also have a 24 hour call line for cleaning oversights which was not used by this guest. Following this guest's departure, the hot tub water was found brown, full of trash, and the tub full of sand. This guest also trashed the cabin, hosted a party, destroyed personal property, and lost a portion of their damage deposit. As this guest is not welcome back at this cabin, the retaliatory review is not a surprise.

FROM SPLASH RESORT 704 WEST

Had fun except for waiting for elevator

5/5
Stayed May 2021
David S.
Everything with the unit was fine. Property ownership needs to add elevators for check in and check out traffic. We had to stand in the suffocating heat for an hour to get an elevator to check out. Finally got on the 18th one that stopped at our floor.
Published Jun 20, 2021

Host's response:
Splash elevator service OTIS completed state mandated service (which could not be pushed to winter) resulting in 50% loss of elevator capacity. As this unit is on a lower floor, the two sets of stairways may be used for shorter trips to the beach or pool. Checking in / out though is a much more difficult issue when only one elevator runs, which stinks. If it helps any, OTIS scheduled their work during the weekdays leaving the busier weekends at full capacity. Also, their work is now complete, and the elevators are back running at full capacity in time for the busy summer season.

FROM SPLASH RESORT 704 WEST

Fun and relaxing stay!

4/5
Stayed Jun 2019
Holly O.
The condo owner was really easy to communicate with. Our unit was nice with a fantastic view as describe on VRBO. The beach service was excite and friendly. The only complaints we have is that the RipTide bar and grill on site was under new management and did not provide a lot to desired and had advertisement still hanging at the RipTide Bar that provided Fat Tuesday products. The pool area was very crowded and the elevators were very slow. The unit floor was very sandy as well as the linens in the beds and the linens need replacing. The stove top did not appear to be cleaned. The condo was decorated nicely and spacious! Overall we enjoyed our stay at this unit.
Published Jul 14, 2019

Host's response:
We are super pleased this guest loved the gorgeous 7th floor Gulf front views, spacious unit, and friendly beach chair and umbrella service. We just purchased two new sets of towels and sheets for this unit so this may have been one of the last guests to use the old sets (which were indeed due to be retired). Also guests should not rely upon the onsite lunch cafe for all their meals, as the menu is extremely limited. Guests should either grill out, prepare meals in the unit, or dine at the 50 plus restaurants available within just a few miles of Splash. Finally, we encourage guests to use the provided 24/7 cleaning service hotline, which is complimentary, for cleaning oversights that are observed at the beginning of their stay,

FROM SPLASH RESORT 902 WEST

Was not clean. No trash bags and a/c didn't work good.

3/5

Stayed Jul 2021

Tashia L.

Was not clean. No trash bags and a/c didn't work good.

Published Aug 4, 2021

Host's response:
All guests are provided a complimentary 24/7 hotline for any cleaning oversights or maintenance issues. This guest did not avail themselves of the complimentary service or contact the owner at any point during their stay. After this guest checked out, and was on their way home, our cleaning crew arrived to service the unit and discovered multiple violations of rules of stay, damaged personal property, and other issues resulting in forfeiture of this guest's damage deposit. We then received this poor review, which is likely tied to the guest's dissatisfaction with the loss of their damage deposit. To be clear - the unit's AC is relatively new, and includes a state of the art dehumidification system. It has and continues to work properly for guests who stayed both before and after this guest stay. All guests are provided starter supplies (trash bags, paper towels, toilet paper, hand soap, dish soap, dishwasher soap, shampoo and body wash). Guests are then instructed to supplement those starter supplies as needed depending upon the length of their stay. This is standard practice in the vacation rental business. Our cleaning crew consistently gets great reviews. Call backs to fix cleaning oversights are available 24/7. Fortunately, damage deposit claims and disputes such as this are extremely rare, which is good news.

Chapter 83

Handling family and friends

In your excitement of purchasing your vacation rental, you post photos on Facebook of you and your family enjoying the new vacation rental and all that it has to offer. You even create a Facebook page for the vacation rental and share it with all your friends and family.

Even if you are super low key about the vacation rental purchase, friends and family inevitably will find out that you headed over to Panama City Beach for Spring Break, and that you have a condo there. They will see your pictures of your kids skiing at Ober Gatlinburg. On each occasion, the questions arise – so where are you staying?

What then inevitably happens is that a friend or family member will ask you to use your vacation rental or will dance around the topic enough in the hopes that you will just offer the vacation rental to them, and during that request, there is no discussion about payment terms, rules, policies, cancellations, or that they can't bring their dog with them. It could happen as casually as your hairdresser asking you about a potential stay over a haircut, or a friend from high school who sees you at a party and then 'hits you up' for the potential stay.

I kid you not – we get some type of roundabout inquiry from a friend, or family member, or someone asking for their friend about potentially staying, all the time. Their hope is that we will simply let them book the vacation rental and stay for free.

First and foremost, you need to remember that when these requests come in, they do not ask to come and stay 'with' you, they just want to use the vacation rental. This is not turning down someone that is trying to spend time with you. In those cases, where the family member or friend is staying with you, the rules are different, and we will discuss those rules shortly.

What is the best way to handle this conundrum? You can't simply let people stay in your vacation rental for free and lose valuable rental income, and potentially expose the unit to wear and tear, breakdowns, and other problems, all on a complimentary basis. You did not set up this elaborate system to not make any money, but still, it's a friend or family member and you want to try and play nice.

Think about it – if you let a friend or family member stay during season for free for a week at the beach during the summer, without you being a part of that stay, the value of that $500 nightly rate alone would be $3500, in the form of lost rental income, during peak season.

You then need to ask yourself, "am I prepared to write an (imaginary) check to this friend or family member for $3500?" The answer is likely no. Again, it is lost income from your pocket, so you are not actually paying the friend or family member, you just end up at the end of the year with $3500 less in gross rental revenues.

Realistically, you probably didn't even give this friend or family member something for Christmas last year, so why in tarnation would you give the friend or family member $3500? If it is an old high school friend, the outrageousness of handing over $3500 to someone you haven't seen in years becomes even more crystal clear. But nevertheless, the requests will come in, in varied forms, and in every shape and manner, on a consistent basis, so be ready.

I recommend the following policies in this area.

If it is a friend or family member, and they want to stay in your vacation rental, and wish to book or reserve way in advance, I recommend that you simply provide them the VRBO listing number, and instruct them to make an inquiry through VRBO. You then send them a custom quote for their stay. You generously provide a 'friends and family' discount in an amount you deem appropriate under the circumstances. However, it is still arm's length. Taxes are still paid. You are using your templates and automated system for booking and the key code. Your cleaners clean as usual.

By the way, NEVER allow a guest, friend, or family member to try and clean the unit following their own stay to save on the cleaning fee. That will absolutely lead to a subsequent guest complaint on the cleanliness of the unit. Further, the guest will not have all the regular starter supplies that your cleaning team provides with each turn.

9 out of 10 times when you just say this is the procedure that we are going to follow, the friend or family member does not follow up, even in those situations where you gratuitously provided a dramatic discount for their stay. Again, they are simply hoping that they can stay for free. When they realize that you do not do that, they drop the request.

There are exceptions. If it is a parent or child, then yes you can allow for an advance reservation and allow them to stay for free. Indeed, I think my parents have stayed at one or two of our vacation properties, but it was only one time in ten years. They really don't have any interest in staying at our properties without us. This is a sign that they want to spend time with us – not 'use us' for our vacation properties.

In addition, you need to avoid those friends or family members who want to do an 'off the books' stay, and they just Venmo you a lump sum, and skip taxes, and skip the damage deposit and so forth.

Do not take the Venmo bait. Let me explain why.

First, you are then setting up a stay outside of the VRBO process, so you immediately lose the $1M in liability coverage if the guest gets hurt during their stay and they try and sue you.

Second, you lose the advantage of having a damage deposit. The guest has zero motivation to follow your Rules of Stay. If there is a problem, you then risk losing the family relationship or friendship if something is broken or torn up during the stay, or if they smoke in the unit, as the friend or family member will not want to pay for the damage or excessive cleaning fee. If you choose to waive reimbursement, the bitterness of the deal could potentially tarnish the family relationship, or friendship.

Third, this guest will then want a myriad of exceptions to rules that are non-negotiable. They will bring other friends or family members that you do not know and may exceed capacity. They will host a party. They will bring their pets. They will shoot off fireworks into the woods. They won't follow check-out procedures and Rules of Stay. So you then are in this situation where you have to tell this 'friend' why they cannot bring their dog, an uncomfortable situation for you to be in, especially since they are your friend. It is hard to tell friends or family members 'No' on issues such as this.

Fourth, taxes are not then paid, and you run the risk of an audit.

Fifth, as soon as you do an 'off the books' rental with the friend or family member, they will expect the same treatment again and again and again in the future.

For the foregoing reasons and many more, do not do 'off the books' rentals. Simply provide a reasonable discount based on your discretion with the person staying, but still run the stay through VRBO.

There will be situations where you stay in your vacation rental, and you have along a friend or family member. In those cases, the guest or family member does not have to pay anything, as they are there to spend time with you and your family, especially if this is a close friend or family member that rarely stays.

For those close family members or friends who stay often or frequently, it may be reasonable for them to cover the cleaning fee, or perhaps take you to dinner or something similar.

The main thing is that you do not pick up a family member or friend who always 'expects' to get the extra room for free every time you visit any given vacation rental. Be wary of that situation as they may not actually be wanting to spend time with you, but rather, are using you for the free accommodation. This is sad but does happen.

What about last-minute stays?

Yes, if it is Friday afternoon, and Friday and Saturday night have not yet booked, the unit is empty, and you are not able to otherwise use the unit yourself, you absolutely may offer it to a friend, client, acquaintance, or family member to use on a last-minute basis for free. However, they must follow all rules of stay, pay the cleaning fees, pay the parking pass fees or any other expenses of stay. I do not recommend extending a free stay to anyone unless they at least pay the cost of the cleaning fee and parking pass. You do not want to lose money by having someone stay for free. You at least want it to be a wash for you if it's a last-minute stay.

Usually, you want to look for that family member or friend who then tries to reciprocate the generosity. They not only pay the cleaning fee and parking pass fee, but during their stay, notice that the coffee maker is broken, and run to Walmart to pick one up and replace it at their own expense.

The staying guest upon their return wants to 'take you all to dinner' and wine and dine you on their own nickel in appreciation for you letting them stay for the weekend.

The guest staying for free methodically washed every quilt in the unit, so that by the end of their stay, everything in the unit had been laundered. It was not a huge deal – they did it in the unit's washer and dryer, but that generous gesture alone is huge to a vacation rental owner. They also did not gripe about having to do it – they 'surprised' you with their generous gesture over dinner and drinks a few days after their stay.

These are the types of guests that you want in your unit on a last-minute basis, as otherwise, it would simply sit empty, so it might as well be used.

However, if you extend the free stay last minute to a friend or family member, and the following happens, don't extend the offer again.

1   They want to bring their dog. This is against HOA rules, and they will inevitably leave dog hair, soil the carpet, or infest your unit with fleas. These people are staying for free. For Pete's sake, they should not ask to bring their dog.

2   They want to bring one or two sets of friends that you do not know. Those friends are then 'grateful' to the person staying for free, not you.

3   They won't commit either way whether they want to stay or not, resulting in your not being able to offer the vacation rental to someone else.

4   They say yes, they want to use it and then never do.

5   They ruin towels or pillowcases with mascara, break a wine glass, and spill red wine on the sofa - and don't fix it.

6   They complain about something in the unit (the batteries are dead in the remote) and don't fix it or do anything about it. They provide you a list of all the things wrong in the unit and call the production of the list to you as their effort to 'help you out.'

7   They insist that they can clean the unit themselves and should not have to pay the cleaning fee.

8   They leave the unit in a mess causing your cleaner to charge you an excessive cleaning fee.

9   They promise to pay the cleaning fee but never do.

10   You ask them to do one thing, to just wash one quilt, and they are too busy during their stay to get around to it and take offense that we even asked them to do that.

11   They get the code, and then let their close friend go and use the unit – someone you don't even know.

12   Even worse, they say they are going to stay, but don't and instead let their teens, or their college kids stay with their friends who exceed capacity and make a mess.

Every one of the preceding examples are possible on last minute gratuitous stays. Be mentally prepared for possibility. If the guest does any of the foregoing, nip it in the bud and never offer the unit again to them on a last-minute basis.

On a final note, you occasionally may have someone ask you to donate a stay at the beach for some worthy cause. I also recently had both a cleaner and a maintenance person ask me if I would let a pastor or missionary and their family stay on a complimentary basis.

As you can probably guess, I don't recommend doing any of that. It is a no-win situation. The staying guest does not know you personally. They will not be grateful to you. If they trash the unit, it may compromise your relationship with the intermediary. It is not worth it.

There are occasional exceptions.

We recently had a bad ice storm in Pigeon Forge, and my cleaning person lost power, and it was 5 degrees on her first night with no heat. Our cabin was empty, and had power, was clean and otherwise rental ready. She did not ask me to stay but I offered our place anyway. She was so grateful.

She made me promise that I would not block off the calendar and agreed that if someone booked last minute that she would immediately vacate and get it cleaned and rental ready in time. She said it once she said it hundred times – do not lose a potential stay because I am here. That was very thoughtful.

Later, after only staying two nights, she then told me she had deep cleaned the whole place in appreciation.

That stay was a 'win win' for everyone.

RULE: For friends and family members wishing to book a vacation in advance, require that the stay be run through VRBO and provide them a small or significant nightly rate discount that is appropriate to the level of relationship. There is a rare exception to this rule if a parent or your children wants to stay. For last minute vacancies, you can let someone stay for free if they cover the cleaning fee and parking pass and reciprocate in some way your generosity.

Chapter 84

Whether to rent to snowbirds, and if so, how to do it

During a vacation rental off season, one may consider a 'snowbird' or longer-term rental.

First, what is a snowbird?

A snowbird is the generic term for an older, retired person who travels from the North to the Southern states to escape the cold and stay in warmer weather during January and February, the slowest months of the year along the beaches.

Why rent to a snowbird?

The goal in renting to a snowbird is to keep the vacation rental occupied and in use, and at least 'break even' during time that the unit typically sits empty.

Let me explain.

January is a notoriously slow month at our vacation rentals along the beaches. If the unit is not rented, the vacation rental operates at a total loss as there is no one staying for the entire month. Ideally, we at least get a snowbird to pay something to help offset that loss, or to at least 'break even.'

There are also other benefits of having a snowbird.

Up at our cabin, during long periods of vacancy, I worry whether the unit might be broken into due to its remote location and extended vacancy, or whether there is a water leak, or some other catastrophe that we do not know about. Believe it or not, the biggest risk of theft is not from your guests, but from those times where someone may break into your vacation rental during a period of extended vacancy.

In essence, having paying guests occupy your vacation rental provides a certain sense of security, versus having the unit sitting empty for an extended period.

For the foregoing reasons, it is great to have a snowbird during the slowest of months. Icemakers are being used instead of freezing over. The air is being circulated and exchanged. The use of the unit or vacation rental keeps it moving and alive and functioning.

Think of the automobile – which tends to deteriorate rapidly when stored and not put to consistent use. The car battery dies. Mildew or mold grows. Tires dry rot.

Similarly, it is better to have your vacation rental occupied rather than sitting vacant for extended periods, if possible.

We list on our property description the following to attract snowbirds:

SNOWBIRDS: Please inquire about our competitive rates, for one of the best units at (list name of resort).

The snowbird will then contact you to check your monthly rate for the months of November, December, January and/or February, the slowest months down on the beaches. We usually get a standard rental for January and February, at minimum.

The snowbird stay cannot bleed too much into March as that is Spring Break and we can make a lot more money off standard vacation rentals, so we try and wrap up all snowbird stays by March 1.

Similarly, we also hope for a Christmas and/or New Year's rental, so start the snowbird stay on January 2 or later.

The snowbird stay can be an awesome deal if you get a great snowbird that doesn't complain, doesn't 'nit-pick' things, and is generally a happy camper.

One of our first snowbirds was a real pickle. The unit wasn't clean enough on arrival. The unit did not have enough blankets and they expected us to buy some extra and *immediately* deliver to them. They complained about amenities being down for maintenance. They were so big and heavy they left giant valleys in our master bedroom bed. They cooked bacon every morning leaving a slimy goo on all our kitchen cabinets and walls. We literally deep cleaned at the beginning of their stay, but then had to deep clean again right after they left – all at our expense. It went on and on from there. I honestly had decided to not do a snowbird rental ever again after that first poor snowbird experience.

We then had new snowbirds in both Panama City Beach, Florida and Orange Beach, Alabama. These snowbirds were cool. They were flexible on the first and last day of stay. They paid for anything they needed that was under $100. I literally never heard a word from them. If a bulb or battery went out, they fixed it.

These snowbirds are still with us today, and are now in their 80's. We only met them for the first time recently, despite over eight seasons with us. This is the type of snowbird that you want. Ideal snowbirds are out there – it may just take a couple tries in finding a good one.

So how do you get a good snowbird?

First, do not be the cheapest unit in the resort. You want someone that is looking for quality, not just the bottom-line dollar. You do not want a penny-pinching uptight snowbird in your unit.

Second, tell the snowbird your expectations. Tell them from the very beginning that this is a 'hands off' rental, that the unit is 'as is,' that there are no refunds, and that anything under $100 is their responsibility. You are looking for a 'happy camper.' Whiners or complainers are not welcome. You do not rent to smokers – even if they smoke outside. They can take it or leave it.

Often, the snowbird inquiry comes a full year before their proposed stay, and there may be an opportunity for them to look at the unit before deciding – let them do that.

Believe it or not, after we show them the unit, and literally 'read them the riot act' about our requirement that they must be happy campers, they accept, and we never hear a peep out of them.

Third, once you get a good snowbird, go out of your way to keep them. Do not rent the unit out from under them for the next season. Always give the good snowbird the right of first refusal for next season.

Typically, as well, I try and never raise their rate and stick with the same rate each year.

Fourth, charge them if their stay starts bleeding over into Spring Break. The monthly rate in January and February is super affordable. However, once they start staying into March, the nightly rates dramatically increase to $200 or $300 per night or higher for Spring Break. Believe it or not, the snowbird will pay a higher rate for March, so go ahead and quote a reasonable rate that is less than the full amount but more than the inexpensive standard snowbird rate. Sometimes they will pay it, even if it is dramatically more than the rate for January and February. If the snowbird balks at the higher March rate, then they need to end their stay on March 1.

The question then becomes whether to run the snowbird stay through the VRBO platform or not. The answer is - it depends.

If you get a signed lease from the snowbird for a leased term, the lease arrangement potentially removes the unit from short term rental status and is then considered a longer-term rental, where lodging taxes do not then have to be paid. This assumes that the term of the monthly lease is of a sufficient minimum length of time (i.e., it's a several month lease not a short-term vacation rental stay) to remove it from being considered as a vacation rental.

Check your local laws to determine how long the monthly term stay must be before it's considered to be a residential lease (where there are no lodging taxes due) versus a short term vacation rental (where lodging taxes are required to be paid).

On VRBO, you simply block the months off for the snowbird and simply correspond with the snowbird directly by email, text, or phone calls.

As this stay would not be booked through VRBO, you definitely want standard Homeowners insurance to pick up any liability claim if the snowbird were injured during their stay.

We check with other owners, and other management companies, to see what the going rate is for snowbird rentals, and match those rates, or maybe go a little higher, as we feel our unit is furnished better, maintained better, and or may have better views than our competition.

What's the snowbird process? It's not an easy answer. Every vacation rental owner may approach this differently.

We require a simple, signed lease from the snowbird (unit is 'as is,' no pets, no smoking, etc.).

We then require 50% down at the time of booking, which is nonrefundable. We then require the balance paid at least 30 days in advance of stay. We also require a refundable damage deposit on their first snowbird stay, but after that, the refundable damage deposit is waived on subsequent stays. We do not charge cleaning fees. It is a monthly term lease with a signed lease - so not a short-term vacation rental, and we state that in the written lease. The guest typically pays by check when the lease is signed and returned. By requiring 50% down and nonrefundable, this means that the guest is serious about staying.

Further, requiring that the last check be received at least thirty days in advance of stay assures that the check will indeed clear. We then send the guest the KABA code for entry after their final payment clears – not before.

I am generally bullish lately on having our vacation rentals booked with a snowbird during the slow months. We have had good results from it, after getting some great snowbirds onto our properties. If you get a whiner or complainer, simply ask them to stay elsewhere next year and wait for another snowbird that may be a better fit.

RULE: Consider a long-term lease with a snowbird or renter for the slowest months of the year. Be very picky about your snowbird – you want a happy camper – not a whiner or complainer.

Chapter 85

How do you conduct a periodic safety review?

After you get your vacation rental up and running, you then need to physically visit the vacation rental in person and perform a safety review.

What is a safety review?

A safety review is where you visit your vacation rental and brainstorm all the different ways that a guest could possibly hurt themselves when staying in the unit. You then do a second sweep and imagine every possible scenario where a child or toddler could hurt themselves when staying in the unit.

Finally, your final sweep is to consider what could possibly happen if your guest was intoxicated, and how they might possibly hurt themselves.

With all that in mind, and after you identify the risks, the next step is to either eliminate the hazard, or if not completely eliminate the hazard, mitigate the hazard. If the hazard cannot be eliminated or mitigated, warn of the hazard.

An effective warning will ideally be both visibly displayed in the vacation rental and provided in your check in instructions.

Accidents happen. However, you want to do everything in your power to prevent a guest from being injured during their stay. Even if you do, you still may have an accident, and someone may still get hurt. This is why it is critical that you have homeowners' liability insurance in place for this contingency, and as an additional layer of protection, run the stays through VRBO for an additional $1M in liability coverage if someone is hurt on premises.

As an attorney, I assure you that if a guest is injured during a vacation rental stay, they will consult an attorney. The personal injury attorney will then determine whether the vacation rental owner was somehow negligent, or made a mistake, that may have caused the guest to be injured. If so, there will be a demand and potentially, litigation. Again, this is why you should carry insurance in case something like this were to ever happen.

When you perform your safety sweep from three perspectives – general risks, a child's risk, and then finally an inebriated guest risk, you then take the steps to eliminate the risk, mitigate the risk, and warn of the risk. The final step is to document the steps that you have taken and efforts you have taken to keep your guests safe.

We recently performed a safety review of our vacation rental in Pigeon Forge, TN and found a series of concerns which we ultimately addressed. We either eliminated the risk, mitigated the risk, and/or warned of the risk, with placards on site, and warnings attached to our check in instructions.

Cabin hot tub

When we purchased our cabin, the owner explained that the hot tub had been replaced but was saddened that the hot tub company replaced the tub with their largest unit, which barely fit on the balcony, and was too big for the space. It was a seven-person hot tub. It was huge.

I immediately was concerned about several things.

The hot tub is on our top balcony three floors up off the ground, on a wooden porch. I was concerned that the weight of the hot tub, when full of water and up to seven adults, may possibly cause the balcony to fail or collapse.

Fortunately, my father is a civil structural engineer, and during a stay, provided me a free inspection of the structural support of the balcony and declared the set up as safe. Whew.

I then looked at the hot tub from a child's perspective.

I quickly realized that due to the hot tub being right up against the railing, a child could easily fall out of the tub, over the railing, and three floors to the ground below if they just sat on the edge of the hot tub. Was it foreseeable for someone to occasionally sit on the edge of the hot tub? Absolutely. The hot tub edge was then just inches from the balcony railing top rail, and the same height.

That proximity to the edge was a major concern. Even if we warned of the danger, we decided that was not enough, as the risk of death or great bodily harm was readily apparent.

In other words, one cannot simply warn away a safety issue when the risk is that severe. One needs to try and eliminate that risk, or at a minimum, dramatically mitigate the risk, not just warn of it when the consequences are that significant.

The second major concern that I had was looking at it if a person was inebriated in the hot tub. If that person stood up, and they lost their balance, which is easy to do in a slippery hot tub, they could fall over and there would be no railing to catch them before falling to the ground three stories below.

These concerns were so serious that I determined that simply warning of the dangers would be insufficient. We needed to mitigate or eliminate the danger immediately.

My first possible fix was to put up an additional railing, but that ran into two issues. It impeded the view. Second, I had to get HOA approval to modify or add to our existing railing.

Becoming increasingly alarmed, and due to the need to move quickly on my concerns, I decided to replace the hot tub with a smaller tub – an $8,000 decision.

By replacing the large tub with a smaller one, there was in turn less risk of a balcony collapse as the total weight of water and tub was dramatically reduced. With a lower tub capacity, the total weight of guests using the tub was also reduced.

With the smaller tub, which has a large space between the tub and the balcony railing, we do not now have to worry about a child crawling or falling over the edge.

We also don't have to worry about a drunk losing their balance and falling over the edge of the railing. If they fell out of the tub, they would simply fall to the balcony floor, as the balcony railing is now too far away from the edge of the smaller tub.

Despite all of this, we still have inherent risks with a hot tub on premises. Older folks, pregnant women or people in poor health could overheat. Children could drown. So, for those risks, we attached those warnings to the check-in instructions for the cabin. We also listed a minimum age for use of the tub and required that children of all ages always be supervised.

Cabin loft ladder

We have a steep, wooden ladder that goes from the second floor to the third-floor loft area. So, let's check the safety of that from three perspectives.

The first perspective is that any given ladder is dangerous. So, we placed a sign or placard by the ladder that says, 'Fall Risk,' and warned of the danger in our check in instructions.

We then knew that kids love to stay in the treehouse loft. We realized that when the kids went up and down the ladder with socks on, the ladder became very slippery.

To mitigate the risk of fall, we then applied nonskid strips on the ladder rungs.

Finally, we looked at that ladder from the perspective of having an inebriated guest try and maneuver it. We could not eliminate the risk (the ladder is necessary to access the ceiling loft), and we mitigated the risk to the extent we could with nonskid strips, so all that we could then was to warn the guests in their check in email not to navigate the ladder if under influence, elderly, not ambulatory, or in poor health.

We also directed that toddlers, babies, and kids of insufficient age, the elderly or infirm not be permitted to use the ladder.

Cabin rocking chairs

We have rocking chairs on both balconies. They are polywood so hold up well, even for a heavier guest (a concern that we should plan for). We don't have to worry about the rockers collapsing, a key advantage that polywood has over a wooden rocking chair.

However, when we sat in the chairs and started rocking, we realized that directly behind the rockers are the cabin's large picture windows.

What would happen if someone rocked back into the window?

So, we weighed whether we should or should not remove the rockers entirely. That was not a workable option as everyone has rockers on their balcony and they are necessary to enjoy the views.

To mitigate the risk, it would entail covering or blocking the large picture window views of the mountains — another difficult choice.

So we simply warned the guests to not rock back into the windows in their check-in instructions, and to keep the rockers positioned away from the picture windows.

In addition, we have instructed the cleaners to make sure the rockers are moved far from the windows and out to the middle of each balcony.

RULE: Perform a safety review of your vacation rental on a regular basis. Brainstorm all the different ways someone could possibly get hurt. After you identify any potential safety issues, eliminate the risk if possible. If the risk cannot be eliminated (i.e., you need a ladder to access the loft), mitigate the risk (i.e., apply nonskid to the rungs). Finally, warn of the risk by physical placard or sign and in your check-in instructions.

Risk of Fall from Balcony Hot Tub Warning

Although this is a beautiful view, the following could happen

- a child could crawl out of the hot tub and over the railing and fall three floors to the ground.
- An inebriated guest could lose their balance in the hot tub and fall over the railing three floors to the ground.
- A guest trying to stand up in the hot tub could lose their balance and fall over the edge three floors to the ground.
- Teenagers horseplaying in the hot tub could cause someone to fall over the railing or push someone over the railing three floors to the ground.

Any one of the foregoing possibilities could result in SERIOUS INJURY OR DEATH as it is a three story drop from the edge of the railing by the hot tub to the ground below.

As a result, please observe (at minimum) the following rules:

1   **Young children, babies and or toddlers are strictly prohibited from using the hot tub.**

2   **Children and Teens are banned from use of the hot tub unless carefully supervised by an adult and warned of the imminent fall risk from the hot tub.**

3   Horseplay by anyone is prohibited (one could easily be pushed over the railing).

4   Standing in the hot tub is prohibited (one could lose their balance and fall over the railing)

5   Excessive consumption of alcohol is prohibited. Loss of balance or blacking out could result in a fall over the edge of the hot tub.

6   Excessive time in the hot tub is prohibited as that could impact one's balance, and potentially falling over the edge of the hot tub.

7   Those with limited physical stamina, in advance age with mobility issues, balance and or strength issues, are prohibited from using the hot tub, due to the risk of losing their balance when using the tub and potentially falling over the edge of the hot tub, or falling when trying to enter or exit the tub.

8   Sitting on the edge of the hot tub is NEVER PERMITTED.

USE OF THE HOT TUB IS AT YOUR OWN RISK. DUE TO THE RISK OF FALL OVER THE BALCONY RAILING, PLEASE CAREFULLY SUPERVISE ALL USERS OF THE HOT TUB. PLEASE MAKE SURE CHILDREN AND TEENS ARE PROHIBITED FROM USING THE HOT TUB UNLESS UNDER STRICT SUPERVISION. EVERYONE IN THE CABIN SHOULD BE WARNED OF THE FALL RISK FROM USING THE HOT TUB. THOSE WITH LIMITED MOBILITY ISSUES SHOULD NOT USE THE HOT TUB DUE TO THE INHERENT RISK OF FALL.

Risk of Fall from 3rd floor Loft / Steep Ladder Warning

There is a third-floor loft, accessed by a steep vertical ladder, available for informal sleeping accommodations.

The loft is one story off the game room level (that's very high), difficult to maneuver and or traverse, and is not designed for toddlers, children, inebriated adults, or those with limited mobility issues.

Due to the risk of fall, babies, toddlers, and younger children are prohibited from climbing any of the ladders in the cabin, using the top bunk, and or using / playing / sleeping in the loft.

Anyone with limited mobility and or strength issues should not use the ladders or loft or top bunk due to the inherent risk of fall from the steep ladders and or accessing these respective spaces.

Anyone who attempts to come down the ladder at night when it is dark runs a SERIOUS RISK OF FALL due to the limited lighting and or their vision without their glasses on or their current sleepy state. Guests should be specifically warned of this danger and should not traverse the ladders unless they are adequately lit, and they are in a condition to be able to traverse the ladders safely.

Anyone under the influence of alcohol or a medication that effects their balance should never attempt to traverse any of the ladders in the cabin.

Due to the risk of fall - luggage, toys, food, drinks, and other personal items are prohibited to be brought up into the loft area. This area is designed to informally accommodate sleeping only.

THE USE OF THE LADDER AND THIRD FLOOR LOFT AND THE LADDER TO THE QUEEN BUNK ARE AT YOUR OWN RISK.

SERIOUS INJURY AND OR DEATH MAY RESULT FROM FALLS FROM THE LADDERS, AND OR LOFT AREAS.

TODDLERS, BABIES, THOSE WITH LIMITED MOBILITY, AND YOUNG CHILDREN ARE PROHIBITED FROM THE LOFT AND OR TOP BUNK.

OLDER CHILDREN / TEENS / AND THOSE WITH SUFFICIENT MOBILITY SHOULD EXERCISE CAUTION ON THE LADDERS AND IN THE LOFT / TOP BUNK AND ONLY WITH COMPETENT SUPERVISION.

DUE TO THE RISK OF FALL, HORSEPLAY IN THE LOFT, ON THE LADDERS AND OR ON THE TOP QUEEN BUNK, IS STRICTLY PROHIBITED.

Rocking Chair Risk of Shattering Balcony Windows Located Behind the Rockers

Although the rocking chairs have epic views, the rockers are all situated or lined up across both balconies and back up to the large picture windows across the front of the cabin.

If the rocking chair is too close to the window behind the chair, and rocks backwards, the back of the rocker could hit the balcony window and cause someone to fall through the glass to the floor below, and or shatter the giant balcony glass causing serious injury or death.

Rocking back into the balcony glass could cause serious injury and or death, from either the broken glass, or falling to the floor below, and or cause substantial monetary damage to the cabin (as replacing a window of that size would be an enormous undertaking).

THERE IS A RISK OF SERIOUS INJURY OR DEATH IF THE ROCKERS BREAK THE BALCONY WINDOWS. GUESTS ARE RESPONSIBLE FOR ANY DAMAGE THEY CAUSE, INCLUDING BREAKING CABIN WINDOWS, REGARDLESS OF WHETHER IT WAS ACCIDENTAL OR NOT.

Due to the risk of breaking the balcony glass on both balconies of the cabin, and the risk of injury or death associated with accidentally breaking the glass, please observe the following rules:

1   Toddlers, young children and infants are prohibited from rocking in the rocking chairs, as they may rock backwards into the windows.

2   Toddlers, young children and infants are prohibited from being on the balcony, as toddlers and young children could climb on the rockers and fall over the railing to the ground several floors below as well.

3   Rocking chair position should be closely monitored by you at all times to be a sufficient distance from the balcony windows so as not to break the large picture windows on the balcony.

4   MOVE THE ROCKERS AND OR SMALL END TABLES to the center of the balcony to avoid hitting the glass behind the rockers.

5   Warn all guests about the risk of rocking backwards into the glass which could break the glass and cause injury or death.

6   Carefully supervise children and teens if they use the rockers and warn them of the glass danger behind the rockers. Horseplay with the rockers is strictly prohibited.

BLACK BEAR WARNING

Black Bears of all sizes live nearby and frequent The Preserve daily.

PLEASE KEEP CAR DOORS LOCKED AND NEVER LEAVE FOOD IN CAR.

ALL TRASH MUST BE SECURED IN THE PROVIDED FORTIFIED BINS
AND <u>LATCHED SHUT</u>.

IF OUTSIDE TRASH BINS ARE FULL (BINS ARE NOT EMPTIED UNTIL YOU
CHECKOUT), OR IF YOU ARE TRYING TO DISPOSE OF FOOD, PLEASE SIMPLY DROP
THE GARBAGE OFF ON YOUR WAY TO PIGEON FORGE, AS FOLLOWS:

Pigeon Forge Free / Drive Thru Garbage Drop
447 Tiger Drive
Pigeon Forge, TN 37863
Monday - Saturday 8:00 am - 6:00 pm
All centers closed on Sunday

PLEASE NEVER LEAVE BAGGED TRASH ADJACENT TO OR OUTSIDE THE FORTIFIED
TRASH BINS UPON DEPARTURE – THE BEARS WILL MAKE A MESS OF IT.

IF BEARS GET INTO YOUR TRASH AT ANY TIME, PLEASE CLEAN IT UP!

SECTION VII: HOW THINGS SHOULD BE

After following all the instructions from this book, you should be able to effectively manage your vacation rental on just a few hours a week or less.

Also, you need to have the vacation rental set up to completely run for any given guest stay without you having to do anything incidental to any given guest stay.

I have said this once and I have said it a thousand times. You don't have a 'business' unless it operates without you when you go on vacation.

Your goal with this book is to get to that point. You want your vacation rental business to operate efficiently *even when you are on vacation*.

My family and I travel frequently to Mexico during the summer. We stay in an all-inclusive resort and travel Riviera Maya, swimming in cenotes, diving in Cozumel, ziplining, swimming with dolphins, learning Spanish, enjoying adventure tours, and amazing all-inclusive theme parks. We typically stay between two and four weeks at a time.

So how do we stay in a foreign country for four weeks at a time, during the middle of peak summer travel season, with four completely booked up vacation rentals? It is peak season back home, and all our vacation rentals are booked solid, with same day turns on nearly every stay. Why on earth would we book a month-long trip to be out of the country during the busiest time of the year?

Assuming you have followed the rules in this book, it should be easy.

Throughout the spring, as each summer reservation trickled in, I generated a KABA code, copy and pasted it into the email template, which have everything the guest needed for their stay, and sent it. That's it. Once that information is sent to the guest, then I am no longer needed.

So, when summer comes, all guests already have everything they need for their vacation. They shouldn't need me for anything. Everything they need is in their welcome email: the keyless entry door code, directions, attachments, Rules of Stay - everything.

As each guest checks out, my cleaner simply inventories and cleans the unit and gets it ready for the next guest. My cleaner uses Resort Cleaning scheduling so they know exactly when to clean. As each cleaning person or company invoices us, my bookkeeper simply electronically pays them from the respective vacation rental account.

If there is a problem, my cleaner will text me. Fortunately, AT&T has unlimited data and phone service in Mexico for Americans, so I am never completely out of touch.

If a guest has an issue during stay, they can call or text me and I can answer their question.

If it's a cleaning issue, I send the cleaner back out. If it's a maintenance issue, I send maintenance out. There really isn't much else that could possibly go wrong during any given stay. All our appliances are new. The HVAC is new. We have solid surface flooring so it's easy to clean. All our quilts are laundered between every guest stay. Nearly anything that a guest would normally complain about has been addressed in a preventative way, in advance.

Realistically, even during peak season with all four vacation rentals booked solid, I am rarely, if ever contacted during that month out of the country on any given issue. I kid you not. It's that easy. Again, it's that easy as everything involving the guest's stay is outsourced. Everything is that easy, because you have put the time in early on to get the vacation rental completely set up correctly.

If I happen to get an inquiry, I respond using the VRBO template, and provide a quote. I can literally answer an inquiry and send a quote in less than 15 seconds.

If I happen to get a booking, I simply confirm that the stay date is not imminent and prepare the KABA code and keycode email upon my return. There really is no rush to send them the keycode, as long as they get it in advance of their stay.

If the stay happens to be imminent, I have my laptop handy, log on to Wi-Fi (or use my phone hot spot), generate the KABA code, and email the guest through VRBO the welcome template with the keycode and everything they need for their stay.

Simultaneous to the booking, the cleaner is alerted through Resort Cleaning that there is an upcoming cleaning. That notification process is fully automated with each booking.

Taxes are either taken out by VRBO, and for those taxes that we pay, we schedule to pay the taxes on the calendar, and my bookkeeper logs on and handles it electronically.

One of the neatest feelings is to be on vacation for a month and get thousands of dollars of new bookings. The phone pings and boom, you have an instant booking. Thousands of dollars have gone into your bank account while you are sitting on a beach in Mexico with your family on vacation.

Follow the rules of this book, and you will get there.

SECTION VIII – ADVANCED TOPICS

Chapter 86

How to approach an upcoming vacancy

by adjusting rates last minute and/or

reducing the nightly minimum to fill any gaps

After your busy season, you should look back over the calendar for the busy months that had an extremely high occupancy rate.

If you have multiple gaps or a low vacancy rate, you may have priced yourself too high. However, we would rather you price your vacation rental too high, rather than too inexpensively, and get your place worn down by wear and tear, so do not beat yourself up too badly.

If the occupancy rate is literally 100% for months straight, you may have priced yourself too low, and/or may consider requiring a longer nightly minimum. A longer staying guest is typically a higher quality guest and results in less risk and less wear and tear on the unit due to a smaller turnover volume.

We tend to price higher than lower when we set our rates each year, and then adjust rates, and minimum night stays last minute for any vacancies.

Once a week, log in to VRBO / Airbnb and take a look at how things are looking for the next two to four weeks. If you have some vacancies, consider lowering the price in hopes of getting a last minute instant booking reservation.

Yes, the price drop will stir up some bargain hunters and they will ask for an even larger discount, so use your discretion on discounting further, or simply send them the template email we discussed earlier, indicating that the latest discount is 'as published,' and leave it at that. Remember it is ok for guests to ask so don't take offense.

The simplest way to adjust rates last minute and on the fly, is to simply go into your VRBO app, go to calendar, highlight the first and last day of the upcoming vacancy, then click on rates, and enter your reduced rate, which may vary depending upon the days of the week (Friday and Saturday nights tend to be higher than weekdays).

We previously discussed sending the 'check in day earlier,' 'check out day later' template email to existing guests to fill gaps between stays. You should send that email roughly thirty days in advance of their stay.

In addition to sending that email thirty days out, and lowering rates as discussed at least two weeks out, also consider reducing the minimum night stay to fill vacancies.

RULE: When you set your prices for the year, err on the side of pricing higher than lower. You can always discount last minute. Fill all gaps in stay by offering existing guests the opportunity to expand their existing stay with your template email, discounting unfilled nights last minute, and reducing minimum night stays to fill any remaining vacancies.

Chapter 87

How to get to the top of VRBO search results

VRBO, and I am sure Airbnb is similar, has a search algorithm or metric that ranks search results based on a series of factors that you should pay attention to and carefully guard, work to improve on, and diligently protect.

Acceptance rate

The first factor is the acceptance rate, which ranks how many times you accept a proposed booking or decline it. As you should be set up on instant reservations, your acceptance rate should be 100%.

Again, we do not recommend pre-approving each proposed guest stay. Once guests decide on a place to stay, they want it to be booked and done, so they can then book flights, or other travel arrangements. Waiting 24-48 hours for an owner to 'accept' their proposed stay is less attractive as an alternative compared to the comparable unit where the guest can instantly book.

As mentioned earlier, you will require a significant damage deposit, so you shouldn't worry about trying to screen every guest stay to detect that one in a hundred bad apple. Also, you can handle a last-minute stay, as you have a smart phone, and can generate a KABA lock code and send your template email on the fly, even last minute, so you don't need additional time last minute to have to approve any given stay.

Also, with our goal of spending as little time as possible running the vacation rental, having Instant Booking set up is one less step for you to have to take in the booking process and saves you time.

Since we do Instant Booking, we have the needed 100% acceptance rate.

Cancellation rate

The cancellation rate is where you cancel a reservation with or without the guest's permission. Don't ever do that, regardless of whether the cancellation is at your request, or the guest's request. Either way, the owner-initiated cancellation will ding your cancellation rate, and in turn, negatively impact your search rankings.

If the cancellation request is by the guest, that is easy.

You simply email the guest and tell them what your cancellation policy is on the cancellation, or that you intend to override any non-refundable policies you have. You then instruct the guest to contact VRBO's customer service line, and they then request the cancellation, and point to the owner correspondence agreeing to the guest's request to cancel.

VRBO will then cancel the reservation.

You will then be prompted to approve a full refund, partial refund, or other penalty. You then simply honor the agreement you made with the guest on what if anything will be done on the cancellation if it deviates from your cancellation policy.

That part is easy.

Be careful though in those situations where the guest is too inept or computer deficient to understand how to cancel the stay from their end, and they simply ask that you handle it for them. Don't take the bait. If you cancel them, even if it is at the guest's request, you may ding your own cancellation rate, which will hurt your search result rankings. Simply supply the guest with the VRBO customer service number and make them request the cancellation from their end.

On the flip side, you should never have to cancel from your end any given reservation. If you do, it is most likely due to an emergency or some type of problem with your vacation rental.

For example, we had a water leak from the unit above us which required extensive drying, sheetrock repairs and painting. These repairs affected an upcoming stay. Rather than simply cancelling the stay, and refunding the guest, I contacted VRBO and explained to them that our unit was not habitable due to the emergency repairs for the water damage.

VRBO then cancelled the upcoming stay and refunded the guest their money and there was then no accompanying ding to our cancellation policy. When this happens, get the customer service representative to assure you that there will be no ding to your cancellation rate. I hate that the guest who got cancelled was really upset and was quite nasty about the whole thing. However, it was totally outside my control, and fortunately, since the guest did not actually stay, they could not leave a negative review.

If there is a situation where you want to stay at your own place for a special weekend, and you failed to reserve it in advance, you could cancel an existing reservation. The choice to do that though would then leave the cancelled guest 'high and dry' due to your own selfishness. If that were the case, you deservingly should then be dinged on this metric.

Always, always, at the beginning of each calendar year, map out all your stays at all your vacation rentals, so that your place is saved for you for those important events, festivals, concerts, family time or whatever trip you may possibly have planned. Err on the side of booking or blocking off stay dates in your favor. You can always lift the block later and the rental will likely still book even at the last minute. The main thing is to not be in a situation where you need your vacation rental for something special and your vacation rental is already booked up.

Plan accordingly.

Average review

Your goal is to have as close to a 5.0 average review rating from staying guests as humanly possible.

How do you get that type of rating?

First, you follow all the steps in this book, without exception. Every one of these steps, especially the initial set up of the vacation rental, as well as the professional interaction you achieve through non-emotional, and carefully crafted, email correspondence with guests (as opposed to texts riddled with misunderstandings, or an angry late-night call), are all critical in getting that great review.

Second, you need to send the special template follow up email to guests that we discussed earlier, every time a guest checks out. The template email that I provided to you earlier works, and consistently generates 5-star reviews. Use it.

The more reviews you have, the less likely the 'one off' 4-star or 3-star review will materially hurt you. The oddball reviews happen occasionally no matter what you do, so use the law of averages and numbers to help offset that.

Most of our units are sitting around 4.8 with roughly 100 or more reviews each, a good position.

Review count

The review count rewards that vacation rental owner with a lot of reviews. Guests routinely look at reviews during their decision process on whether to rent any given vacation rental. So, VRBO wants each of their properties to have plenty of reviews and plenty of feedback for a prospective guest to see.

In addition, you also want plenty of reviews so that you can offset that one random negative review that may come in at some point.

Again, the way to generate those reviews is to make sure that follow up template email that we discussed earlier, is sent to every guest, every time, following every guest departure. That template email will generate a volume of five-star reviews, which will in turn help 50% of the controlling metrics for higher search result rankings. It is that important.

The million-dollar follow up email to get

5-star reviews and a lot of them

Review again the previously discussed follow up template email that you send to each guest following every departure. Use it Every. Single. Time.

Response time

Although VRBO does not list response time as a factor affecting your ranking in search results, I am suspicious that it may also be a factor.

Even if rapid response time is not a factor, you need to go to great lengths to promptly respond to guest inquiries and questions. The old saying 'the early bird gets the worm,' is true. Studies show that the owner who promptly responds is dramatically more likely to get the reservation than those owners who are slow to respond.

As discussed earlier, you should have a smart phone with the Airbnb and or VRBO app installed, with notifications turned on. You should get your inquiry response template set up, so that you can answer questions quickly and efficiently.

Further, have multiple email template options to respond to the most common inquiries - the last-minute special, the first responder discount, and others.

Assuming you get these metrics going, you will eventually be recategorized into a 'Premier Host,' which is a special badge that is placed on your listing. Although helpful, I am not sure if getting that badge results in more reservations or not. Ranking in the top of search results is what really matters.

RULE: Focus on the four contributors or 'pillars' that will increase your listing position in search results. Allow instant booking. Never cancel a guest. Get 5-star reviews. Get a ton of reviews. Use our special email template and send it to every guest following every guest departure to get both 5-star reviews, and a ton of them, which in turn will dramatically increase your rank in search engine results. Respond quickly to inquiries.

Chapter 88

VRBO Power ups – what they are

and how best to use them

After your first year with VRBO, you will earn with each booking, points called 'power ups.' These earned points can then be used to boost your listing ranking in the VRBO search results for your resort or area. You start accumulating the points immediately following each guest stay, but there really isn't enough to work with right out of the gate, so just wait until the points build up a bit, which may take a few months to a year.

When you are ready to cash them in, simply go to your dashboard in VRBO. Scroll down and to the right is a section called 'power ups.' You then choose to redeem the points, and you can choose which dates you want the 'power ups' to be applied towards, on any given future vacancy.

Obviously, you would not want to apply the 'power ups' to dates where the vacation rental is already booked. Rather, you would apply them to dates where the unit is currently vacant.

As you apply 'power ups,' VRBO will then show your listing ranking move up. Each time you apply power up points, you may move roughly 20 positions higher. Apply 100 power up points and move from 100th to 80th. Apply another 100 powerup points and move your search position to 70th.

Unfortunately, you do not have unlimited 'power ups' and need to spend or spread them wisely to get as much value out of them as you possibly can. Therefore, you need to employ some type of strategy that works for you to get the best results out of the power ups you have available.

I have found that if you use even minimal power ups, just one set of them, that you can dramatically increase your listing results in the off season, moving you to the top of the search results. In other words, your listing ranking is dramatically increased while using very few of your available 'power ups.'

For the time on either side of peak season, this is where I apply the most 'power ups' to increase my listing position. In other words, I want to be at the top of the search results during shoulder season, which is the time before and after peak season.

For peak season, I do not use any power ups.

Let me explain why.

The problem is that it takes many 'power ups' to get ahead of your competition and you can easily burn through your entire 'power up' supply in short order, if trying to get even close to a higher search engine position in the middle of peak season, and especially big peak season, holiday weekends.

Regardless of whether I use 'power ups' or not for a higher position in search engine results in peak season, it always books, as everything gets sold out during peak season anyway. Eventually, regardless of my search listing position, our unit will move to the top simply because we end up being one of the few left available to book. It always books during peak season, so don't waste power ups on that period of time.

This in part is because we price our unit so high for peak season, and are willing to wait and see, even up until the last minute, if someone will bite and book the unit at the high rate. We do not need 'power ups' under that type of strategy. We are typically the 'last one standing' and the only availability for peak season, and fortunately, it books every time at that super high rate, because we held out.

If during peak season we get a vacancy, we simply use the techniques discussed in previous lessons and it always books, even last minute.

So, under this strategy, you use minimal 'power ups' to get you to the top position in search engine results in the dead of winter, or slowest season. For us, that is December, January, and February.

You then also are in the top position in search engine results in the fall and spring as well, which for us is September, October, and March, April, and May. Yes, pushing our listing to the top during this time will likely sap most of our available power ups.

For peak season between say, Memorial Day and Labor Day, you do not worry about your search engine results, as your vacation rental will book no matter what happens.

After applying all available power ups with this strategy in mind, you should then be ranked in the top five of search engine results for approximately nine of the twelve months of the year. That's the goal.

Think about it. Your listing ends up in the top 5 search results, in roughly nine of the twelve months of the year. That is pretty cool.

Note that the 'power ups' do expire. You need to use them within a year or so of them being earned. Typically, I simply log on to each vacation rental listing each January and use up all the 'power ups' for the year, and simply do that annually in January. If you do not use them all up, they will start expiring.

It seems silly to have to go through the time-consuming process to boost your search result placement, but it is what it is. The good news is that it's only a once per year task – so worth the hassle.

RULE: Use up all your 'power ups' each January to boost your position in search engine results throughout the year and apply them in a strategic manner. Apply 'power ups' during off season and get huge 'bank' for the use of the 'power up.' For shoulder season, use power ups to get your position in search engine results into the top 20, 10 or even 5. Do not waste 'power ups' on peak season. Keep your unit priced high compared to your peers and as things sell out, your unit will end up at the top of search results anyway, and your vacation rental will book during peak season, even last minute.

Chapter 89

Choosing the most effective marketing techniques for your vacation rental

As discussed previously, your goal is to land at the top of the VRBO search engine results by focusing on a strong acceptance rate, a low cancellation rate, five-star reviews, and plenty of them. By doing that, you will graduate to 'Premiere Host' status and be placed high in search engine results.

Once you get through the first year, you will then strategically use your 'power ups' to further boost your listing position in search engine results nine out of the twelve months each year.

Doing the two foregoing things are the two most important ways to successfully get your vacation rental marketed and booked. Simply being listed on VRBO and/or Airbnb is huge. Both platforms aggressively advertise and have become staple names in the vacation rental market. They even run ads now in the Super Bowl. They, in essence, are already doing the bulk of the marketing for you. This is why you need to be at the top of their search results, to take advantage of the masses being lured to their website through their advertising.

We also already discussed in a previous lesson on how to create a YouTube video of your vacation rental, resort, and area. The three- or four-minute video is then posted to YouTube, and linked to your photo carousel so that prospective guests can watch your promotional video.

I kid you not. Thousands of views may be generated of people searching YouTube for a vacation rental, and having the video is a terrific way to drive traffic to your VRBO or Airbnb listing. Creating a YouTube video with a visible link to your Airbnb or VRBO listing is thus an extremely cost effective and inexpensive way to drive a ton of traffic to your listing. It costs nothing to store the video on YouTube. The hardest part is getting the video created and uploaded. Once that is done, people will watch the video, want to stay in your vacation rental, and then will go to the VRBO or Airbnb site and book your unit. It is thus an absolute 'must have' marketing tool.

Other marketing techniques discussed below are helpful, but not nearly as controlling or as significant as getting ranked on top of the VRBO and/or Airbnb search engine results or having a terrific (and free to list) YouTube video linked to your vacation rental listing.

Facebook Vacation Rental Page

You should create a vacation rental page on Facebook. Simply list your VRBO website link with your listing ID number, your phone number, email and so forth.

After creation, you then populate that new listing with the 50 or so photos that you used for your VRBO listing in the form of posts. You then 'pin' the post at the top of your Facebook feed a post that has the ten most essential VRBO photos, so that newcomers to your page always see that set of photos at the top of your Facebook page.

In addition, you provide a link to the Facebook page in the follow-up email that you send to guests following every guest stay. This is where you ask departing guests to 'tag' their photos to your Facebook page.

Each time we are down at the vacation rental, we snap photos and post them to the Facebook page.

If there is a closure or amenity update or some type of construction, we post those updates to the page. If a hurricane narrowly missed the resort, we post that we were spared and open for business – that sort of thing.

You can also post a 'special' or 'coupon' with a specific keyword that they use and tell them to contact the owner in order to tell them that special keyword. The prospective guest will then get a discount stay, by mentioning that code. That may generate a booking or two as well.

Over the years, we would occasionally 'boost' a post on the vacation rental, which highlighted pretty pictures of say the beach chair service, waterpark, lazy river, views and so forth. A couple thousand people would see the boosted post, and we would get some comments, but again, I am not sure how much of that traffic resulted in a reservation.

Despite years of having Facebook pages on each of our vacation rental listings, we only have a couple hundred followers on each one. I am not sure what if any business we get off them so this may or may or may not be worth your time to do. I would characterize the results of the paid 'boosted posts' on Facebook as mixed.

Google Listing / Maps

At one point, we tried to get each of our vacation rental listings listed on Google so that we would appear on their maps section of search engine results.

To do so, Google requires that a Google post card be sent to the vacation rental physical address, and received there, to verify that we were actually located at the address claimed.

At Splash, we to this day do not have a mailbox key, as all our mail goes to our office. I think we got around that somehow by having maintenance locate the special post card – cannot remember.

At the cabin, we do not have a mailbox at all. We had to drive to the post office to pick up the postcard from the mail person. It was a real hassle.

In the last few months, all our map's listings were taken down by Google, as we were not 'open' for business in the sense of having a desk or something where a customer could walk in and book the unit. We then were prompted to go through the entire mail verification process again, so we just gave up.

The other problem with getting a maps listing was that it did not necessarily drive any traffic to our VRBO listing.

Rather, guests would call our maps listing number looking for directions to the resort, or they were a guest staying in the resort, and called us thinking we were the front desk, wanting assistance with any given problem they were having. Again, a total pain. I do not recommend a Maps listing at this point.

Google Ads

If you want to spend some money marketing, consider creating a Google ads account, and then set up some inexpensive ads that will appear in the primary geographic where your guests come from.

For example, we have run inexpensive Google ads in a two state radius of Florida, in an effort to capture those guests looking to vacation in Florida. We will run the ads in Louisiana, Alabama, Mississippi, Tennessee, Georgia, North and South Carolina. The ads will then show up whenever a prospective guest located in those states type in 'Splash vacation rental.'

Your targeted ad both in geographic focus, and keyword specific, will then appear with a link to your VRBO or Airbnb listing.

General Google ads that target the entire country without targeted, specific keywords, would be a waste of money. You must have a targeted demographic, with very narrow, specific keywords that would then trigger your ad to appear. Otherwise, your budget is burned up with nothing to show for it.

Remember, even if you make the targeted ad super narrow and super specific, always set a daily limit for your budget. Do not go overboard with marketing as it can get expensive very quickly.

We have had some good results with a small budget dedicated to Google ads along those lines for each unit. Like Facebook ads though, we are not sure how many of those leads converted into an actual booking. We budget around $50 per month or so for Google and or Facebook ads for each unit – not a huge expense.

In sum, focus on getting your listing at the top of the VRBO and/or Airbnb search engine results. That is the main priority. The second priority is to get a promotional three-minute video shot of your vacation rental, the resort and area. That promotional video should visibly list the URL for them to book your unit on VRBO or Airbnb. Then, link that video to your photo carousel. If you do those two main things, you should be good.

Yes, create a Facebook vacation rental listing page, and run some inexpensive ads to boost posts on that site. That may drum up some traffic to your listing. It certainly cannot hurt.

Yes, create some Google ads that target specific geographic territories near your vacation rental, with targeted specific keywords for those looking to book a vacation rental either in your resort or area.

The Facebook and Google ads are the best 'bang for your buck' at this point. Do not go overboard though and spend too much, as the actual results may or may not be there. This is why, at minimum, you should focus on getting the top of the search engine results within your listing platform and have a free YouTube video that visibly lists your URL in the video and linked to your VRBO photo carousel. Those are truly the drivers of traffic to your site. Facebook and Google are just backups to that primary plan.

Yes, embrace new apps and new systems as the method on how vacationing guests find listings evolve. Always find new and creative ways to get your listing seen by prospective guests. It is a never ending and evolving process. Embrace change. Adapt.

RULE: Focus on securing the highest position possible in VRBO and/or Airbnb results. Become a 'Premier Owner,' use 'power ups,' or any other tricks within the platform's system to get your listing position as high as possible. Make sure you have a YouTube video highlighting your vacation rental, resort, and area attractions, with a visible URL or link to your VRBO or Airbnb listing. A Facebook page with an occasional boosted post may also be helpful. As long you do not spend too much, an additional Google narrowly focused ad to a targeted geographic area, may also be helpful.

Made in the USA
Middletown, DE
14 September 2023

38523791R00197